'The future of marketing is to enable a business to make sustainable profits by selling good products and services whilst respecting planetary boundaries – or sustainable marketing. If you are a marketer, this is an inspiring vision because it shows how you can shape a better world. To understand how to make this vision a reality, read this book.'

James Perry, Co-Chairman, COOK and Co-Founder, B Lab UK

'I thought I knew a great deal about this subject until I read this book. If you didn't believe in the power of sustainable marketing before; you will after you read this – but more importantly you will also know how to *do* it.'

Sarah Walker-Smith, CEO, Shakespeare Martineau

'At a time when society is looking to organizations to be a catalyst for positive change, and the need to communicate effectively could not be more important, this book demonstrates the critical role marketing plays in driving change and building trust. Not only does *Sustainable Marketing* inform, it also provides practical advice and actionable plans on how the marketing function can engage, both internally and externally, in taking on the biggest challenge that the world faces.'

Chris Daly, Chief Executive, CIM

'This book drives you to reappraise the role that sustainability plays, both internally and externally. It moves your perceptions from a consumer trend or something mentioned in a CSR policy, to an integral way in which we can drive "profit with purpose" in all we do. *Sustainable Marketing* is a practical guide on how to authentically drive change from board alignment to daily implementation.'

Abigail Dixon, Founder & Director, Labyrinth Marketing

'A thoughtful, informative and practical guide that will transform businesses for the better. Every business leader needs to read this.'

Victoria Page, Founder, Victoria Page Communications

'*Sustainable Marketing* provides a rounded and comprehensive view of key issues such as sustainable supply chain management, packaging, and responsible marketing. With case studies and practical advice on how to drive business transformation, it is a must-read book given the importance of the issues covered for consumers, employees and governments.'

Chris Bartley, Innovation and Partnerships Director, MedShr

'As we reach a tipping point in society that links our resiliency to the way the economy works, this book is a timely reminder that clear commitments and accountability around sustainability become essential components of a future fit business model.'

Chris Grantham, Executive Director, Circular Economy, IDEO

'Want to support your organization to build a better world? This easy-to-digest book is packed with the latest trends, facts and statistics to help the experienced marketer, those pivoting their careers or just starting out.'

Catherine Weetman FRSA FCILT, author of
A Circular Economy Handbook

'A valuable handbook for marketers at all levels of seniority to lead sustainable change in their organizations. By balancing research and pragmatic analysis, the authors provide clear action steps to turn a daunting endeavour into an exciting sustainability roadmap.'

Lucie Montel, Founder & Director, Project Integrity Ltd

'*Sustainable Marketing* is a Swiss Army knife of a book, engagingly weaving research-based frameworks, compelling case studies and practical ideas on how to promote and drive sustainability within business. Sustainability is an issue for every person on the planet and this book shows you how to ensure that it gets on everyone's agenda.'

Rob Baker, Founder and Director, Tailored Thinking
and author of Personalization at Work

'Through a number of case studies, *Sustainable Marketing* offers an opportunity to gain a crucial understanding of sustainable practices and is a great tool for anyone aspiring to venture into this very relevant field.'

Caroline Heinz, Senior Sustainability Consultant, Sofies

'A well-researched, balanced and action-oriented primer for marketing professionals looking to understand sustainability and what it means for them.'

Lisa Dittmar, Circular Economy Practitioner

'If you're looking to understand what sustainable marketing means and how to introduce this effectively into your business, the contents of this book will give you a Formula 1 start. Each chapter unwraps the complexities of sustainability, giving the reader a definitive understanding of why this all matters. Every company is moving towards a more progressive future where both people and the planet benefit from sustainable endeavours and an overriding commitment to change. *Sustainable Marketing* should be top of every marketeer's reading list because it gives you all the know-how you need to go forward and make it count.'

Richard Rawlins, CEO, Finn

Sustainable Marketing

HOW TO DRIVE PROFITS WITH PURPOSE

MICHELLE CARVILL,
GEMMA BUTLER AND GERAINT EVANS

BLOOMSBURY BUSINESS
LONDON · OXFORD · NEW YORK · NEW DELHI · SYDNEY

BLOOMSBURY BUSINESS
Bloomsbury Publishing Plc
50 Bedford Square, London, WC1B 3DP, UK
29 Earlsfort Terrace, Dublin 2, Ireland

BLOOMSBURY, BLOOMSBURY BUSINESS and the Diana logo are trademarks
of Bloomsbury Publishing Plc

First published in Great Britain 2021

A catalogue record for this book is available from the British Library

Library of Congress Cataloguing-in-Publication data has been applied for

ISBN: 978-1-4729-7913-1; eBook: 978-1-4729-7912-4

2 4 6 8 10 9 7 5 3 1

Typeset by Deanta Global Publishing Services, Chennai, India
Printed and bound in Great Britain by CPI Group (UK) Ltd, Croydon CR0 4YY

Every effort has been made to ensure that this book has been produced in a sustainable way.

The FSC® label means that materials used for the product have been responsibly sourced.
The Forest Stewardship Council® (FSC®) is a global, not-for-profit organization dedicated
to the promotion of responsible forest management worldwide. FSC defines standards
based on agreed principles for responsible forest stewardship that are supported by
environmental, social, and economic stakeholders. To learn more, visit www.fsc.org

This product has been printed at CPI Books Ltd using renewable energy.
CPI Books Ltd is committed to reducing its impact on the environment
as part of its ISO14001 environmental management objectives.

To find out more about our authors and books visit www.bloomsbury.com
and sign up for our newsletters

Contents

CHAPTER TWELVE

Preface

Welcome to *Sustainable Marketing*! We know there are so many other business and marketing books you could have chosen, so we are truly grateful you selected this one!

Sitting at the heart of brand, communications, stakeholders and product development, we believe that marketers have a significant role to play when it comes to promoting and driving sustainability, whether it's within your organizations, with your consumers or within the wider world.

We also believe that the key to delivering meaningful, tangible change is focusing on providing practical education and help to your colleagues, partners and customers wherever possible, and that whilst you can undoubtedly improve *all* areas of your business, it is ineffective to try to change everything at once. As marketers, we also need to recognize that we are a key part of the problem itself – the products and services we so expertly research, develop and market inevitably require resources, many of which are highly likely to produce some waste.

The authors of this book are all experienced marketing practitioners, who, hopefully like you, are passionate about developing their knowledge of sustainability and what 'responsible marketing' really means when it's put into practice, to practically make a real difference. No longer can the marketing and commercial professions ignore their impact on the environment. In an age of growing authenticity and consumer demands for more transparency, it is more important than ever for brands to communicate their responsible and sustainable practices, stand up for things they're passionate about, and importantly, follow through on the promises they make.

We were inspired to write this book following numerous conversations with fellow marketing professionals and business leaders, increasing numbers of whom are seeking to embrace a profits-with-purpose approach to their marketing strategy – whilst still naturally keen to ensure that their companies continue to grow. Our intention in this book therefore is to both educate and bring awareness of the current realities we face and provide some ideas and benchmarks for what best practice in sustainability looks like for modern marketers, as well as how to embrace a cause-led strategy. Ultimately, we want to help you grow, whilst at the same time learning how to leave the world a better place!

We will explore a variety of related and highly relevant issues – from the current global picture on sustainability and gaining true boardroom 'buy-in', to offering practical day-to-day advice to enable marketing professionals to take the lead in driving sustainable practice within their company. The book also details inspiring examples of best practice and direct interviews from companies from all over the world that are using sustainability as a source of brand loyalty and competitive advantage.

As we look back in time, as authors, we're hopeful that following the period of coronavirus the 2020s will be the age in which boardrooms around the globe wake up to the reality of running a business focused on making profits with purpose, with an authentic desire to take a more sustainable approach. Indeed, headlines report that climate change is a hot topic in every boardroom, and this isn't surprising. As we entered the 2020s, climate change manifested itself through the Australian bush fires, some of the worst ever experienced, providing a chilling wake-up call. It should be noted, however, that whilst Greta Thunberg, David Attenborough and other prominent activists align these catastrophes with climate change – and a body of climate scientists would agree with them – there is also, of course, a smaller body of climate scientists who would argue that it's got nothing to do with the climate. Nevertheless, in general terms, consumers are waking up and becoming ever more conscious of these issues, which are projected into our everyday lives by all forms of media. For instance, we've all viewed the scenes of miles of floating plastic in our oceans and heard terrifying facts and statistics related to the rising temperature of our planet and the many contributing factors (some of which we've shared throughout this book). This can mean we sometimes experience a very real and heavy weight of total hopelessness.

In consequence, sustainability has never been more important, yet marketing sustainability in a business sense is no easy task. As marketers ourselves, we are all fully aware of the challenge of influencing boardrooms and creating real change across an organization. Our view, however, is that there's no one better placed to educate, communicate, and drive and effect hope than a marketer with a responsibility to drive sustainability within their organization. For this reason, this book is aimed at marketers. Marketers are the champions of both brand and the consumer – so there's real opportunity to create change, make an impact and use powerful influencing skills to drive profit with purpose. That said, whilst we've positioned this book for marketers, seeing them as a key conduit to effect change and connect with customers, it's not solely for marketers. Indeed, this book is just as valuable for business owners, CEOs, leaders, and any other responsible humans concerned about what's happening to our planet and who are also keen to drive and effect real change.

How this book is structured

In Chapter 1 we'll take a look at 'where we are' on the topic of sustainability in business. We'll touch on brand, brand values, the alignment with corporate responsibility and introduce a number of the key sustainability frameworks and targets. In Chapter 2 we will tackle head-on the need for clear leadership, and the crucial aspect of developing personal accountability and ownership for change. Chapter 3 will dive into how to navigate all of your other stakeholders in the mix, including the importance of gaining boardroom buy-in and employee engagement as well as connecting with one of your biggest stakeholder groups – your customers. Chapter 4 explores issues of managing global supply chains and sources of manufacture within your cost base. Chapter 5 will examine how many leading companies are already moving beyond the basic principles of corporate responsibility and implementing incredible business-wide initiatives – with marketing taking the lead in sustainability strategy and implementation. Chapter 6 addresses the significant issue of waste, and looks at strategies to reduce waste produced in your marketing practice – from using less paper to offering better options in your offices and locations. Chapter 7 is devoted to guidance on the urgent need to address the plastic crisis that is enveloping the earth, whilst Chapter 8 offers help and ideas on how to reduce your company's overall carbon footprint. Chapter 9 will explore the plethora of sustainable energy sources available – renewables and innovations to help improve your operations and lessen your impact. Talking of lessening impact, Chapter 10 will focus on the significant issue of packaging – how to improve how you handle it, reduce and reuse it, packaging innovations and options to drive competitive advantage. Chapter 11 extends out into how to work with partners – particularly with NGOs – and how partnership can expand your approach, before Chapter 12 pulls everything together to summarize your next steps, including our model that outlines a cohesive 10-step action plan for change.

Each chapter will follow a common structure. First we will provide all of the key background you need to get a feel for your options in a given area. From there, we'll try to give you a balanced view on their reality. Tackling sustainability is not perfect; there are negative impacts to producing and marketing products and services everywhere you turn, so we will endeavour to give you both the positive and negative aspects in order for you to make your own judgements. To bring best practice alive for you, we'll include lots of examples and case studies and also interviews from practitioners from all over the world, before ending each chapter with some practical steps and actions you can take to progressively develop your approach to embedding sustainability into your marketing strategy.

So, with a lot to get through – let's get going!

CHAPTER ONE

Where are we ... situation analysis

1.0 Chapter introduction

It has become increasingly clear that, as marketers and business owners, we all need to take responsibility for the impact our companies and their activities have on the environment. What is clear is that when it comes to sustainability and responsible marketing, it is an inherently conflicted and difficult space to navigate, and this book won't try to hide that in any way. However, it is also clear that even some of the smallest changes – from making your packaging recyclable or reducing single-use items, to how you interact with your wider partner network – can all have a substantial beneficial impact on your company and the wider world.

This book aims to introduce the principles that will help you evaluate your company's current sustainability approach; help you develop, 'own' and lead the creation of a purpose-driven marketing approach in your organization; and ultimately achieve a company-wide philosophy of running a company with a true 'profits with purpose' approach. Our intention is to give you a mix of the theoretical bases that underpin different strategies and schools of thought on a variety of subjects – from branding and corporate social responsibility to managing your supply chain in the production of the goods and services you offer. We will also endeavour to provide you with both sides of the argument, fully acknowledging this is inherently conflicted and difficult, and – let's be honest – rather murky territory for any marketer or their company to navigate.

1.1 Where are we?

Any good book on marketing usually begins with a discussion of the role of branding – and understanding the basic concepts of branding is crucial in order to then become a brand aligned with and known for its sustainable approach.

What exactly *is* a brand?

The most often-cited American Marketing Association definition of a brand is as a: 'name, term, design, symbol, or any other feature that identifies one seller's good or service as distinct from those of other sellers'. Of course, the branding of goods and services is not a new phenomenon at all; it has been around for as long as commerce itself, which is centuries. Billions of farmers, traders and craftspeople have sought to demonstrate ownership and recognition of their goods through marking them with a unique, identifiable name or sign – in fact the word 'brand' originates from the Nordic word for burning a mark on to cattle as a sign of ownership (Holland, 2017). Perhaps not surprisingly, it is therefore a bit of a loaded term – with as many negative as positive connotations to differing consumers. These components need to be actively managed on a day-to-day basis by all marketing leaders. De Chernatony et al (2010) propose four dimensions that can act as a key bridge for us to discuss the concept of a consumer's view on a company:

Table 1.0 Components of the brand (de Chernatony et al, 2010)

Culture	The basic assumptions underlying an organization's values and behaviour.
Relationship	The quality of relationships that a brand has with its customers.
Reflection	A brand as a communication tool for consumers.
Self-image	Internal reflection.

From a marketing perspective, it is clear that many of the key aspects shown in Table 1.0 can assist in understanding how the image of a company, and how it asks for consideration of its products and services, is manifested. This operates in both its consumers' and employees' minds, and helps explain how it adds value, its vision and how it establishes its value system – all of which are essential to understanding its position regarding sustainability.

In our ever-increasingly digital world, proactively managing brand strategy is arguably more important than ever, if only because brands are now more *accessible* than ever. The prevalence of interactive technology has increasingly meant direct interaction between an organization and its stakeholders on a daily basis – meaning greater effort is required in order to maintain and strengthen an effective brand strategy in any marketplace. With an exponential increase in content, promotions and advertisements from brands, we are constantly being bombarded and asked to evaluate, both consciously and unconsciously, an ever-widening range of goods, services, companies, countries and individuals. With all of them seeking to reach their target audience, it is a crowded market place – as *Entrepreneur* magazine (Griffith, 2019) has branded this time, it is 'a war for attention' – and the environmental practices of a company are now the subject of greater focus and visibility than at any time in the past.

Although technology increasingly encourages and supports our choice between alternative brands and their options, any buyer must now also search through a great deal of potentially relevant information surrounding their choices, some of which they might even perceive to be 'fake news', in an attempt to evaluate their various options in order to reach the best decision for them – essentially making everyday consumer behaviour an increasingly complex area for marketers to understand and manage.

Trust and consumer behaviour

When a consumer seeks a new product or service, they are likely to be seeking a solution to a problem (perceived or real), or at least to improve an otherwise adverse situation. These purchase decisions can range on a continuum from low- to high-level risk (in terms of factors such as psychological, financial or social risk), and will vary in the amount of time devoted to information searches and the number of brand alternatives considered (Stankevich, 2017). Consumers will also be anxious to feel that they have not made a mistake in any aspect of their decision – and the qualities of a brand in allaying this fear will therefore play an essential role in helping consumers mitigate any feelings of risk by providing reassurance and security.

It is perhaps not surprising that the most important concept of all for any brand – especially in the subject of sustainability – is trust. Dall'Olmo Riley & de Chernatony (2000); de Chernatony (2002, 2003, 2010) suggest that 'the concept of the brand has evolved from a firm's products, to that of a relationship based on trust'. Brands use tangible devices such as logos or slogans in their advertising, such as McDonald's golden arches or the Nike swoosh, to create the feeling they are a strong brand that the customer trusts and believes will always deliver on their promise (Kotler and Pfoertsch, 2006). At the same time, they also leverage intangible assets, which together represent the dynamic interrelationship between an organization's activities and its customers' interpretations – essentially 'a cluster of functional and emotional values that enable a promise to be made about a unique and welcomed experience' (de Chernatony et al, 2010: 17).

Another essential element to consider in developing a sustainability marketing strategy is the growing important of 'authenticity', reassuring the consumer, supporting their perception of 'risk' reduction and acting as a key communication device. The perception of a brand identity can also be considered to be analogous to the identity that a person has about themselves. Brand researcher Aaker (1996) proposes that

consumers unconsciously, or consciously, consider the importance of
the following questions:

- What do I stand for?
- How do I want to be perceived?
- What personality traits do I want to project?
- What are the important relationships in my life?
- What are my core values?

Brand and corporate social responsibility

Whilst product brands can be seen primarily as needing to appeal to a
limited group of stakeholders who buy and use the product – namely,
their customers – corporate brands increasingly recognize how they are
perceived by a far wider group of stakeholders – including current and
potential employees, their suppliers, potential investors, governments
and the media. As such, there is a clear link between corporate brand
and corporate reputation (Fombrun, 1996).

Corporate reputation is the continuing assessment of an organization's
activities by all of these stakeholder groups, based on their perception
of what the company is, how well it meets its commitments, and how
it conforms to stakeholders' expectations. Brand and reputation are
closely interrelated assets for any company, yet they are not always
synonymous. Ettenson and Knowles (2008) argue that a trustworthy
corporate reputation is a *precondition* for stakeholders to consider
doing business with an organization, whereas it is the brand being
marketed that *drives* the purchase decision.

The growth in the digital environment has enabled organizations to
more actively create and manage interactive ongoing relationships in
real time – whether they be with individual customers, market segments
or other key stakeholders. Social media has significantly changed the

relationship between the consumer and producer, enabling consumers to be far more proactive in the search for more granular product information or the position an organization takes when it comes to sustainability. With the number of relevant digital platforms increasing daily – from traditional media houses to blogs, forums and wikis, as well as social media such as Facebook, YouTube, Twitter, LinkedIn, Instagram or Tumblr – managing brands is now more complicated than ever.

1.2 Why do companies need to do something about this now?

The focus on managing a brand's reputation has been closely related to the rise of 'corporate responsibility' (CR) or 'corporate social responsibility' (CSR), which has become a major topic of debate and a growing boardroom issue for organizations and their leadership teams, is something we'll explore in greater detail in Chapter 5. By contrast, business ethics, and a concern with the role of business in society more generally, is not a new area of debate and contention. The role of how to appropriately run a business in society has been noted as far back as the 1st century BC, evidenced in Cicero's arguments on 'controlled greed' (Blowfield and Frynas, 2005).

The 'business case' for corporate responsibility

Key for business leaders to take action and address their role in tackling environmental problems has been the emergence of the 'business case' for corporate responsibility. Research undertaken by consulting firm IO Sustainability compared CSR programmes within organizations against the rest of the company's operations. Their study found that a winning strategy is one whereby a company identifies areas of social impact that fit with its core strategy, products or services and operations, and makes a commitment to dedicating resources, sets clear key performance indicators (KPIs), and connects and engages with stakeholders. According to the research, companies that stick to this three-pronged approach showed significant returns, including: enhanced sales, by as much as 20 per cent; increased productivity, by 13 per cent; reduction in employee turnover, by half; and an increase in the company's share price by up to 6 per cent (Kline, 2018). The same study also realized the direct impact on consumers, splitting customers into two categories: 1) 'aspirationals' – those customers who think of a brand as part of the cultural fabric they identify with, (39 per cent); 2) 'advocates', those customers who proactively promote a brand and support its values (20 per cent). I'm sure any marketer, or savvy business person, would agree that faced with such statistics, the case for proactively engaging in effective CSR activities can be good for the planet and the wider stakeholder group, such as employees, and the wider business community. What's more, the commercial benefits seem to stack up, too. A body of earlier research (Margolis and Walsh, 2003), examined 127 empirical studies from 1972 to 2002 measuring the relationship between social and financial performance and concluded that they have a positive association – helping the business case for corporate responsibility. Porter and Kramer (2011) describe this as developing 'shared value' – which argues that firms can simultaneously implement policies and operational practices that increase their competitiveness whilst also advancing the economic and social conditions in the communities in which they operate.

As marketers, we design, develop and undertake market research in the pursuit of the creation and development of 'unique selling propositions (USPs),' manifesting and identifying points of differentiation that can lead to competitive advantage. Sustainable approaches can support such differentiation, and as we'll demonstrate throughout this book, can create an attractive and aligned proposition in the market.

CSR and translating the United Nations' Sustainable Development Goals

When we talk about sustainability and CSR, there are many interpretations of corporate social responsibility. As a result, aligning an organization's CSR goals with wider global sustainable goals not only makes sense from the point of us all pulling together in the right direction as a collective, but also provides a practical framework to determine areas of focus and priority. The United Nations' Sustainable Development Goals (SDGs) have set out 17 goals to 'transform our world', with targets set for 2030. These goals provide organizations with a comprehensive framework, covering a broad spectrum of issues aligned with global sustainable development, from which to align CSR activity. Whilst each goal has its own objectives and targets (and more specific detail on each one can be found via www.UN.org), the titles of the 17 goals are pretty self-explanatory:

1) no poverty;
2) zero hunger;
3) good health and well-being;
4) quality education;
5) gender equality;
6) clean water and sanitation;
7) affordable and clean energy;
8) decent work and economic growth;
9) industry innovation and infrastructure;
10) reduced inequalities;
11) sustainable cities and communities;
12) responsible consumption and production;
13) climate action;
14) life below water;
15) life on land;

16) peace, justice and strong institutions;

17) partnerships for the goals.

Research from PricewaterhouseCoopers (PwC) found that 71 per cent of businesses surveyed planned to develop measures to meet the SDGs, and that 78 per cent of consumers stated that they would be more likely to make a purchase of goods or services from organizations that have formally committed to the SDGs. When it comes to CSR, many organizations choose perhaps one or a few areas to focus on and develop specific targets – and from a practical perspective you can understand why, as there are some significant issues to address. However, PwC advises against cutting corners, and states that by only committing to a fraction of the SDGs, organizations demonstrate to consumers that their support for sustainable development is superficial, and is more likely to be interpreted as a self-interested PR campaign rather than a genuine reflection of the company's brand and values (Preston and Scott, 2015).

1.3 Things that need to be acknowledged as not perfect

Schemes, schemes and more damned schemes

So far, we've mentioned just two of the key frameworks aligned with organizations and sustainability: CSR and the SDGs. However, within each of the 17 SDGs there are often numerous associations and specialized agencies championing and designing their own frameworks and targets around individual goals. For example, the United Nations Industrial Development Organization (UNIDO) is the specialized agency of the United Nations that promotes industrial development for poverty reduction, inclusive globalization and environmental sustainability (www.unido.org). As of 1 April 2019, UNIDO is made up of 170 member states, which regularly discuss and decide UNIDO's guiding principles and policymaking to promote and accelerate inclusive and sustainable industrial development in member states, taking an integrated approach towards meeting the 2030 SDGs. UNIDO have CSR centres and run CSR research, projects and programmes supporting governments and organizations, including small- and medium-sized enterprises (SMEs), around the world with implementation. For a full picture of all that CSR encapsulates, UNIDO's CSR Framework (*see* Figure 1) showcases the business as the nucleus, sometimes referred to as the 'consciousness' of the business, and then the range of direct stakeholders, and the wider economic, social and environmental responsibilities.

Within Figure 1 there are 24 key elements to consider – each of which could be broken down even further and each of which has its own set of complexities, targets and frameworks. For example, let's take the thorny topic of diversity; this one element alone covers activities

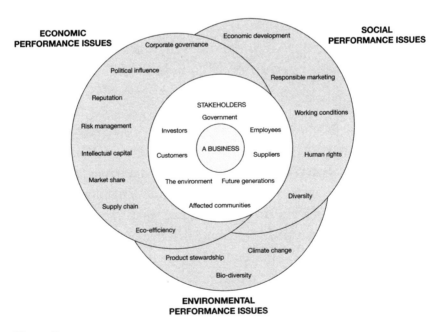

Figure 1

pertaining to gender, race, ethnicity, socio-economic status, physical abilities, religious beliefs and political beliefs, to name but a few.

Throughout this book we will reference a wide range of associations, groups, bodies and frameworks – the Paris Agreement, the Ellen MacArthur Foundation's 'Pledge', the World Health Organization's guidance, the World Wide Fund for Nature (WWF) and many other global and local associations aligned with plastic, energy, packaging and climate change. All are worthy and relevant but illuminate a key challenge as regards the clarification and simplicity of target setting, measurement and, importantly, accountability. As we conclude consistently, whilst there are numerous 'schemes', there are also significant challenges in finding a central point of reference, and this creates disparity and challenge and enables organizations to interpret guidance in ways that don't necessarily align with the 'triple bottom line': people, profits and planet.

The concept that companies might be using sustainability as a smokescreen for irresponsible behaviour has been given names such as 'greenwashing', 'social washing' and 'blue washing' – describing the idea that action is misleadingly reported and overhyped. Whether we agree or disagree with these types of arguments against corporate responsibility, their relevance for companies and their marketing teams cannot be ignored.

We're all in this together

It's also worth noting at the outset of this book that the word 'corporate' has the obvious connotation of being related to larger private sector businesses, typically owned by shareholders and run by managers. However, the principles we discuss in relation to CSR and profit with purpose are equally appropriate to SMEs, and also to the public sector, the third sector, NGOs and charities. It can be argued that larger companies are more visible due to their size and therefore also more vulnerable to public criticism than smaller ones and, indeed, research conducted with a variety of stakeholders often suggests that they mistrust the motivation of businesses that engage in a debate about corporate responsibility, and question the credibility of their social and environmental reporting (Mohr et al, 2001; Kolk, 2008; Pomering and Dolnicar, 2009). The negative accusations concerning CSR are perhaps understandable in some context – no company or individual can ever be perfect. However (and you won't be too surprised to read this!), we feel strongly that, regardless of the challenges, the myriad schemes and associated complexities, creating objectives that place positivity and sustainable proactivity at the fore is key to the growth – and, in some cases, survival – of business as well as the planet we all live on. And understanding some of the less-than-perfect aspects of the views of CSR and the nuances of the different schemes and complexities with regards to target setting is also essential for marketers to recognize and use in their own strategy, as there will be common objections and barriers to progress. Awareness and education from a marketer's perspective is key.

Throughout this book we'll shine a light on organizations – some deemed as 'pioneers' in the sustainable marketing landscape, and others that are setting out with sustainability at the heart of everything they do. Regardless of whether there's a long-term heritage of sustainable practice or they're just starting out, they are organizations stepping up to the challenge of navigating their way through the bureaucracy of the 'schemes and targets', taking action and, importantly, leading with a people, profit and planet focus.

1.4 Case study – Ben & Jerry's

Ben & Jerry's can be seen as a pioneer in many areas of corporate responsibility. The ice-cream brand opened its first shop in Vermont, USA, in 1981 and went public in 1984. As well as wanting to make excellent ice cream, the founders were also determined to build a company that gave back to its community and its stakeholders. In the process of establishing Ben & Jerry's as the global brand it is today, the company's two co-founders, Ben Cohen and Jerry Greenfield, have also repeatedly set the standard in defining what a responsible employer and company can be: for example, Ben & Jerry's was the first major corporation to allow an independent social audit of its business operations way back in 1989 – long before such activity became more of a norm.

In addition to various initiatives focused on treating their employees well – including events hosted by its 'Joy Gang' ('2006 Social & Environmental Assessment Report'), a team responsible for supporting its employee-first culture – the company also put a very early emphasis on using Fairtrade, non-GMO ingredients and investing time and money in social mission causes and improving the environment. Greenfield has been quoted about this philosophy on business: 'Businesses can lead with their values and make money, too. You don't have to simply be purely profit-driven. You can integrate social and environmental concerns into a business, be a caring business, be a generous business, and still do very well financially.' (Petrone, 2015)

The company also retains an independent board of directors ('The B.O.D.') to act as a governing body that is empowered to ensure that the company's social mission is supported through their role to 'protect and defend Ben & Jerry's brand equity and integrity and product quality', and also make sure 'entry level folks come into the company making a livable wage'.

Despite its ownership now by global giant Unilever, Ben & Jerry's has continued to base much of its strategy on placing stakeholder concerns at the heart of its business model. This is reflected in the firm's mission statement to this day, and clearly demonstrates it is holding true to its original brand values:

Ben & Jerry's mission statement

Ben & Jerry's operates on a three-part mission that aims to create linked prosperity for everyone that's connected to our business: suppliers, employees, farmers, franchisees, customers and neighbours alike.

Product mission: to make, distribute and sell the finest quality all-natural ice cream and euphoric concoctions with a continued commitment to incorporating wholesome, natural ingredients and promoting business practices that respect the Earth and the environment.

Economic mission: to operate the company on a sustainable financial basis of profitable growth, increasing value for our stakeholders and expanding opportunities for development and career growth for our employees.

Social mission: to operate the company in a way that actively recognizes the central role that business plays in society by initiating innovative ways to improve the quality of life locally, nationally and internationally.

(Ben & Jerry's, 'Our Values' 2020)

We feel this mission statement is a fantastic articulation of what a fully realized corporate responsibility strategy can be. Crucially it is also then actively used in planning: 'it guides our decision making ... with a continued commitment to incorporating wholesome, natural ingredients and promoting business practices that respect the Earth and the environment' ('How We Do Business', 2020). Through this strategy, Ben & Jerry's stays true to its brand and goal, which authentically shine through as part of the DNA of the company, internally and externally.

1.5 Chapter summary

In this chapter we have discussed the role and relevance of brand and reputation, and its inextricable link to developing a corporate responsibility strategy in your business. Although different pressures apply to various organizational context, it is clear that its active management is essential in any business.

We have broadened the view to consider how CSR initiatives need to align with the wider work around sustainability as part of SDG goals, and the practicalities and indeed challenges of aligning measurable activities. Whilst we've explored how sustainability performance can be measured across environmental, economic and social domains, this is a theme that we will continue to explore in further detail throughout the rest of the chapters, alongside topics such as the challenges and complexities of the multitude of schemes, reporting structures, performance measurement, benchmarketing and accountability.

The key outcome from this chapter should be for you to begin your journey towards more sustainable marketing practice by developing a clearer understanding of its wider business role – and hopefully be enthused by the profits-with-purpose efforts of pioneers such as Ben & Jerry's (and other examples we will share with you throughout this book). We recognize this path is not a simple one and a key part of effective implementation will require balance; there will be sometimes seemingly conflicting positions and responsibilities arising out of how your company has 'always done it'. You may – OK, probably will – be met with cynicism at times, as well as having to face colleagues who will struggle to see the value in being more sustainable. Many will consider it a 'lost cause' and believe that anything you do will not have an impact. However, as we will consistently demonstrate, this could not be further from the truth. However, we will continue to fully acknowledge the good and bad parts of the sustainable marketing practices on which we offer perspectives. Ultimately, our companies, by producing products and services, will always have an environmental impact. Such impacts may often be hidden and surprising, but equally there are significant ways in which you and your company will be able to contribute towards a more sustainable stance.

To support you in achieving this, at the end of each chapter we offer practical actions you can undertake to begin to use sustainability as a source of competitive advantage. These are designed to help you actively embed sustainability in your marketing plan and day-to-day activity, and ultimately support your company in becoming a truly 'authentic' brand in the market.

The key takeaway we hope you have is that making a difference with the company you are working for is the right thing to do. Whether you work in, or lead, a company in the private, public or non-profit sectors, sustainability relates to many different arenas of your marketing and company activity. This can be an internal perspective of how people interact and are treated in the workplace; how your business recognizes and contributes to its local community and the wider marketplace you operate in; or how you create a framework to ensure that your performance in social, environmental and economic domains is maximized.

You're not on your own – we are well and truly with you on this journey.

1.6 Action points to consider

As Chapter 1 has focused on background perspectives, the suggested actions we have for you centre around understanding where you and your company are right now, and how your reputation, based on your actions, might be perceived. Try these activities to get started:

No.	Action	Considerations	Next step
1	Review your company's current publicly stated CR/CSR position (whether it is in annual reports etc).	What areas does your company focus on? What does it not mention?	Write down three areas in which your company is making good progress – and three in which it is not.
2	Review your competitors' current CR/CSR positions.	How do you differ? Is there anything you can learn from – or seek not to do?!	Write down a key observation from each of your competitors that warrants further investigation or an issue in your own business that this work has highlighted you need to address.
3	Put yourself in your customers' shoes – what would they think about your current reputation?	Would your customers consider you to be an ethical brand? Would they be aware of your impact on the environment?	Do a simple SWOT analysis of your company's current position from a customer perspective. What are your strengths and weaknesses from their perspective? Where do you have opportunity to do more? What threats do you see?
4	How is CR/CSR reflected in your internal culture?	What initiatives do you have internally that reflect your publicly stated strategy?	Write down three initiatives that would really improve your company's working environment.
5	Are you clear on the UN's SDGs, the Paris Agreement and the Ellen MacArthur Foundation's 'Pledge'?	Can you develop a deeper awareness of and education about what's expected regarding key targets and challenges?	Start researching the wider concepts and target sustainable goals. Run a quick audit internally to understand awareness of these from your colleagues and leadership team. Commit to developing an awareness communication.
6	What would be your equivalent of Ben & Jerry's three missions?	What would your product, social and economic mission be in your ideal view?	Write down draft versions of your company's new mission in the three areas.

1.7 Chapter 1 references

Aaker, D. A. (1991) *Managing Brand Equity: Capitalizing on the Value of a Brand Name*. San Francisco: Free Press

Ben & Jerry's (2020) 'How We Do Business'. Available at: https://www.benjerry.co.uk/values/how-we-do-business (Accessed: 28 June 2020)

Ben & Jerry's (2006) '2006 Social & Environmental Assessment Report'. Available at: https://www.benjerry.com/about-us/sear-reports/2006-sear-report (Accessed: 9 August 2020)

Blowfield, M. and Frynas, J. G. (2005), Editorial: 'Setting new agendas: critical perspectives on Corporate Social Responsibility in the developing world'. *International Affairs*, 81: 499–513. doi:10.1111/j.1468-2346.2005.00465.x

Dall'Olmo Riley, F. & de Chernatony, L. (2000) 'The service brand as relationships builder'.
British Journal of Management, 11 (2), 137–50

De Chernatony, L., McDonald, M. and Wallace, E. (2010). *Creating Powerful Brands: Fourth Edition*. A Butterworth-Heinemann Title

Ettenson, R. & Knowles, J. (2008) 'Don't confuse reputation with brand'. *MIT Sloan Management Review*, 49 (2), 19–21

Fombrun, C. J. (1996) *Reputation: Realizing Value from the Corporate Image*. Boston: Harvard Business School Press

Griffith, W. (2019). 'Every Minute Online Is a Battle for Consumer Attention'. Available at: https://www.entrepreneur.com/article/330726 (Accessed: 28 April 2020)

GivingForce.com (2018). 'Why you should align your CSR with the UN's Sustainable Development Goals'. Available at: https://www.givingforce.com/sustainabledevelopmentgoals/ (Accessed: 21 May 2020)

Holland, T. (2017). 'What Is Branding? A Brief History'. Available at: https://www.skyword.com/contentstandard/branding-brief-history/ (Accessed: 28 May 2020)

Kline, M. (2018). 'How to Drive Profits with Corporate Social Responsibility'. Available at: https://www.inc.com/maureen-kline/how-to-drive-profits-with-corporate-social-responsibility.html (Accessed: 28 May 2020)

Kolk, A. (2008). 'Sustainability, accountability and corporate governance: Exploring multinationals' reporting practices'. *Business Strategy and the Environment*, 17 (1) (2008), pp. 1–15

Margolis, J. D., & Walsh, J. P. (2003). 'Misery loves companies: Rethinking social initiatives by business'. *Administrative Science Quarterly*, 48(2), 268–305

Mohr, L. A. & Webb, D. J. & Harris, K. E. (2001). 'Do consumers expect companies to be socially responsible? The impact of corporate social responsibility on buying behavior'. *Journal of Consumer Affairs*, 35. 45–72

Preston, M. and Scott, L. (2015). 'Make it your business: Engaging with the Sustainable Development Goals'. PwC. Available at: https://www.pwc.com/gx/en/sustainability/SDG/SDG%20Research_FINAL.pdf (Accessed: 21 May 2020)

Petrone, P. (2015). 'Ben & Jerry's Employer Brand Recipe: It's About More Than Just the (Cookie) Dough'. Available at: https://business.linkedin.com/talent-solutions/blog/2015/06/ben-jerrys-employer-brand-recipe-its-about-more-than-just-the-cookie-dough (Accessed: 28 April 2020)

Pomering, A., & Johnson, L. W. (2009). 'Advertising corporate social responsibility initiatives to communicate corporate image: Inhibiting scepticism to enhance persuasion'. *Corporate Communications: an International Journal*, 14(4), 420–439

Porter, M. E. and Kramer M. R. (2011). 'Creating Shared Value'. *Harvard Business Review*, Vol. 89, No. 1, 2011, pp. 2–17

Stankevich, A. (2017). 'Explaining the Consumer Decision-Making Process: Critical Literature Review'. *Journal of International Business Research and Marketing Volume 2, Issue 6*, 2017. Available at: https://researchleap.com/wp-content/uploads/2017/10/01_Explaining-the-Consumer-Decision-Making-Process.pdf (Accessed: 28 May 2020)

CHAPTER TWO

Sustainability and Leadership

2.0 Chapter introduction

'Today, more than ever, the world needs leadership in environmental sustainability'.

Kevin Johnson, CEO, Starbucks (Cuff, M., 2020)

When it comes to a writing a book about marketing sustainability within and across organizations, there's no escaping the fundamental role that leadership plays. If there is buy-in and commitment from 'the top', then the task of bringing about sustainable change being championed and driven from the front, is undoubtedly going to make the task easier.

Over recent years, there have been a number of pledges made by senior leaders and CEOs around the globe committing to effect change. In 1992, the Rio Earth Summit saw 130 leaders come together to discuss key environmental challenges. In 2016, 195 world leaders signed the Paris Agreement, an agreement within the United Nations Framework Convention on Climate Change (UNFCCC) dealing with greenhouse gas emissions mitigation, adaptation and finance. More recently, in October 2019, almost 200 CEOs from some of the leading US organizations came together as part of Business Roundtable to make a pledge to move away from being purely focused on serving shareholders and maximizing profits to rather focus endeavours on investing in employees, delivering value to customers, dealing ethically with suppliers and supporting outside communities. This represents an important step change towards the triple bottom line, sometimes referred to as the three Ps: people, purpose and planet.

As mentioned in our introduction, there are a number of factors driving this change of heart. Organizations that have focused attention on the triple bottom line are now seeing and reporting tangible financial benefits – and so organizations are waking up to the realities of how a focus on profit with purpose is having a positive impact on both the planet and the bottom line. And as we'll explore, there's a growing collective pressure from a more conscious consumer base, too, provoking and expecting leaders and organizations to take a stand. Climate change in particular has become a matter of global urgency, hotly discussed and predicted to be high up on the majority of boardroom agendas throughout the coming years.

In this chapter, we'll look specifically at the role leadership plays in successfully marketing sustainability. We'll draw on case studies from inspirational leaders from a variety of organizations that focus on leading with purpose. We'll dig into the practicalities of what it takes to be a sustainable leader and consider leadership responsibility and accountability. Whether you're the leader at the top, someone who has been tasked with educating the board, the person responsible for leading sustainability within your organization, or a responsible marketer frustrated by the pace of change within your organization with an appetite to better educate your organization about what they can be doing to make real change, our focus is to arm with you enough advice, facts, inspiration and insights to both inspire and challenge you.

2.1 Where are we?

Whether you think it is a good thing, or a bad thing, CEO activism is a real thing!

There are an increasing number of CEOs taking a stand on political and social issues. Their view is that a company should have a higher purpose beyond maximizing shareholder value, and that they can use their position of power as a force for raising awareness and doing good. Marc Benioff, CEO of Salesforce, has written extensively on the topic. In his latest book, *Trailblazer – The Power of Business as the Greatest Platform for Change* (Benioff, M., 2019. Currency), he tells the story of how he founded Salesforce with a clear sense of purpose, and from inception built in a pledge that 1 per cent of profits would go towards doing good. He is quoted in *Time* magazine, (Steinmetz, K 2016) as saying: '... today CEOs need to stand up not just for their shareholders, but their employees, their customers, their partners, the community, the environment, schools, everybody.' In effect, this stance is one of taking responsibility not only for the organization and direct shareholders, but for wider societal communities too.

Benioff is far from alone in holding those views. Jeff Immelt, the former CEO of General Electric, has said: 'I just think it's insincere to not stand up for those things that you believe in. We're also stewards of our companies, we're representatives of the people that work with us and I think we're cowards if we don't take a position occasionally on those things that are really consistent with what our mission is and where our people "stand"' (Chatterji, A.K. Toffel, M.W.).

Patagonia is an organization that has long been at the forefront of the profit with purpose movement. Since its inception, Patagonia has donated 1 per cent of sales to environmental non-profit organizations, and in 2016 it gave 100 hundred per cent of Black Friday sales (approximately $10 million) to environmental groups.

Beyond funding, there's also education. Patagonia consult with private and large public companies on best practices for reducing production and packaging waste, lowering greenhouse gas emissions and using innovative technologies – e.g. turning recycled bottles into polyester. In 2009, it partnered with Walmart to create a Sustainable Apparel

Coalition (www.apparelcoalition.org), an industry collaboration transforming the apparel, footwear and textile industry. Members – including Nike, Gap and Adidas – are committed to measuring and improving social and environmental sustainability impact. One of the coalition's founders, Yvon Chouinard, has championed Patagonia to be a catalyst for lasting change and since 1985 Patagonia is reported to have donated more than $100 million to environmental causes. Furthermore, in 2013 it launched a venture capital fund that invests in start-ups that focus on environmental issues.

Until recently led by CEO Rose Marcario, Patagonia has stepped up its environmental focus even more, with a commitment to finding solutions to the environmental crisis and changing the face of capitalism. To share the intent and transparency of its commitment, in 2018 it changed its mission statement to: 'We're in business to save our home planet'. In her article in *Time* magazine in 2019, Marcario stated: 'Everyone that I work with, from CEOs of big public companies to private companies, recognize that things need to change. And capitalism needs to evolve if we're going to have a healthy planet and we're going to have healthy people on the planet. Today's customers want their dollars to go to companies that will use their money to make the world a better place. Companies are realising that their customers and their employees expect them to take a stand' (Semuels, 2019).

Indeed, when it comes to leaders taking a stand, Patagonia sued President Donald Trump's administration in 2017 after it reduced the size of the Bears Ears National Monument in Utah, claiming the move was illegal. That same year they also successfully led a boycott of the Outdoor Retailer Trade Show in Salt Lake City after Utah's government urged President Trump to make the reduction to the monument. The next year, Patagonia teamed up with Levi's to launch the Time to Vote initiative, which led to 400 companies granting time off so that their employees could go out and vote (Semuels, 2019). More recently, Rose Marcario announced that Patagonia would only take on new corporate clients for customized Patagonia products if the company had a significant sustainability plan as part of its mission (Berger, S. 2019).

These purpose-driven leaders are just a few of the many trailblazing CEOs who are taking on the role of 'activist'. And of course, when they get together, collective action can have a greater impact than companies acting alone. For example, in 2015 the CEOs of 14 major food companies – including Mars, General Mills, Coca-Cola, Unilever, Danone, The Hershey Company, Ben & Jerry's, Kellogg's, PepsiCo and Nestlé – co-signed an open letter calling on government leaders to address the reality of climate change. In 2016, more than 160 CEOs, including those from Apple, Facebook, Salesforce and Google, signed a letter by the Human Rights Campaign opposing a North Carolina bathroom law, which discriminated against the LGBTQ community. The law was repealed. Then, in 2017, 100 CEOs co-signed a brief to overturn an executive order banning citizens from Muslim countries from entering the US.

Another example occurred in August 2019, when Business Roundtable, which since 1978 has periodically issued Principles of Corporate Governance to US corporations, announced the release of a new statement on the 'Purpose of a Corporation'. This was signed by 181 CEOs, each committing to lead their companies for the benefit of not just shareholders, but also all its stakeholders – customers, employees, suppliers and communities (Chatterji and Toffel, 2018).

More leaders seem to be taking a stand and focusing attention on getting back to the basic foundations of what organizations were historically created for: 'social enterprise', supporting their employees, their employees' families and the wider community, often building hospitals, schools and resources for communities and generally contributing to the health, well-being and wealth of society at large.

The CEO of Unilever, Alan Jope, cites purpose as one of the most exciting opportunities he's seen in the industry in his 35 years of marketing. Speaking at the Cannes Lion Festival of Creativity in 2019, he said: 'Done properly, done responsibly, it [leading on purpose] will help restore trust in our industry, unlock greater creativity in our work and grow the brands we love' (Unilever.com).

In that interview, he also showcased that Unilever is disposing of brands that don't stand for something and stated the intent that *every* Unilever brand is to be a brand with purpose. This is a pretty powerful statement to stand by given the number of brands within the Unilever umbrella. However, there's commercial wisdom behind this stance. In that interview, he also explained that the Unilever brands that focus on taking action for people and the planet grew 69 per cent faster than the rest of their business in 2018 – and that's a significant number. From a marketing perspective, Unilever is committed to investing more of its marketing spend on communications that are explicitly purposeful (Vizard, S., 2020). Unilever is finding that leading on purpose is good for growth and profitability. Jope's view is that purpose is a consumer-led phenomenon and consumers hold the key to identifying the right purpose – one that balances the need to do good with commercial gain.

It's interesting, then, to try to understand what's driving this change. Is it that organizations and their leaders have generally become more conscious, the rise of the conscious consumer and consumer activism is driving change, or that leading on purpose is good for business – or a combination of these factors?

2.2 Why do companies need to do something now?

Two professors, Aaron K. Chatterji and Michael W. Toffel, conducted an experiment in 2018 to assess the influence of CEO activism on US consumer behaviour. They asked a nationally representative group of respondents about their intent to buy Apple products in the near future. They randomly arranged the 2,176 respondents into three segments.

They gave a statement to the first segment in which they described CEO Tim Cook's opinion that Indiana's religious freedom bill was discriminatory against LGBTQ individuals. To the second segment, they gave a generic statement about his management philosophy. To the third segment they provided no associated statement about the CEO. What they discovered was that in the segment exposed to the statement about CEO activism there was significantly higher intent to purchase Apple products in the near future than there was in the other two groups. Learning about the CEO's activism also increased intent to purchase amongst supporters of same-sex marriage, but did not impact intent amongst its opponents.

Their results indicated that CEO activism can generate goodwill for the company and drive purchase intent but need not alienate those who disagree with the CEO. Some leaders may feel that they do not understand the issue well enough or may be reluctant to speak out for fear their view may be unpopular. However, as advised by the report from *Harvard Business Review* and the Deloitte Human Capital Research, it's advised the CEOs should expect employees, the media and other parties to question why the CEO has not spoken out, and be ready to explain the rationale. And of course, as more leaders maintain a clear sense of purpose and may choose to speak out on political and social matters, those who appear disengaged are likely to face harsh headlines and negative attention on social media.

Belief-driven buyers

When it comes to deciding upon which brand to align with, belief-driven buyers are those who choose a brand or organization based on its position on social issues. According to Edelman's 'Brands Take a Stand' report (Ries, Bersoff et al, 2018), borne out of a survey of 40,000 consumers, one in two people are now belief-driven buyers, with 67 per cent buying a brand for the first time because of its position on a controversial issue and 65 per cent not buying a brand because it stayed silent on an issue they felt it had an obligation to address. More recently, the '2019 Edelman Trust Barometer Special Report' (Ries, Edelman et al, 2019) showcased that 64 per cent of consumers are now belief-driven buyers, choosing to switch, avoid or boycott a brand based on its stand on societal issues. Consumers expect brands and leaders to act – believing that brands can be a powerful force for change and their wallet is their vote, with ethical drivers proving to be three times more important to engendering trust in a company than competence.

In the '2019 Edelman Trust Barometer Special Report', 75 per cent of consumers stated that they want to buy products that stand with their beliefs and 73 per cent agreed that a company can take actions that both increase profits and improve conditions in the communities in which it operates. And when it comes to changing the face of capitalism, 56 per cent agreed with Patagonia's leader Rose Marcario, asserting that capitalism as it exists today does more harm than good in the world.

The power of the consumer most certainly plays a part and Gen Z (those born between the mid- to late 1990s and the early 2010s) and younger millennials (those born between the early 1980s and the mid- to late 1990s) are leading the way. For the first time in mature markets, young people believe that their lives will be worse than their parents' – and they are actively questioning the core premises of corporate behaviour and the economic and social principles that guide it. Some 86 per cent of millennials think that business success should be measured in terms of more than just financial performance (Agarwal et al, 2018, 'Global Human Capital Trends'). And of course, with millennials currently making up 50 per cent of the workforce around the globe, and predicted to be 75 per cent by 2050 (Hall, M., 2017), their power and influence as hyper-connected individuals will continue to grow.

Research from Weber Shandwick and KRC Research (Polansky, A. et al, 2018), found that a large percentage of millennials, whether employees or customers, believe that CEOs have a responsibility to speak out on political and social issues and stated that CEO activism is a key factor in their purchasing decisions.

Other catalysts driving change

The 'Global Human Capital Trends' report (Agarwal et al, 2018), cites the 2008 financial crisis as being a catalyst to increasing people's expectation that business leaders do more for society. And whilst there's been economic recovery in the world since that time (which may of course have been undone by the coronavirus pandemic), many people continue to feel frustrated that reported financial gains and stability have failed to improve individuals' lives, address social problems and support political stability. People today have less trust in their political and social institutions than they had in previous years and are now turning to the private sector with the expectation that business leaders should fill the void.

Pressure from financial investment is also driving change. In January 2020, BlackRock – the world's largest asset manager, with investment funds valued into the trillions ($7tn in assets) – shook the business world when they advised that they were shifting their investment strategy to focus on sustainable investing. CEO Larry Fink stated that: 'Climate change has become a defining factor in a companies' long-term prospects,' and said in his letter to chief executives: 'I believe we are on the edge of a fundamental reshaping of finance' (Henderson et al, 2020). And BlackRock are not alone in this significant shift in focus. In the same month, BlackRock joined Climate Action 100+ (www.climateaction100.org), a group of 370 asset owners and managers that advocates for environmentally friendly shareholder proposals and pushes companies to align their businesses with the Paris Climate Agreement (Henderson et al, 2020).

From a 'leading on purpose' perspective then, there are a number of drivers:

1) the expectation and pressure of consumers;
2) the fact that purpose is driving growth of products and brands;
3) changes in financial investment and measures of success aligned with responsibility to deliver on goals aligned with improving social and environmental issues in the world.

These drivers are shifting motivation away from historical measures of success dominated purely by financial success and shareholder value.

Measurement and accountability

When it comes to measurement and accountability beyond financial and shareholder value then, what reporting benchmarks around sustainability are in place for leaders?

Globally, the focus on leading with purpose and sustainable leadership aligns with Global Goals (you'll find we mention these a number of times throughout this book). In 2015, 193 governments around the world came together and agreed to 17 Global Goals, creating targets and pledging to make necessary shifts to meet those targets. The goals are officially referred to as Sustainable Development Goals (SDGs). The focus of the goals is to create a better world by 2030. The goals target poverty, fighting inequality and addressing the urgency of climate change.

However, from a leadership perspective, although there are SDG goals in place, there aren't any central reporting mandates or formal stipulated reporting frameworks via governments. Without a central reference point, measurement and assessment of levels of accountability and responsibility is almost impossible.

Nevertheless, many organizations do independently report on social impact. Since 2001, for instance, Starbucks has been publishing an annual 'Global Social Impact Report' (www.starbucks.com/stories/2019/2018-starbucks-global-social-impact-report/). This is one of the longest-running reporting commitments of any public company, which clearly sets out their commitments pertaining to packaging, supply chain, deforestation, waste management and eco store management. However, whilst a good example of transparency, many leading lights in this area are calling for a central framework for measuring adherence and performance aligned with SDG goals. For example, Malcolm Preston, former Global Head of Sustainability Services at PwC, was cited as saying: 'When 193 governments came together to agree and achieve 17 goals tackling major world issues, it only seems sensible that business aligns its strategy and reporting against the same objectives' (Scott and Midgeley, 2020). In addition, Andrew Staines, the UK's deputy ambassador to the United Nations in Geneva, is urging more companies to use the United Nations guidance on core indicators for SDG reporting, to enable organizations to clearly demonstrate their contribution to sustainable development (UNCTAD, October 2019).

To positively support the importance of sustainable investment, and in line with the British government's focus on tackling climate change, new rules enforced in October 2019 mean that pension funds are now required to consider environmental and social factors when making investment decisions. Further, a joint paper between leading pension provider Royal London and law firm Herbert Smith Freehills showcased the growing risk of legal challenge by The Pensions Regulator to trustees and pension providers that fail to take account of Environmental, Social and Governance (ESG) factors, stating: 'ESG is no longer an optional extra for trustees, pension providers and asset managers, it's essential that trustees and providers are able to demonstrate that they are taking ESG factors seriously and that they don't just treat this as a tick-box exercise' (Daniel, 2019). A focus on ESGs is measurably good for business. When financial return is measured alongside ESG levels and aligned with the findings that revealed that organizations that focus on sustainability are performing better financially, research from the same report again showed that companies performed much better financially when they had a higher ESG.

2.3 Things that need to be acknowledged as not perfect

When it comes to the role of the leader and sustainable leadership, leaders need to balance their own values, the organizational values, short-term goals and priorities with long-term goals that embrace a wider focus on improving social and environmental issues in the world. Maintaining financial performance clearly still needs to be a driver, but not the sole driver, with ESGs and SDGs providing new benchmarks for success.

The '2019 Edelman Trust Barometer Special Report' cites that 73 per cent of employees expect to be heard and want the opportunity to shape the future of society; 92 per cent of consumers expect CEOs to speak out on societal issues; and 74 per cent believe that CEOs should take the lead on change rather than waiting for the government to implement it (Ries, Edelman et al, 2019). These shifts mean that leaders are increasingly being held to account by both their employees and their customers. They are expected to be more visible, more transparent, more collaborative and inclusive and display more traits of 'activism' – thereby bringing to light just a few of the skills and competencies required by an effective sustainable leader.

According to the 'Sustainable Leadership: Talent requirements for sustainable enterprises' report (Russell Reynolds Associates, 2019), when it comes to competences, characteristics of successful sustainable leaders include:

- valuing the interests of stakeholders rather than using people for individual gain;
- focusing on long-term goals and not being dissuaded by pressure from parties with different and competing goals, whilst being aware there is no long-term success without short-term delivery;
- inspiring others and working together in the pursuit of a vision – combining doing what they love and loving what they do with being deeply immersed in the world;
- making decisions in uncertain conditions, unhindered by an overload or lack of information;
- demonstrating honest and moral values in both their professional and personal life so that stakeholders see sustainable leaders as role models;
- displaying an unprejudiced attitude towards new ideas and the beliefs of other stakeholders.

Working with people from different backgrounds and cultures is also cited, together with a diverse background and experience of different cultures, living internationally and a thirst for continuous education and learning. We feel that the latter is especially critical, particularly when it comes to navigating the sustainable landscape. Many of the characteristics mentioned align with those we associate with the challenges of leadership today, particularly given that we are living in what is often referred to as a VUCA (volatile, uncertain, complex and ambiguous) world.

The report further cites eight key areas that sustainable leaders should be focusing on:

1) Promoting the company's vision – crafting a long-term strategy that focuses on serving the triple bottom line and developing policies to meet those goals.

2) Operationalizing corporate social responsibility (CSR) – turning policies into actions by integrating them into everyday processes and procedures.

3) Obtaining top management support – getting buy-in for actions that create visibility for and awareness of global responsibility, both inside and outside the company.

4) Engaging diverse stakeholders – aligning cultures and systems to create balanced relationships characterized by reciprocal commitments, responsibilities and benefits.

5) Empowering and developing stakeholders – enhancing the power of individuals to implement CSR, being open to new ideas, providing training activities and challenging assignments, and acting as a coach or mentor.

6) Communicating with stakeholders – actively supporting and developing a culture of shared information amongst stakeholders about corporate sustainability.

7) Measuring performance – holding individuals and groups within the organization accountable for their work through feedback, formal appraisal and reward policies. Helping to ensure accountability amongst external stakeholders through regular reporting and external audits.

8) Setting ethical standards – setting an example to stakeholders, within and outside the organization, by behaving with integrity in both professional and personal life.

However, the report also outlines that the number of leaders with a 'sustainable' focus isn't growing quickly enough, citing two reasons: 1) the demand for and the supply of sustainable business leaders is limited; and 2) most companies are not looking for sustainable business leaders, either explicitly or implicitly. As part of their research, they analysed more than 1,300 position specifications and found that fewer than 5 per cent required candidates to possess any kind of sustainability mindset. Key terms such as 'SDGs', 'climate change', 'social impact' and suchlike hardly ever appear in position specifications in the private sector. And of the clients who do position themselves as sustainable, only

27 per cent require candidates to have a sustainability mindset in some shape or form. Compare this to diversity and digital, where the figures are significantly higher at 50 per cent and 33 per cent respectively.

So why the mismatch? If there's growing concern and demand for leaders to drive sustainability to meet consumer, employee and growing legislative and investment requirements, why are so many leaders hesitant to embrace sustainability?

The report found that many leaders don't feel the intrinsic motivation and even if they do, they are worried about their short-term financial results, career, status and resistance from others. Again, there's a commitment required to long-term measurement and reporting. And this leads us nicely to another key trait: courage.

Courage is an essential trait of a sustainable leader. It takes courage to stand up to investors. It takes courage to make a commitment to doing more than focusing on short-term shareholder profits (as demonstrated by those CEOs who came together around the Business Roundtable). Research by a Harvard Business School senior fellow cites courage as the defining characteristic of great leaders, stating: 'Courageous leaders take risks that go against the grain of their organizations. They make decisions with the potential for revolutionary change in their markets. Their boldness inspires their teams, energises customers, and positions their companies as leaders in societal change' (George, B., 2017). Paul Polman, former CEO at Unilever, is cited as a courageous leader. He has supported the shift to sustainable leadership for years, saying: 'CEOs cannot be slaves to shareholders'. *Harvard Business Review* branded Polman 'Captain Planet' due to his redesign of Unilever's business model to contribute to society and the environment instead of hurting them – a legacy that Polman's successor, Alan Jope, continues (Werft, M., 2018).

From a practical perspective, Carmine Di Sibio, EY global chairman and CEO, calls for leaders to move from ambition to action and to accountability by: 1) engaging your people; 2) measuring and reporting on long-term value; 3) engaging your business community;

and 4) supporting your communities and protecting the environment. His inspirational message to leaders is: 'This is a pivotal moment for business. It's clearer than ever before that success is about more than our bottom line today; it's also about helping those around us thrive in the long term. CEOs don't have to choose any more between doing what's good for business and good for their stakeholders. They can – and must – do both' (Carmine Di Sibio, 2020).

Interview – Sarah Walker-Smith

As part of our research about leadership and sustainability, we interviewed Sarah Walker-Smith, chief executive of leading law firm Shakespeare Martineau. Sarah is a firm believer that business can be both purposeful and profitable at the same time … and that one leads to the other. She told us:

'I increasingly see the need for alignment of people's personal values with their organizations', and their roles having capacity to make a difference in order for them to feel truly happy and fulfilled at work. This isn't just a generational thing although it's increasingly prevalent in people coming into the workforce for the first time. We see it in the questions we are asked before people join, through to the traffic on our digital presence and the activities people want to engage in when they are here. This equally applies to clients who want to work with brands who share at least some of their values and who they are proud to be associated with. For a while now I've referred to this intersection of purpose and commercialism as "good business"; indeed the recent CBI manifesto also alludes to this – they call it a "new kind of inclusive capitalism". Put simply, I believe purpose will enable organizations to remain competitive in an increasingly volatile and competitive market given the changes in social attitudes and demographics.'

What practical challenges have you had to overcome to take a stance on 'profit with purpose'?

'Short-term versus long-term is perhaps the biggest mindset shift. Too many businesses and business commentators react to annual profit cycles rather than trends. Explaining that purpose is commercially essential and not a "fluffy aspiration", ensuring that purpose is shared and more than just generic. And aligning purpose with someone's role, their values and those of the organization – that's where you can use purpose to drive motivation and therefore competitive advantage through people.'

Is there enough pressure on leaders to take a more responsible sustainable approach?

'They shouldn't need pressure. I do worry that the wrong kind of pressure will lead to a superficial response. Business leaders need to see the genuine medium- to long-term business benefits in this to make the response meaningful.'

(The full interview with Sarah Walker-Smith can be found on pp. 282–86).

2.4 Chapter summary

When it comes to being a sustainable leader and leading on purpose, whilst we've demonstrated throughout this chapter that taking a stand to focus on more than just driving shareholder profit is proving to be good for business, that 'purpose' starts at the top, and that the views and values of the leader can and do have a dramatic effect on organizational culture, impact and action around a long-term focus on sustainability, there are challenges – hence sustainability really needs to be an organization-wide responsibility, led from the top. Everyone within the organization needs to work together to make sustainability an essential business model. This means either leading on purpose or, where the leadership team isn't doing enough, others prodding and provoking them to share clarity about organizational values that align with sustainability and SDG goals and, importantly, taking action and being accountable.

Here are some useful questions to put to yourself as a leader or to your leadership team.

Leaders

- Are you clear about your purpose and if so, does it include alignment with the triple bottom line?
- Is your organizational purpose clear?
- Are purpose, vision and values clearly communicated across the organization? And importantly, what level of accountability against them is in place?
- Are people drawn to work for your organization to be part of something that's making a difference?
- What CSR activities are in place?
- Is your CSR activity a tick-box exercise or is activity genuinely aligned with SDGs and making an impact?
- Are you aware of and clear about the SDGs?
- What actions have you taken to enable your organization to achieve SDG targets?
- Which SDGs are you most concerned about and on which ones could you be most influential?
- Does your reporting include tracking development of SDG targets?
- If there were no barriers to implementation, which SDG targets would you like to invest the remainder of your career pursuing?
- What is your personal sense of purpose?
- What differences have you made so far?

- What difficulties have you faced and how have your dealt with them?
- As the leader of an organization, what are you doing to communicate your organizational values, and how easy and accessible are they for employees and customers to engage with?
- How important is it for you as a leader that your personal sense of purpose aligns with organizational values?
- Do you see yourself as a CEO activist?
- How are you researching the views and values of your customers and your employees?

For those championing sustainable leadership

- What is your personal sense of purpose?
- How does your leader stack up against the stance of your competitors when it comes to leadership sustainability?
- How are you researching the views of your customers?
- Do you do any customer research into views and values that align with organizational purpose?
- Ask yourself many of the questions above, too – they are equally as applicable.

2.5 Action points to consider

Chapter 2 has focused on the perspective of leadership in sustainability, and the suggested actions we have outlined encourage you to ask questions and drive action. Here are some suggested actions:

No.	Action	Considerations	Next Step
1	Explore SDGs in more detail.	Where are your knowledge gaps when it comes to SDGs and how do they apply to your company? Make a list of what more you need to be doing, prioritize them and then take courageous steps to drive change.	Make one target a commitment to continuously learn.
2	Develop a sustainability action group.	Identify those within the organization who are driven to make change aligned with SDGs, collaborating and sharing responsibility, and who have a sense of purpose across the organization.	Set clear targets and accountability and work as a collective task force.
3	Review your reporting model	How are you reporting on sustainability and SDGs now?	Consider how to embed SDG targets into your reporting.
4	Research best practice.	Look at practice by other organizations in your industry, and further afield.	What are three practical lessons you can apply to your business based on what others are doing?
5	Create or join a leadership best practice task force.	Find ways to collaborate with other leaders from other organizations to share best practice and continuous learning.	Reach out to three people on LinkedIn whom you respect in the area of SDG and invite them to join a call to discuss the issue.

And we'll leave this chapter with the wise words often attributed to Gandhi, but formally credited to Arleen Lorrance (Lorrance, A. 1974): '*Be the change you want to see in the world*'.

2.6 Chapter 2 references

Agarwal D., Bersin J., Lahir G., (2018). 'The rise of the social enterprise, 2018 Deloitte Global Human Capital Trends'. Deloitte. Available at: https://www2.deloitte.com/content/dam/insights/us/articles/ HCTrends2018/2018-HCtrends_Rise-of-the-social-enterprise.pdf (Accessed: 28 April 2020)

Berger, S. (2019). 'Silicon Valley, Wall Street set may need a new favorite uniform as Patagonia shifts policy on its famous fleece'. CNBC. Available at: https://www.cnbc.com/2019/04/03/patagonia-shifts-policy-on-co-branded-products-silicon-valley-loves.html (Accessed: 28 April 2020)

Bloomgarden, K. (2019). 'How Purpose-Driven Companies Address Business's Greatest Challenges'. Fortune.com. Available at: https://fortune.com/2019/06/19/purpose-driven-companies-ceo-initiative (Accessed: 28 April 2020)

Chatterji, A. and Toffel, M. (2018). 'The New CEO Activists'. *Harvard Business Review.* Available at: https://hbr.org/2018/01/the-new-ceo-activists (Accessed: 28 April 2020)

Cuff, M. (2020). 'The World Needs Leadership: Starbucks pledges to become "resource positive"'. Available at: https://www.businessgreen.com/news-analysis/3085105/starbucks-pledges-to-become-resource-positive (Accessed: 20 May 2020)

Daniel, A. (2019). 'More Companies Urged to report how they help meet SDGs'. United Nations Conference on Trade and Development (UNCTAD). Available at: https://unctad.org/en/pages/newsdetails. aspx?OriginalVersionID=2223 (Accessed: 28 April 2020)

Di Sibio, C. (2020). 'Four actions business leaders can take now to embrace long term value creation'. EY.com. Available at: https://www.ey.com/en_gl/wef/ four-actions-business-leaders-can-take-now-to-embrace-long-term-value-creation (Accessed: 28 April 2020)

George, B. (2017). Op-Ed: Courage: The Defining Characteristic of Great Leaders, Harvard Business School. (Accessed: 29 June 2020)

Hall, M. (2017). 'What the Ideal Workplace of the Future Looks Like According to Millennials'. Available at: https://www.forbes.com/sites/markhall/2017/11/08/what-the-ideal-workplace-of-the-future-looks-like-according-to-Millennials/#1ceb78bc4228Millennials/ (Accessed: 29 June 2020)

Henderson, R., Nauman, B. and Edgecliffe-Johnson, A. (2020). 'BlackRock shakes up business to focus on sustainable investing'. *Financial Times.* Available at: https://www.ft.com/content/57db9dc2-3690-11ea-a6d3-9a26f8c3cba4 (Accessed: 28 April 2020)

Lee, M. and York, B. (2019). 'The 2019 GlobeScan/SustainAbility Leaders Survey'. GlobeScan. Available at: https://globescan.com/unilever-patagonia-ikea-sustainability-leadership-2019/ (Accessed: 28 April 2020)

Livingstone, S. (2019). 'What Brand Purpose Really Means & Why It Matters'. Available at: https://blog.globalwebindex.com/marketing/brand-purpose/ (Accessed: 28 April 2020)

Lorrance, A. (1974). Quote Investigator https://quoteinvestigator.com/2017/10/23/be-change/ (Accessed: 6 July 2020)

Oligschlaeger, A. (2019). 'Rise of the Conscious Consumer'. Available at: https://www.walnutunlimited.com/rise-of-the-conscious-consumer (Accessed: 28 April 2020)

Polansky, A., Richards, M., Heimann G. et al (2018). 'CEO Activism Inside Comms and Marketing'. Weber Shandwick and KRC Research. Available at: https://www.webershandwick.com/wp-content/uploads/2019/01/CEO-Activism-Inside-Comms-and-Marketing.pdf (Accessed: 29 June 2020)

Ries, T. et al '2019 Edelman Trust Barometer: In Brands We Trust?'. Available at: https://www.edelman.com/sites/g/files/aatuss191/files/2019-06/2019_edelman_trust_barometer_special_report_in_brands_we_trust.pdf (Accessed: 29 June 2020)

Ries, T., Bersoff, D. M. et al (2018). 'Brands Take a Stand Report'. Available at: https://www.edelman.com/sites/g/files/aatuss191/files/2019-07/2019_edelman_trust_barometer_special_report_in_brands_we_trust.pdf (Accessed: 28 April 2020)

Russell Reynolds Associates (2016). 'Sustainable leadership: Talent requirements for sustainable enterprises'. Available at: https://www.russellreynolds.com/insights/thought-leadership/sustainable-leadership-talent-requirements-for-sustainable-enterprises (Accessed: 28 April 2020)

Russell Reynolds Associates (2018). 'Call to Action: Accelerating Sustainable Business Leadership Report'. Available at: https://www.russellreynolds.com/insights/thought-leadership/call-to-action-accelerating-sustainable-business-leadership (Accessed: 28 April 2020)

Semuels, A. (2019). 'Patagonia Is Climbing to the Top – and Reimagining Capitalism Along the Way'. Available at: https://time.com/5684011/patagonia/ (Accessed: 28 April 2020)

Steinmetz, K. (2016). *Time*. 'Salesforce CEO Marc Benioff: "Anti-LGBT Bills are Anti-Business"'

Sustainable Apparel Coalition (2020). Available at: www.apparelcoalition.org/ (Accessed: 28 April 2020)

Vizard, S. (2020). 'Unilever doubles down on purpose'. Available at: https://www.i-com.org/news-articles/unilever-doubles-down-on-purpose-we-know-it-drives-short-and-long-term-growth (Accessed: 20 May 2020)

Werft, M. (2018). '10 Reasons the world needs sustainable leadership'. Global Citizen. Available at: https://www.globalcitizen.org/en/content/0-reasons-the-world-needs-sustainable-leadership/ (Accessed: 28 April 2020)

CHAPTER THREE

The Importance of Stakeholder Engagement

3.0 Chapter introduction

Over the last two decades, the definition of a stakeholder has evolved as business has evolved from the traditional definition: 'Any group or individual who can affect or is affected by the achievement of the organization's objectives' (Freeman, E., 1984) to: 'A person such as an employee, customer, or citizen who is involved with an organization, society, etc. and therefore has responsibilities towards it and an interest in its success (Cambridge Dictionary, 2020). Whilst certain traits of stakeholders remain consistent – such as stakeholders all have an interest or impact on an organization's performance – other areas have evolved. For example, the range of those who are included or recognized has become broader and the increase in focus on sustainability means accountability now sits not just with internal stakeholders but also external ones.

3.1 Where are we? Stakeholders – the shift

We have seen a significant shift in stakeholder behaviour and in the engagement and impact they are having on the chain. Societal and environmental factors play a large part in this. The start of 2016 saw the UN Sustainable Development Goals (SDGs) come into force following buy-in from world leaders in September 2015. It states in the

2030 Agenda for Sustainable Development that: 'They are integrated and indivisible and balance the three dimensions of sustainable development: the economic, social and environmental' ('Transforming our world: the 2030 Agenda for Sustainable Development', United Nations General Assembly, 2015). And, as discussed in the previous chapter, further commitments were made in August 2019 when 181 CEOs recognized and agreed to a fundamental commitment to all stakeholders, signing a statement at Business Roundtable that spoke of delivering value to all (not just shareholders) to ensure the future success of their companies, the communities and their countries.

Sustainability is extremely complex due to the number of interconnected challenges that need to be understood and addressed. Nothing can be fixed in isolation and it will take a global effort, as shown by the UN SDGs, across multiple systems, people, companies and society in general in order to effect change. Effective engagement (which is a core part of marketing) is essential if an organization is to succeed in its financial, social and environmental aims.

Organizations are increasingly being seen as the leading driver of change when it comes to sustainable development. There has been a growing move from shareholder capitalism, which focuses primarily on the shareholders, to stakeholder capitalism, which serves the interest of all stakeholders, including employees, customers, communities and the environment. Research and data also show that companies that serve the interest of all stakeholders generate better returns and results across their various stakeholders. There are many examples of organizations today that serve the interests of all stakeholders, some of the larger ones of which include Starbucks, Apple and JP Morgan.

Investors

If we go down the stakeholder chain and look at some of the significant shifts then we should start with investors. Sustainable investments are not new. However, as the focus on the environment increases and the impact becomes more critical, there has been an increasing shift in the investment chain towards longer-term investments and sustainability. Significant global announcements hit the headlines in 2020, including one by the founder of BlackRock announcing in January 2020 in an open letter that: 'BlackRock had a number of initiatives to place sustainability at the centre of their investment approach'. He also stated that: 'climate risk is investment risk' (Fink, L. 2020), sparking debate and discussion that investors have no choice but to take sustainability seriously.

Global networks such as the Investment Leaders Group (ILG) facilitated by the Cambridge Institute for Sustainability Leadership (CISL) are working with investors and multiple organizations. Their vision is 'an investment chain in which economic, social and environmental sustainability are delivered as an outcome of the investment process and as investors go about generating robust, long-term returns' (https://www.cisl.cam.ac.uk, 2020). They, like other networks, want to deliver positive outcomes in line with the UN SDGs. In their work to support investors, the ILG launched an Investment Impact Framework in 2019 ('In Search of Impact', 2019), which translates the SDGs into measurable indicators that are calculable and easily understood and implementable by investors. Networks such as the IGL are crucial in enabling investors to make informed choices when it comes to their investments.

The growing movement we are seeing is investors wanting to know where their money is going and what companies are really doing when it comes to sustainability. It is no longer enough to treat sustainability as a tick-box exercise; ESG investing and socially responsible investing (SRI) are now under more scrutiny. If companies are to prove to investors that they are serious about sustainability, they need to have a clearly defined understanding of the issues and an action plan that supports and delivers against it.

Consumers

Another significant shift in the stakeholder chain is the impact and growing voice of consumers. With public interest in the environmental and societal issues we face increasing, so does their influence, and this affects all parts of the stakeholder chain. We are all more informed than ever and the rise in conscious consumerism enabled by advancements in technology, unlimited access to information, and the growth of social media cannot be ignored. We live in a fully connected world where conversations are happening all the time. It's no longer about just hearing what brands want to tell you. As previously mentioned, 75 per cent of the public are consciously modifying their behaviour when it comes to consumer items (Oligschlaeger A., 2019). Knowledge that informs your decisions comes in many forms, from social media conversations to effective labelling, but often it's those around us who are the most influential. According to the Brandwatch Consumer Trends report for 2020, the top factor when making a purchasing decision is hearing about experiences from your friends, family or colleagues (33 per cent).

Marketing has been defined as 'the social process by which individuals and organizations obtain what they need and want through creating and exchanging value with others' (Kotler P., 2010). Never more so than now are we seeing the value exchange with consumers becoming the top priority for organizations. Start-ups and disruptors such as Monzo are a great example of brands working directly with their customers. Monzo's aim is simple – build a better bank – and in 2018 they launched Monzo Labs, a place where they share their product roadmaps and new features and allow customers early access. Customers then share their feedback and any ideas, enabling Monzo to build a bank with the help of customers, based directly on their needs. Monzo states that: 'community is at the core of everything we do. And as we grow, we want to make sure more and more of you can be part of it' (www.monzo.com, 2020). By putting consumers at the core, they can not only find out what they want, but by the very nature of the connected, conscious consumer, they know that their customers will naturally become advocates, which in turn leads to more customers. They let their customers do the talking for them and with more consumers now basing their purchasing decisions on how much value a brand gives them and the wider environmental and social impacts associated with the product or the values of the organization, not prioritizing consumers in the stakeholder chain will impact the business long term.

Employees

It's a fact that people want to work for organizations that have a strong social conscience and a sense of environmental responsibility. They want to work for organizations that match their own values, make them feel motivated and, most importantly, feel like they are contributing and making a difference. Workplace culture as it is commonly called is high up on the agenda. ('Human resources' is not a departmental name you hear as much these days – HR has been renamed or rebranded in many organizations, using words such as 'people', 'engagement', 'talent' and 'workplace', which are more inclusive and, well, more human.) Organizations are fiercely competing to create 'employer brand', building the best workforce with the best talent. Having an actionable proposition that focuses on sustainability and incorporates your workforce is critical. Marks & Spencer's 'Plan A' is a good example of this in practice, and they utilize the plan as a catalyst for even greater engagement: 'To build our relationships with the communities around us and contribute to the development of an inclusive business able to attract the best talent'. Marketing can play a pivotal role in how a company communicates to its employees to ensure they are informed, included and understand their part in the company's sustainable development plan. Regular communication of what your organization is doing when it comes to sustainability is important to ensure that employees understand the direction and actions in place. If employees fail to see or do not have access to the right information then they can't build an understanding of it.

Successful brands that recognize this are aligning marketing more closely with HR. Take the example of Heineken, which in 2016 executed their full-blown HR campaign 'Go Places'. The campaign mirrored a consumer marketing campaign, with the objective to engage current employees and attract future talent. 'Go Places' continues to run today and was revamped as 'Go Places 2.0' in 2019. Companies that recognize their internal stakeholders are their strongest asset create a better culture, which in turn enables a more united workforce who deliver greater impact.

3.2 Why do companies need to do something about this now?

Trust

Trust is at an all-time low. As discussed in the introduction, the most important concept of all in brand, especially when it comes to sustainability, is trust. The 'Edelman Trust Barometer 2020' reveals that no societal institution, business, government, NGOs or media outlet is completely trusted, stating: 'The four existential issues of the next decade: income inequality, sustainability, information quality and artificial intelligence will require higher levels of co-operation among our institutions; no single entity can take on these complex challenges alone' (Ries, Edelman et al, 2019).

When we look at the roles stakeholders play in relation to environmental and societal issues, governments should be the ultimate controlling authority, responsible for putting in place laws and regulations that protect the environment and the citizens who live in it. However, as we write in 2020 this is far from the case. Whilst scientists are saying one thing, government leaders are saying another, and when it comes to who is more trusted, global research released in 2020 by SAP Qualtrics on public opinion (Snell, 2020) shows that more than half of global respondents trust what scientists say about the environment and believe that governments should be doing more. NGOs are generally more trusted than any other stakeholders, but they are not effective enough on their own to lead change. NGOs need to partner with organizations and government if they are to deliver change. Collaboration is key to progress.

Despite the results of the 'Edelman Trust Barometer 2020' report, business is seen as the leading catalyst for change. However, it is only through effective partnerships with government and NGOs and engagement through the entire stakeholder chain that business can rebuild trust and effect change. As we have been discussing throughout this chapter, customers and employees are hugely significant. Further results from the Trust Barometer report support this, with 87 per cent of respondents stating that: 'customers, employees, and communities are more important than shareholders to a company's long-term success' (Ries, Edelman et al, 2020).

Conscious consumerism

As touched upon at the start of the chapter, consumers are increasingly more conscious when it comes to purchasing decisions and the organizations they engage with, enabled by the connected world we live in. Global focus on sustainability has highlighted the negative impact industries are having, one such being fast fashion. Alarming reports and figures show the damage: water pollution, high levels of waste into landfill and a heavy carbon footprint. Then there's the food industry, which is probably one of the most high-profile, due to public interest in animal welfare. Figures reported on food consumption reveal that Europe is responsible for approximately 30 per cent of total greenhouse gas emissions, with meat generally having a considerably higher carbon footprint than plant-based food (Petrovic et al, 2015). Consumer behaviours have started to shift, and 2018 saw plant-based products become a leading economy in the UK, and product launches in the category soared. Poll results suggest that over the next year, 2.2 million people will adopt veganism, increasing the vegan population to around 2.9 million (Rae, 2020).

Consumers are more aware of the issues and more mindful of their actions, and thus behaviours are changing. People are reviewing their values, spending habits, frequency of purchase, what they eat, and what they wear. We are more aware of packaging and supply chains, and questions are now being asked that were not asked before. Organizations that recognize this are responding. For instance, some fashion brands are reacting by offering customers services such as recycling, whereby consumers can take their clothes along to their stores, whether they purchased them from that brand or not. Clothes are also being made using recycled materials. H&M is a company leading the charge, aligning its goals to the UN SDGs. Its sustainability report 2019 stated that 57 per cent of all materials it uses in its products are recycled or from sustainably sourced materials. It launched the 'Take Care' concept, which offers customers hands-on support in how to take care of their garments, so they last longer, in turn reducing waste. And, in 2019, it started a pilot rental service in Sweden whereby members can rent up to three items for a fixed cost. Outside of fashion brands, the resale market is growing at an accelerated rate. In the US, it's predicted to grow from $24 to $51 billion in the next five years, while in the UK, industry reports forecast the market could overtake fast fashion by 2029. ThredUP, which launched in 2009, is now the world's largest fashion resale marketplace, their message being that they offer: 'the best way to shop clothes with the smallest impact to the planet, your time and your wallet' (www.thredup.com). Reselling and reusing garments via sites such as these allows people to experiment with styles and access a huge range of brands, while also addressing overconsumption and reducing waste.

Beware fake news and misinformation

With all the focus and noise around sustainability, one of the biggest contributing factors in the decline in trust is fake news. The 'Edelman Trust Barometer 2020' report highlights the concerns when it comes to false information, with a staggering 75 per cent of respondents worrying about fake news being used as a weapon (Ries, Edelman et al, 2020). Building and, more importantly, retaining trust isn't easy, and with so much more information available it's almost impossible to navigate through what is fact and what is fiction. Recent research published by the Global Fashion Agenda in the 'Pulse of the Fashion Industry: Update 2019' report shows that: 'consumers mostly acquire information about sustainability issues through online search (35 per cent), social media (31 per cent) and non-digital print media (29 per cent)' (Lehmann, M., Arici, G., et al, 2019). And, for the second year running the 'Edelman Trust Barometer 2020' report showed: 'engagement with news has surged with 50 per cent of people not only consuming news once a week or more, but also routinely amplifying it' (Ries, Edelman et al, 2020).

Consistency and transparency throughout the stakeholder chain will go some way to tackling the growing issue of fake news and misinformation, but it is up to government and industries to come together and collectively agree on how they measure and report their sustainability objectives and results with complete transparency and in a balanced way. Making the reporting of sustainable objectives mandatory and consistent across industries is critical. There also needs to be accountability; more organizations are reporting their achievements, but few paint the whole picture. If we take fast fashion again, whilst the industry is making progress in its efforts to address the impact on the environment, it did in fact do so at a slower rate in 2019 according to the 'Pulse of the Fashion Industry: Update 2019' report. This means that collectively the industry could fail to meet its UN SDGs targets. On the other side, the media also need to be more balanced when reporting on both the positive and negative sides of progress. As more people engage in online conversations it's important that facts are available as proof of progress. Fake news thrives on lack of evidence and facts. Marketers need to take responsibility for their communications and engagement on social channels and ensure that the conversations they have about sustainability are based on facts, in order to stem the tide of opinion and misinformation, and also to present a true picture to consumers.

3.3 Things that need to be acknowledged as not perfect

The messages

Following on from the need for more consistency, whilst there are a lot of headline messages, facts and figures regarding sustainability and actions being taken by organizations, it is almost impossible for any stakeholder to understand and compare these headlines. This is often where trust can break down and it is therefore an area where action needs to be taken. If we take retail as an example, specifically the pledges being made by UK supermarkets on the reduction of plastic, we can see the issue. 'Asda stated that nearly one-third of its plastic packaging would come from recycled sources by the end of 2020 and all should be recyclable by 2025'; 'Waitrose said it had removed 90 per cent of the 2,291 tonnes of black plastic'; and 'Tesco pledged to remove 1bn pieces of plastic from products for sale in UK stores by the end of 2020' (Vidal, 2020). Whilst powerful in isolation, none of these pledges is actually measurable by consumers. They can't be compared, and there is no central point of reference to allow informed conclusions to be drawn. This highlights that whilst all the above organizations are working on sustainable development, from a consumer level it is very hard to work out which retailer to engage with in order to make a difference. Also, the reporting that should support these pledges and demonstrate the progress also comes in different formats, again making comparison difficult.

So, what can companies do? Shaping sustainability credentials and communicating them effectively and, more importantly, consistently to your stakeholders is far from easy. However, if we can take a moment, let's acknowledge the value marketing can bring to this area, because it is vast, and the impact can be long-lasting. When it comes to communicating societal issues, there are clear examples where marketing has already had an impact, such as raising the awareness of the dangers of obesity and smoking in healthcare and educating people about the growing issues surrounding mental health. In these instances, marketing is evolving in its role as a force for good in the world. Another more recent example that we've touched upon is veganism; marketing has been a catalyst in making veganism mainstream. However, for marketing to be as effective as it can be in its communication and for the messages to be understood, consistency and transparency when it comes to what organizations are actually doing, why they are doing it and the results of their actions must be a key requirement – whether the message is an externally facing one or an internally facing one.

Sustainability reporting

The purpose of reporting is to create greater transparency and accountability and allow stakeholders to make better-informed decisions. Over the years, sustainability reporting has become more widely practised, but making them more comparable and trusted is something that continues to need attention. The sheer weight of metrics makes it difficult to know what to report on, which tools to use and how to effectively communicate them. Whilst there are many independent organizations that provide support when it comes to reporting, there is still no unified global approach, which continues to make sustainability reporting difficult to navigate and understand. When it comes to reporting on ESG issues, the most well-known companies are the Global Reporting Initiative (GRI), an independent international organization that has been pioneering sustainability reporting since 1997; the Sustainability Accounting Standards Board (SASB); and the International Integrated Reporting Council (IIRC). The SASB and IIRC frameworks are more weighted towards investor-focused reporting whilst the GRI framework allows for multiple stakeholder-focused reporting, including customers, employees and NGOs. As of 2020, 93 per cent of the world's largest companies use the GRI standards (www.globalreporting.org).

Engagement

Sustainability reporting has moved some way from being a box-ticking exercise for a lot of organizations. They understand the importance of it, and we are seeing it far more widely practised, with information and the quality of the data getting better all the time. However, issues remain. The complexity and size of the reports mean not only do they lack appeal, but they are also difficult to understand. We know from research that people prefer more bite-sized, digestible information. Engagement with social media platforms and the internet has changed behaviours; people have become used to engaging with just headlines or sites and platforms where key information is highlighted for you, so you don't have to read everything.

Content

Whilst the content of reports may provide a full and balanced picture of an organization's sustainability position, it is often the case that they highlight the positives and bury the negatives. Without looking at both a real view on progress either over time or against specific goals, the sustainability position can be difficult to judge, and that can make the information redundant. There is also an issue with sustainability reports being difficult to compare – so there aren't any clear benchmarks. And, whilst the SASB and IIRC have been working on trying to make reports more comparable across industries, until this happens, stakeholders – more specifically consumers and employees – will realistically be unable to make informed decisions.

Communication

How reports are communicated is also an issue we need to address. On the whole, they are generally just placed on company websites for consumers or other stakeholders to download. Research from the GlobalWebIndex showed that when it comes to actively searching for environmental information on brands and products, the main sources consumers use are social media platforms (41 per cent), followed by the product/brand sites (34 per cent) (GlobalWebIndex, 2019). Where you place your sustainability information is important; if consumers cannot navigate your site and find the information they are looking for easily then your sustainability development and values are at risk of not being seen or heard. This can have a negative effect on the levels of engagement with potential or existing customers, affecting acquisition and retention and potentially driving your customers to your competition if they happen to be communicating more effectively. In short, if you don't amplify your report through the relevant channels your audience engages with then the valuable content within the report just stays within the report as opposed to being the powerful agent for change it should be.

Marketing's value

Marketers can add value in multiple areas: in the creation of the reports through providing insights on customer sentiment and what's important to them; informing on the areas to amplify; and advising how to bring the data and the story together in a way that resonates and is digestible. Marketing can also shed light on what the competition is doing and how they are progressing, enabling a more comparable report that informs decision-making as opposed to just stating facts and figures. Marketing can also add value by suggesting means to take the report to market, informing the business on the best way in which to communicate it and which channels to use to get engagement. It can then measure engagement and feed it back to internal stakeholders so it can be used to improve further sustainable development actions, keep the conversation going and furthermore provide marketing with insights about areas such as future proposition development and campaigns to drive long-term performance.

An agent for change

It is important that we keep working towards better reporting and make it a priority. If done the right way, it can be a powerful agent for change, and here's why: with more data comes more information and the connected world we live in will only get more transparent and continue to fuel the conversations being had. What and how companies report will become increasingly more important. As outlined previously, the level of misinformation is growing, and sustainability reports are a way to ensure evidence and facts are presented clearly to all stakeholders and receive better engagement. Getting the data and insights within the reports in front of consumers will enable them to make informed decisions about who they engage with and where they spend their money. Reporting can also help your company attract and retain employees, and a motivated workforce means better company performance. Information can make the company more attractive to NGOs and foster stronger partnerships. And, for investors, effective reporting will help them identify those companies that are well positioned to meet their sustainability goals now and in the future, giving them confidence and your company the investment funds it needs to grow.

3.4 Case study – Marks & Spencer – Plan A

Throughout this chapter, we have discussed how the stakeholder chain consists of many different elements: investors, leaders, partners, employers and society (consumers and communities) – all of whom play important roles. It is only when all elements come together that a true sustainability action plan is enabled.

Marks & Spencer launched its sustainable 'Plan A' in 2007 and became the first UK retailer to become carbon neutral in 2012. It is surprising given all we have and will be discussing that Marks & Spencer do not shout louder about their truly impressive sustainability plan. Aligned to 15 of the United Nations SDGs, Marks & Spencer have built a plan that places sustainability at the heart of its business. They recognize the importance of stakeholder engagement and their 2019 updated report is a clear demonstration of an inclusive strategy.

When it comes to reporting, they are clear that they use their own assessment with the GRI Standards as a secondary index: 'In October 2016 the UN Global Sustainability Standards Board (GSSB) introduced new GRI Sustainability Reporting Standards to replace the previous G4 version by July 2018. Since we launched the Plan A sustainability programme in 2007, our reporting has been based on our own assessment of materiality used to create Plan A with GRI as a secondary index. We've taken the same approach with GRI Standards and this report is GRI-referenced. We have retained a content Index to assist those who wish to use this report for benchmarking purposes' ('M&S Plan A Performance Update', 2019). The report clearly lays out their sustainability goals and shows whether they are 'on plan' or 'behind plan'.

Stakeholder engagement is important, and the 'Transformation Underway: M&S Plan A Report 2018' report (found at www.corporate. marksandspencer.com/sustainability) shows how they have clearly identified their stakeholders, how they listen to them, what the feedback is and what actions they have taken. Their employees are Plan A champions who not only take the strategy on board and drive it throughout the organization, but also voice the wider societal issues and concerns back to Marks & Spencer, which is crucial to shaping an effective sustainable development plan.

External stakeholders such as suppliers, NGOs, government and regulators are all included in Plan A, and Marks & Spencer work with them supporting environmental standards, participating in tenders and surveys, and ensuring that all parts of the chain are included.

As discussed throughout this book and highlighted by Sustainable Business Director for Marks & Spencer Mike Barry: 'transparency, once a matter of choice for some businesses, is increasingly becoming a basic social expectation, prompting greater public debate and accelerating action on issues such as the gender pay gap and modern slavery' (Marks & Spencer, 2019).

Plan A sets a high standard for sustainable development. The only criticism is that not enough people know about it.

3.5 Chapter summary

In this chapter we have discussed the importance of stakeholder engagement and the shifts in focus and impact that investors, employees and consumers now have. Although each part of the chain has different reasons for engagement and different levels of impact it is clear that no single stakeholder can effect change in isolation. It takes engagement, collective action and collaboration at every point across the stakeholder chain when it comes to sustainability.

We have acknowledged that environmental and societal issues are at the forefront of conversations and there is a concern that business is being seen as the leading driver of change. In addition, we have highlighted areas that are presenting challenges when it comes to a collaborative approach, such as decline in trust, the increase in fake news and the need for more consistency and transparency if business is to be effective.

The key outcome from this chapter is to recognize the impact and value marketing can bring as both a facilitator and an enabler in delivering a company's sustainability development to all parts of the stakeholder chain. Marketing has to be involved and is a catalyst for change. Its role to inform and educate through taking information and making it relevant to the different stakeholder groups is critical. Whether it's bringing internal stakeholders together by explaining the direction in which the company is going in its sustainability objectives or giving consumers context and reasons to engage with your brand – because it will ultimately have a positive impact on the planet – the role of marketing is an important one.

Sustainability is a broad and complex issue. However, for business, whilst it comes with many challenges, it also presents a huge opportunity for growth and long-term return on investment. We acknowledge that the amount of information that needs to be understood and communicated effectively can at times feel overwhelming. At any given moment, the landscape can change, and it doesn't take much to lose the attention and trust of your stakeholders. Overconsumption, which we'll look at in more detail, is a behaviour that marketing is responsible for and has developed over many years, yet it is unlikely to change overnight. Change will take time, but that it is in no way an excuse to not act, nor is it acceptable to think someone else will do it for you. With the change from shareholder capitalism to stakeholder capitalism being acknowledged, marketing has the attention of all stakeholders, so now is the time to communicate and collaborate.

3.6 Action points to consider

No.	Action	Considerations	Next Step
1	Collate a list of all internal stakeholders connected to your organization.	Consider which departments should be involved in developing your sustainability strategy. Should it be all of them? Add them to a visual plan to help you map all stakeholders.	Begin to identify the key stakeholders who can help sponsor change in your organization.
2	Collate a list of all external stakeholders connected to your organization.	What groups and individuals may have an active interest in how your company approaches developing your sustainability strategy? How do they connect to your internal stakeholders?	Begin to decide whether and how the external stakeholder will be involved – will they be an active participant or just informed of your plans?
3	Create a stakeholder communications plan.	Once you have mapped all of your stakeholder groups, develop a plan for how, and with what media, you will aim to engage with them throughout the next year.	Have you considered your customer yet? How are you going to engage with them in this process? Remember – give your consumers context and reasons to engage with your brand. Remember that your internal customers are just as important as your external customers.
4	Create an engagement timing plan.	Consider whether it is useful for your company to have a calendar of events, including key meetings, to ensure that sustainability is being considered.	What other meetings should sustainability be a part of? For example, is it a standing item on your management team/ board meeting?

No.	Action	Considerations	Next Step
5	Create an annual impact summary for your stakeholders on your company's progress in meetings.	Remember, your role is to act as a catalyst for change – establish your key KPIs and track them to show that you are progressing and the company is effecting change.	Consider whether bringing all stakeholders together to discuss your annual summary might help you further explain the direction of your sustainability objectives.

3.7 Chapter 3 references

CISL team led by Dr Jake Reynolds (2019). 'In Search of Impact'. Available at: https://www.cisl.cam.ac.uk/resources/publication-pdfs/in-search-of-impact-report-2019.pdf/view (Accessed: 19 January 2020)

Fink, L. (2020). 'A Fundamental Reshaping of Finance'. Available at: https://www.blackrock.com/corporate/investor-relations/larry-fink-ceo-letter (Accessed: 19 January 2020)

Freeman, E. (1984). 'Strategic Management: A Stakeholder Approach. What is a Stakeholder?' – Definitions of a Stakeholder Available at: https://www.stakeholdermap.com/what-is-a-stakeholder.html (Accessed: 18 January 2020)

Lehmann, M., Arici, G., Boger, S., Martinez-Pardo, C., Krueger, F., Schneider, M., Carrière-Pradal, B. and Schou, D. (2019). 'Pulse of the Fashion Industry: Update 2019'. Available at: http://media-publications.bcg.com/france/Pulse-of-the-Fashion-Industry2019.pdf (Accessed: 26 January 2020)

Marks & Spencer (2018). 'Transformation Underway' Plan A Report. Available at: https://corporate.marksandspencer.com/annual-report-2018/mands_plan_a_2018.pdf (Accessed: 23 January 2020)

Marks & Spencer (2018). 'Transformation Underway: M&S Plan A Report 2018'. Available at: https://corporate.marksandspencer.com/annual-report-2018/mands_plan_a_2018.pdf (Accessed: 26 January 2020)

Marks & Spencer (2019). 'M&S Plan A Performance Update 2019'. Available at: https://corporate.marksandspencer.com/documents/reports-results-and-publications/plan-a-reports/plan-a-performance-update-2019 (Accessed: 25 January 2020)

Oligschlaeger, A. (2019). 'Rise of the Conscious Consumer'. Available at: https://www.walnutunlimited.com/rise-of-the-conscious-consumer (Accessed: 19 January 2020)

Oliver, R. (2019). 'The Rise of Veganism in the UK in Numbers – Update for 2019'. Available at: https://trulyexperiences.com/blog/veganism-uk-statistics/ (Accessed: 26 January 2020)

Petrovic, Z., Djordjevic, V., Milicevic, D., Nastasijevic, I. and Parunovi, N. (2015). 'Meat Production and Consumption: Environmental Consequences'. *Procedia Food Science*, Volume 5 (2015), pp. 235–38. Available at: https://www.sciencedirect.com/science/article/pii/S2211601X15001315 (Accessed: 25 January 2020)

Ries, T. et al (2019). '2019 Edelman Trust Barometer Special Report: In Brands We Trust?'. Available at: https://www.edelman.com/sites/g/files/aatuss191/files/2019-06/2019_edelman_trust_barometer_special_report_in_brands_we_trust.pdf (Accessed: 18 January 2020)

Ries, T. et al (2020). 'Edelman Trust Barometer 2020'. Available at: https://www.edelman.com/sites/g/files/aatuss191/files/2020-01/2020%20Edelman%20Trust%20Barometer%20Global%20Report_LIVE.pdf (Accessed: 25 January 2020)

Snell, S. (2020). 'How To Use Citizen Experiences To Build A Better World'. Forbes. Available at: https://www.forbes.com/sites/sap/2020/01/23/how-to-use-citizen-experiences-to-build-a-better-world/#34a730d074d5 (Accessed: 26 January 2020)

ThredUP. Available at: www.thredup.com (Accessed: 26 January 2020)

United Nations General Assembly (2015). 'Transforming our world: the 2030 Agenda for Sustainable Development' A/RES/70/1. Available at: https://www.un.org/ga/search/view_doc.asp?symbol=A/RES/70/1&Lang=E (Accessed: 25 January 2020)

Vidal, J. (14 January 2020). 'The solution to the plastic waste crisis? It isn't recycling'. *Guardian*. Available at: https://www.theguardian.com/commentisfree/2020/jan/14/plastic-waste-crisis-recycling-consumption-environmentally-friendly (Accessed: 26 January 2020)

CHAPTER FOUR

Sustainable Supply Chain Management

4.0 Chapter introduction

A reality for marketing practitioners today is the ever-growing weight consumers give to the companies they buy from for acting in a sustainable manner. Research conducted ahead of the 2020 HRH Sustainability Summit by GlobalWebIndex (Ernest-Jones, 2020) found that the majority (80 per cent) of Internet users in the UK are 'concerned' about the future of the environment. The research also confirmed the top reasons that alienate people most from a brand:

1) poor environmental track record (84 per cent);
2) unsustainable packaging (83 per cent);
3) poor compliance record (82 per cent);
4) irresponsible sourcing of materials (82 per cent);
5) poor human rights track record (82 per cent).

As consumers begin to make more substantial efforts in their own life to adopt circular principles of recycling more waste, reusing products and materials and acting in a more conscious manner, it is increasingly incumbent on business to do the same in order to retain their loyalty. Equally, though, it is still a reality that not all segments of your customers care as much as others. This makes it hard for a company to persuade its investors and shareholders to agree to take action on sustainability, let alone see it as a method from which they could yield something approaching a conventional positive return on investment.

The need for more sustainable marketing practices naturally leads us to the need to examine our business's supply chain. Apart from a small handful of hyper-local producers, the majority of marketing practitioners work for a company that is part of an often vast network of other producers and manufacturers that supply the constituent parts to create the final products and services that we develop and sell. As we have pointed out throughout this book, we acknowledge the difficulties of the duality of our business's survival relying on this whilst asking practitioners to make changes. This is acknowledged as a difficult enough process locally in your own business, never mind also having to address it in your supply chain partners. However, gaining a true understanding of how your suppliers are acting, how their behaviour ties into your brand and whether you can influence it to align with your own values is becoming increasingly important to continued survival and growth, not just to align with targets around SDGs, but also to meet consumer awareness and desire.

4.1 Where are we?

A decade ago, renowned marketing writer Philip Kotler wrote: 'Marketers in the past have based their strategies on the assumption of infinite resources and zero environmental impact. With the growing recognition of finite resources and high environmental costs, marketers need to re-examine their theory and practices. They need to revise their policies on product development, pricing, distribution, and branding. Companies must balance more carefully their growth goals with the need to pursue "sustainability"' (Kotler, 2011).

So, how much have we moved on over the past 10 years?

Changing consumer attitudes

Whilst many marketing practices may not have moved forwards especially progressively in this area, consumers definitely have. Ensuring the environment is protected and nurtured is a growing topic of interest for consumers. A 2019 survey by social media platform Pinterest that discussed the underlying trends around sustainability and the planet found that younger groups such as millennials and Gen Z were each twice as likely to search for sustainability ideas compared to 'Pinners' over the age of 38. Furthermore, searches for 'sustainable living for beginners' were up by 265 per cent since 2018, as its users searched for advice on sustainable living, sustainable travel options and carbon footprint reduction (Pinterest 100, 2019).

But what of business? As discussed in Chapter 2 and Chapter 3, the leadership teams of major global brands are undeniably beginning to look at their sustainable practices and listening to their stakeholders' perspectives. Connected to this, many organizations are waking up to the fact that it is their partner business in their supply chain that may be greatly contributing to the challenges they are looking to make a positive contribution towards. Increasingly, it is clear that if requirements that products are sustainable are not met, consumers will look elsewhere. Many 'business cases' for sustainability still all too often only look at their own companies' energy efficiency in order to appear to be tackling climate change. That said, other business cases are emerging that recognize the need for careful management – with companies risking not only their brand reputation but also the future earnings of their business – and acting in a more sustainable manner, which can also improve a business's competitive context (Oliveira and Sullivan, 2015). Others are embracing strategic philanthropy and creating 'shared value' (Porter and Kramer, 2011), with increasingly numbers of business proactively trying to profile themselves as responsible organizations (Sadler and Lloyd, 2009). For example, voluntary reporting on social dimensions has grown considerably in recent years, as has the number of companies joining initiatives such as the GRI. These changes have all contributed to a growing focus on the supply chains of every company.

The role of brand in B2B relationships

Business-to-business (B2B) organizational buying was first defined by Webster and Wind (1972). Organization buying can be defined as 'the decision-making process by which formal organizations establish the need for purchased products and services and identify, evaluate and choose among alternative brands and suppliers'.

Today, the B2B context differs in its natural emphasis on a different model of demand; there is a significantly lower number of customers for a manufacturer's products, however there may be in turn a larger sales demand over time if the relationship involves a significant volume of purchases. This in itself lends B2B supplier-client relationships to naturally becoming longer lasting and partnership based. In larger businesses, the purchasing task is typically handled by a centralized procurement function, whereby dedicated teams and individuals lead the evaluation of alternative options and select the optimum supplier (Kotler and Pfoertsch, 2007) often due to the proliferation of similar products being available from a wide variety of sources.

Working with NGOs

Research published by the global PR firm Edelman claims that non-governmental organizations (NGOs), such as World Wide Fund for Nature (WWF), Amnesty International and Greenpeace, are amongst some of the most trusted institutions globally – far more so than many businesses, media institutions and government (Ries, Edelman et al, 2020). When adopting a more contemporary, strategic and integrated approach to corporate responsibility in a global supply chain context, companies typically begin to engage and work more closely in partnerships with both NGOs and government. Peloza and Falkenburg (2009) suggest that business leaders should seek to structure collaborative relationships by aligning their economic/strategic objectives to their corporate responsibility activity.

Corporations can be increasingly guided by a variety of codes and standards such as:

- United Nations Global Compact (principles in the areas of human rights, labour, the environment and anti-corruption);
- International Labour Organization (ILO) global labour standards and the decent work agenda;
- International Standards Organization (ISO) 26000 social responsibility standard;
- Social Accountability SA8000 standard on decent workplaces.

Developing supply chain sustainability (SCS)

The conventional view of a company's supply chain connects together the process for producing and delivering goods – from 'inputs' to 'outputs'. Whilst discussion about supply chain analysis was traditionally more about the literal logistics of where and when goods moved to their final destination, the most recent rise of the 'digital supply chain' has allowed companies to have greater transparency through a growing ability to gather and analyse data regarding each component of their supply chain.

Academic and corporate awareness of sustainable supply chain and logistics issues has increased significantly in recent years (Ahi et al, 2016; Köksal et al, 2017). Today, supply chains offer multiple aspects, one of which is the achievement of business sustainability, particularly as this aspect covers a range of areas for improvement. Most crucial to improving a company's sustainability position is that organizations can identify the actual source of raw materials, the manufacturing process and differing tiers of production, and understand the true conditions of the workers involved in every process of production. For large companies outsourcing their manufacturing function, this has led to the rise of the concept of 'responsible sourcing' and also client companies encouraging the different companies in its supply chain to be more sustainable through the development and sharing of knowledge transfer and best practice. This in turn has allowed manufacturers and service providers to be able to more clearly demonstrate compliance with the highest standards of worker welfare, a reduction in environmental impact (including waste, overall carbon footprint, deforestation, emissions and air pollution), as well as the overall health and safety of the working conditions of their employees, and ultimately to show that they are running an ethical, responsible business.

Therefore, supply chain sustainability (SCS) describes taking a more holistic view of a company's supply chain – from improving its processes, logistics and technologies to addressing social, environmental, economic and legal aspects of a supply chain's components. SCS aims to balance the view that for companies, having a sustainable supply chain should be based on producing both socially responsible products and practices that should minimize environmental impact for the good of the planet and the people making and receiving them, and their subsequent contribution towards building positive brand awareness and improving the long-term profitability of any company.

4.2 Why do companies need to do something about this now?

The Intergovernmental Panel on Climate Change (IPCC), a scientific body established by the United Nations, defines global targets for companies producing consumer products in their sustainability strategies, recommending that they reduce their greenhouse gas emissions by up to 44 per cent in order to own a 'fair share' of overall global reductions before 2030, in line with the UN's SDG targets. However, the current picture is bleak.

At the Conference of Parties (COP) 21 in Paris on 12 December 2015, parties to the UNFCCC reached a landmark agreement to combat climate change and to accelerate and intensify the actions and investments needed for a sustainable low-carbon future. However, a 2018 landmark report by the IPCC from some of world's leading climate scientists (Watts, 2018) warned that there had been little progress, and the world only has until 2030 for global warming to be kept to a maximum of 1.5°C (2.7°F), beyond which even 'half a degree will significantly worsen the risks of drought, floods, extreme heat and poverty for hundreds of millions of people'. It also stated that although its recommendations were both affordable and feasible, urgent – and unprecedented – changes are needed to reach the target, which lies at the most ambitious end of the original Paris Agreement pledge to keep temperatures between 1.5°C (2.7°F) and 2°C (3.6°F).

The business case for sustainability

The business case for sustainability has been more widely discussed in various books, such as: *Capitalism as if the World Matters* (Porritt, 2005, Routledge); *The Triple Bottom Line* (Savitz and Weber, 2006, John Wiley & Sons); *Green to Gold* (Esty and Winston, 2006, John Wiley & Sons); and *The New Sustainability Advantage* (Willard, 2012, New Society Publishers). Furthermore, according to the Global Living Asset Management Performance (LAMP) Index, firms that adopt more sustainable strategies financially outperform those that don't (www. lampindex.com).

A key challenge in this is the reality that corporate supply chains are bigger and more complex than ever before, and open markets have now enabled companies to outsource production and source materials from suppliers in developing and emerging economies. Whilst, if done correctly, this can deliver significant benefits in the form of reduced costs, enhanced profitability and shareholder value, it can also contribute to economic and social development in those countries, resulting in higher standards of living for millions of workers and their families. However, there is now a general acceptance that this exchange cannot be carried out to the continued detriment of the environment and continued negative working conditions. Public scrutiny and weak implementation is now naturally forcing companies to address issues outside of their own company locations but inside their own supply chain.

Environmental, Social and Governance (ESG) criteria

According to the UN Global Compact, which aims to mobilize a global movement of sustainable companies and stakeholders, companies that incorporate ESG thinking into their supply chain management can deliver a range of business benefits ('Supply Chain Sustainability: The Business Case', 2020) including:

- better anticipation and management of risks, as risk is spread out across different players;
- reduced operational risks, such as disruption to supply, increased cost and lack of access to key raw materials;
- 'social' licence to operate within communities, legal systems and governments that otherwise might be antagonistic;
- reduced costs and enhanced efficiency and productivity;
- improved working conditions, which can reduce turnover and improve quality and reliability;
- improved efficiency and profitability as a result of increased environmental responsibility;

- protection of corporate brand and values, and enhanced consumer confidence and loyalty;
- greater process and product innovation uncovered by empowered suppliers;
- potential increase in shareholder value as shown by examples from leading companies with good supply chain management.

Chen (2020) also notes that the pressure to achieve more sustainable outcomes comes not only from NGOs and end customers, but also from investors. As outlined in Chapter 3, ESG criteria are becoming more of a key method from which investors are evaluating companies.

Creating long-term relationships for long-term value

Marketers must proactively work with their procurement and supply chain colleagues to move beyond short-term financial objectives to instead build mutually rewarding relationships that deliver long-term value for all parties involved in a company's entire supply chain, by incorporating sustainability into all of a company's sourcing and purchasing practices.

We highly recommend seeking out other brands that are also taking sustainability seriously and seeing if there are ways you can collaborate with each other and your respective sustainable suppliers. For example, consider how you might combine resources between manufacturers in a way that can collectively reduce waste and environmental impact. It is also fair to explore how this might also enable cost savings, such as sharing of logistics and fulfilment to ensure maximum capacity.

Although historically many consumer companies paid relatively little attention to how suppliers managed the environmental and social impact of their business activities, this is now beginning to change. A number of leading consumer businesses, along with civil-society institutions, have begun to create an array of best practices and tools that are shared with their suppliers to begin to jointly lessen their environmental impact. According to McKinsey (Bové and Swartz, 2016), Walmart originally pledged that by the end of 2017, 70 per cent of the goods it sold would come from suppliers that meet the company's Sustainability Index ('Walmart's Sustainability Index Program', 2019). Key to this was identifying critical issues across the whole supply chain and linking the company's supply chain sustainability goals to the global sustainability agenda. It must be recognized that many industry supply chain issues are due to systemic problems. As such, companies are more responsible than ever for communicating, and providing training, infrastructure and tools to help their suppliers improve and embed sustainable change through a combination of promoting supplier accountability, supporting supplier diversity and holding suppliers accountable.

We will explore carbon offsetting in greater detail in Chapter 8, but this is becoming a growing issue in the context of a sustainable supply chain. Many global companies are seeking to impose much stricter carbon offsetting initiatives on their supply chain – recognizing their total impact when producing goods and services. For example, Apple (2019) have been taking significant measures towards achieving a smaller carbon footprint, and indeed have reduced it by 35 per cent since 2015. This has been achieved by taking into account hundreds of their suppliers' and millions of their customers' devices. The significant improvements include all Apple facilities worldwide running on 100 per cent renewable energy, with the company supporting others in their supply chain in emerging markets to find ways to make renewable energy available.

Supply chain sustainability KPIs

In a recent survey by The Sustainability Consortium (TSC) – a non-profit organization that is dedicated to improving the sustainability of consumer products – less than one-fifth of the 1,700 respondents said that they have a comprehensive view of their supply chains' sustainability performance. More than half reported being unable to determine sustainability issues in their supply chains, and clearly, until consumer companies identify the sustainability problems in their supply chains, they cannot begin to work with their suppliers on solving those problems.

Unlike some areas this book covers, thankfully there is an increasingly growing consensus of how companies can measure their improvement in supply chain sustainability. As well as TSC, multiple other organizations, such as the WWF and the SASB, have proposed KPIs and guidelines that can help any consumer business achieve their desired environmental goals. Active management against targets is a factor in understanding whether your efforts have been successful, as well as a coherent methodology on which marketing practitioners can also adapt their company's strategy. We would highly encourage a target-setting approach; as marketers will be used to measurement and tracking of success, so including a set of sustainability KPIs around supply chain (and other areas) is a key action to take. We'd also recommend keeping updated through a combination of understanding the latest scientific recommendations, sharing of resources, and adopting best practice and government regulations.

There are also a number of platforms you can use to manage and benchmark your company's supply chain performance. For example, EcoVadis SAS – considered the world leader in business sustainability ratings for global supply chains – is a useful resource. Having received significant funding, it is leveraging it to help scale globally and 'engrain sustainability, fair labour practices and ethics into enterprise supply chains and business commerce' (CVC, 2020). Using software tools and platforms such as EcoVadis SAS can really help companies in terms of accountability throughout the process of auditing and optimizing their supply chain, allowing them to track the impact of their sustainability goals and progress updates.

4.3 Things that need to be acknowledged as not perfect

As we have covered in Chapter 3, every company needs to recognize that external and internal pressures on the supply chain towards sustainability come from a wide variety of regulatory, organizational, media and community stakeholders. The inherent challenges and contractions for sustainable development within the global supply chain cannot be ignored, and the nature of global commerce makes this a highly charged discussion.

The challenges of creating a sustainable, multinational supply chain has been a significant focus for academic researchers (Lieb and Lieb, 2010; Marchet et al, 2014; Piecyk and Björklund, 2015), as well as practitioners. Whilst the urgent environmental reasons to make progress in this area are (hopefully!) clear, there are many issues at play. These include the need to improve environmental standards through purchasing contracts for local and global suppliers (Simpson et al, 2007). Furthermore, there are challenges when it comes to applying green energy and pursuing ethical and social responsibility, alongside which come uncertainties and cost increases that any industry can face in the sustainable development of its supply chains (Xia and Tang, 2011; Abbasi and Nilson, 2012).

As well as internal reasons and pressures for sustainability arising from regulation by government and other stakeholders, it is also essential to understand the possible conflicts amongst the members of a company's sustainable supply chain due to inevitable tensions between achieving cost-effective operational efficiency versus efforts towards greater sustainability by reducing pollution. There's a lot to consider when streamlining a sustainable supply chain, so let's explore some of these tensions in more detail to understand some of the pay-offs your company is likely to need to balance.

4.4 Balancing corporate responsibility and employee rights

Employees of companies, and how they are treated, can quite rightly be seen as the centre point of much of the implementation regarding corporate responsibility. Connected to this concept is the benefit of strong corporate responsibility in enhancing a business's ability to attract and retain high-performing employees, as well as improving commitment and well-being for all team members (Bhattacharya et al, 2008). Having a happy workforce is also, of course, linked to maximizing productivity – and despite its topicality, this is not a new phenomenon. Industrialists such as Henry Ford and George Cadbury are recognized as imposing the reality of 'enlightened self-interest' – in that, when the housing and workplace conditions of their employees improved, so did productivity. However, tensions between representing the well-being of an employee and their right to a 'voice' and seeking to maximize efficiencies and profits continues to exist across the majority of industries.

However, when creating a truly sustainable supply chain, the concept of enlightened self-interest must also be extended to the employees of your supplier, too. Over the last few decades, multiple global brands have come under scrutiny with regards to the working conditions of companies in their supply chains, particularly in developing nations, including accusations of the use of 'sweatshops', child labour, multiple health and safety issues, and abuse of human rights. Whilst such practices are not justifiable, they have arguably come out of a culture of driving cost-based outsourcing to manufacturers willing to produce items for less.

Despite the increased scrutiny, many companies still do not offer true equal opportunities – from fair pay and conditions, to security of employment and freedom of association, to occupational health and safety, pension schemes and health benefits.

It is essential to remain cognizant that many of the principles of corporate responsibility in the workplace in markets such as Western Europe are based on legal protection for employees being enshrined and comprehensively covered in law, as well as often comprehensive social welfare (e.g. medical provision). Of course, markets such as the US are somewhat different, with several major corporations mirroring these benefits – for example Starbucks' voluntary provision of healthcare benefits for full and part-time employees ('Empowered to Live Well', 2020).

Ultimately, any company's ability to compete globally is dependent on effective cost management, which means production in different markets will remain attractive, but those that want to truly deliver on their corporate responsibility objectives need to consider all employees throughout the supply chain in their thinking and implementation if these objectives are to truly become a reality.

Balancing cost versus sustainability

Abbasi and Nilsson (2012) summarize the challenges in achieving sustainable supply chain management (SSCM) into five major areas:

1) cost increase;
2) operationalization of sustainable development;
3) changing cultures and mindsets;
4) strains in control and management of uncertainties and trade-offs;
5) complexity of problems.

As evidenced, actually operationalizing sustainable development can be challenging – especially when it is against the 'inertia' of how things have always been done, and is open to interpretation if not carefully managed: 'A fear of change connected to difficulties of interpretation, the complexity involved, and the underlying business logic with its clear focus on financial aspects, all contribute to the inertia in reaching sustainable supply chains' (Abbasi and Nilsson, 2012, p. 526). As such, real meaningful change also requires adjustment of mindset and prevailing culture in an organization from leadership teams as well as their employees.

Companies need to be constantly and consistently vigilant about the inherent challenges of delivering a global business on a national and international level, and the complexity of this makes sustainability difficult. For example, the choice of fuel, type of transport and routing of vehicles (to name just a few) all require negotiation of environmental impact. With an ever-competitive environment, the need to deliver on brand promise and customer expectations can necessitate making several non-environmentally-friendly trade-offs, with a drive for lower cost and customer desire for a lower price inhibiting organizations achieving critically important environmental goals. However, adopting more sustainable practices in logistics is possible. For example, Amazon announced in 2019 that they have ordered 100,000 electric delivery vehicles – the largest-ever order of electric delivery vehicles – from Rivian, a producer of emissions-free electric vehicles based near Detroit. 'We're trying to build the most sustainable transportation fleet in the world' outlines Ross Rachey, director of Amazon's global fleet and products (Patel, 2020). The order is part of 'The Climate Pledge', Amazon's commitment to meet the Paris Agreement 10 years early (Amazon, 2019, 2020). The pledge, which we'll refer to in a few chapters throughout this book, calls on its signatories to target achieving net zero carbon across their businesses by 2040 – a decade ahead of the Paris Agreement's goal of 2050 (Coyle, 2020).

Supply chain management impacts business and the economy, the global population and the environment. It is a logistical and operational exercise that faces many challenges along the way. Not only is executing this process difficult, but trying to do it in a sustainable manner is even more of a challenge. But just because it's a challenge, this shouldn't stop organizations from making a start – as there are many benefits. As we've covered in this chapter, managing costs against revenues is still the main driver in the development of any supply chain, so any sustainability initiatives must stand up to commercial scrutiny (Abbasi and Nilsson, 2012). However, it can be argued that real collaboration in regard to sustainable goals between client and supplier as partners can result in cost-effective activities. Areas such as collaborating on waste reduction and environmentally sound innovation are achievable. Key to this is that all partners in a supply chain work together with long-term objectives in mind, and ways to evolve a win-win strategy are key. In this situation, sustainable goals have a positive and direct impact on performance, and also improve trust and mutual co-operation. However, enabling this requires the purchasing companies to walk a fine line of inspiring proactive environmental strategies that lead to competitive advantages for companies (Carter and Jennings, 2002; Lopez-Gomero et al, 2010).

Clearer supplier requirements

Villena and Gioia (2020) also note that corporations can, and must, be clearer with their suppliers in terms of sending a more consistent message that it is not just about the economic requirements that are all-important to them. It is essential that their procurement teams also bear this in mind, and in contract negotiations seek to create incentives for suppliers to pursue not only economic goals, but also their environmental and social goals. As such, teams must be responsible for taking a hands-on approach to collecting and monitoring data about suppliers' sustainability performance, and ensure they are seeking to continuously improve. They also note that companies must seek to work directly with their suppliers' own procurement units to 'disseminate sustainability requirements throughout their supply networks'.

4.5 Case study – Intel – Sustainable Supply Chain Excellence

Global microprocessor manufacturer Intel is arguably one of the most well-known and highly valued brands in the world – and one that puts supply chain responsibility at the centre of its strategy. A large proportion of Intel's success can be seen in how it treats all of its stakeholders in the value chain – not just those suppliers manufacturing its products, but also how it manages its relationships with other stakeholders, such as retailers, wholesalers and employees. Intel has a complex programme of initiatives across multiple areas of its global supply chain of more than 11,000 suppliers in over 90 countries, promoting a strategy of 'Building a responsible, resilient and reliable supply chain'. Of its supplier relationships, it has commented: 'We hold them to strong standards of operation in order to have a positive impact on the world around us while building better technology' ('Supply Chain Responsibility at Intel', 2020).

The company tracks its progress through the publication of its Corporate Social Responsibility Report that details the steps it is taking to ensure 'a responsible, resilient, and reliable supply chain'. The key activities that Intel work on to optimize sustainability in their supply chain include:

Combating slavery and human trafficking

Intel have worked with suppliers to implement a robust system designed to detect and address forced, and bonded, labour in their supply chain. Of this, it states: 'We maintain a firm position on human rights issues and managing our responsibility to respect human rights through our global operations and value chain. We're dedicated to combating slavery and human trafficking and committed to respecting human rights throughout our supply chain'. In 2020, these policies have resulted in $14 million in fees returned by its suppliers to their workers.

Sourcing conflict-free minerals

Since 2008, Intel has maintained a track record of developing responsible mineral-sourcing options for itself and the wider microprocessor industry, and has been manufacturing its microprocessors responsibly since 2013.

Reducing environmental impact

Intel focuses on setting clear expectations on its suppliers for the reporting and reduction of greenhouse gas emissions, with 100 per cent of its suppliers now submitting carbon footprint data.

Supporting supplier diversity

Intel sees the diversification its supply chain brings as being key to increasing innovation in its business, and has spent some $777 million creating a more responsive and competitive supply base – representing significant progress towards its goal of $1 billion in annual diverse spending in 2020.

Holding suppliers – and itself – accountable

Intel believes assessments are an integral part of its management process, auditing 100 per cent of high-risk supplier sites. As a co-founder and full member of the Responsible Business Alliance (RBA), it utilizes its standards to identify compliance gaps and support their suppliers in both immediate action and future planning to resolve them. Intel also holds itself accountable to the same RBA criteria as its suppliers.

Providing training and support

Intel supports its suppliers in providing training, infrastructure and tools to help them grow and improve, and implement their own broad-reaching and sustainable change.

Intel Code of Conduct

Intel has a Code of Conduct designed to support delivering integrity, and guiding the actions of its employees, directors, and business partners as it seeks to build trusted relationships around the world.

Intel is not done yet either, and with the advances of technologies its product power, the company is also focused on playing a key role supporting the UN's wider goals. Suzanne Fallender, director of corporate responsibility at Intel, has been quoted as saying: 'We also expect to see increased discussions of how technologies such as artificial intelligence, internet of things, and 5G can be leveraged by multi-stakeholder groups to advance progress toward the UN Sustainable Development Goals' (McPherson, 2019).

An impressive set of initiatives, and one that demonstrates the value of taking a holistic and co-ordinated approach to growing joint value amongst all companies and individuals involved.

4.6 Chapter summary

This chapter has discussed at length the clear need to ensure that supply chain sustainability is a board-level topic at any company that works with external partners to deliver its end product or service. The need for companies to address their impact on the environment is pressing, with less than 10 years to make a genuine impact through material reduction in carbon emissions and waste. It is also clear that companies need to do this not just because it is 'the right thing to do', but also for sound commercial reasons. Companies need to be extremely cognizant of their brands' reputations amongst shifting consumer attitudes – especially those of a new generation of buyers who expect sustainable practice to be at the centre of the companies they are buying from. If they continue to neglect this issue, they will struggle to exist in the future.

However, it is clear that, by looking at the end-to-end process of manufacturing, logistics and distribution, the subject of sustainable management of supply chains rapidly becomes a daunting task and will require marketing practitioners to dive deep into operational parts of the business. We feel this is highly appropriate due to the brand and customer impact of the production of the items the company sells. The business case for sustainably managing your supply chain is also a complex one. All companies need to approach partnerships from a sound commercial basis of course, but it is clear that the best sources of manufacture cannot only be based on the lowest cost base – it is incumbent on markets to ask the question: 'Why so low'? It is imperative to ensure best practice in sustainability is built into contracts, and key areas include human rights, modern slavery and not just 'turning a blind eye' to possible issues in this area from suppliers. It is clear from the companies featured in this chapter that it is possible to achieve a radically more sustainable supply chain with effort and focus.

This is, however, the result of a company and its leadership team having established long-term sustainability goals. Examples such as Intel's 'Code of Conduct' should also inspire marketers to take ownership of communicating this in simple-to-understand language.

Work with your HR/people teams to ensure you have the equivalent guides for the actions of your employees and business partners.

Another key aspect covered by this chapter is the need to ensure that your company upholds strong integrity from its own actions, and that of its suppliers – ultimately seeking to build trusted relationships through the supply chain. Key to this is constantly learning from the actions of other companies, and also sharing information you have and transferring knowledge that can help other organizations.

There will be challenges, and these should be acknowledged and embraced; as you begin to develop your sustainable supply chain strategy, you will likely find it a struggle to persuade all of your suppliers – and their suppliers (and probably their suppliers' suppliers!) – that sustainability makes sound commercial sense. As we have recognized, ultimately business is often about making a profit (whilst delighting your customers of course!), but this does not need to mean people or the environment should suffer as a consequence of your supply chain.

As a first step, we recommend that marketing practitioners take a lead in bringing all departments in your company together to discuss this issue, and to emphasize its overall importance. From there, drive an agenda of creating a suite of mutually beneficial measures that your companies should consider adopting that will act as a method to measure your progress. Good luck; remember it all counts.

4.7 Action points to consider

We want to help you market the importance of embedding sustainability in your supply chain – both strategically and in terms of day-to-day activity as part of your journey to be an 'authentic' brand, and ultimately to use sustainability as a source of competitive advantage. The suggested actions we have for you centre on being clear about what supply chain represents to your business:

No	Action	Considerations	Next Step
1	Review your company's current supply chain sustainability objectives and KPIs.	What areas does your company focus on? What does it not mention?	Write down three areas of supply chain sustainability where your company is making good progress – and three it could do more on. Try to set targets to measure against wherever possible.
2	Review your company's current publicly stated supply chain sustainability position (whether it be in annual reports etc).	How much are you publicly committing to changes or new standards over the next year?	Write up a new summary of what you are doing as a business for your board to approve to release as public information.
3	Consider how you currently work with your procurement function on supply chain sustainably.	Are you ensuring that your procurement team consider your impact on the environment?	Come up with a practical way you can ensure that supply chain sustainability is a regular topic that is discussed – for example, set up a standing meeting on it with your procurement team each month.
4	Consider the Intel case study – how are you auditing your suppliers and sharing sustainability best practices?	What initiatives could you create internally that set your company up for future success|?	Write down three ways technology might support the future growth of your company – how can they be used to improve your sustainability position?
5	How are you working with your company's employees and the employees of your suppliers on sustainability?	What would be your equivalent of Intel's 'Code of Conduct' that guides the actions of their employees, directors and business partners?	Work with other members of the senior leadership team to create your own 'code of conduct' for how your company expects itself and its partners to act.

4.8 Chapter 4 references

Abbasi, M., Nilsson, F. (2012) 'Themes and challenges in making supply chains environmentally sustainable'. *Supply Chain Management: An International Journal.* Vol. 17, No. 5, pp. 517–530

Ahi, P., Jaber, M. Y. and Searcy, C. (2016). 'A comprehensive multidimensional framework for assessing the performance of sustainable supply chains'. *Appl. Math. Model.* 40(23–24), 10153–10166 (2016). Available at: https://doi. org/10.1016/j.apm.2016.07.001 (Accessed: 28 April 2020)

Apple (2019). 'Climate Change – Taking big steps towards a smaller carbon footprint.' Available at: https://www.apple.com/uk/environment/our-approach/ (Accessed: 28 April 2020)

Bhattacharya, C. B. and Sen S. (2004) 'Doing Better at Doing Good: When, Why, and How Consumers Respond to Corporate Social Initiatives'. *California Management Review* 47, no. 1 (fall 2004): 9–24

Bové and Swartz (2016). 'Starting at the source: Sustainability in supply chains'. McKinsey. Available at: https://www.mckinsey.com/business-functions/ sustainability/our-insights/starting-at-the-source-sustainability-in-supply-chains (Accessed: 28 April 2020)

Carter, C. R., & Jennings, M. M. (2002). Social responsibility and supply chain relationships. Transportation Research Part E: Logistics and Transportation Review, 38(1), 37–52. https://doi.org/10.1016/S1366-5545(01)00008-4

Chen, J. (2020). 'Environmental, Social, and Governance (ESG) Criteria'. Available at: https://www.investopedia.com/terms/e/environmental-social-and-governance-esg-criteria.asp (Accessed: 28 April 2020)

Circular Online (2020). 'Retailers feeling pressure from consumers to prioritise sustainable packaging'. Available at: https://www.circularonline.co.uk/ news/retailers-feeling-pressure-from-consumers-to-prioritise-sustainable-packaging/ (Accessed: 28 April 2020)

Coyle, M. (2020). 'Go behind the scenes as Amazon develops a new electric vehicle'. Available at: https://blog.aboutamazon.com/sustainability/go-behind-the-scenes-as-amazon-develops-a-new-electric-vehicle (Accessed: 28 April 2020)

Crane, A. Spence, L. and Matten, D. (2014). 'Four Types Of Workplace'. Available at: https://www.researchgate.net/publication/228123773_ Corporate_Social_Responsibility_In_Global_Context (Accessed: 28 April 2020)

CVC (2020). 'EcoVadis secures c.$200m investment from CVC Growth Partners'. Available at: https://www.cvc.com/media/press-releases/2020/ecovadis-secures-200m-investment-cvc-growth-partners (Accessed: 28 April 2020)

Ernest-Jones, S. (2020). 'CSR trends that can make or break a brand'. Available at: https://blog.globalwebindex.com/marketing/csr-trends-2020/ (Accessed: 28 April 2020)

GRI (2020). 'About GRI'. Available at: https://www.globalreporting.org/Information/about-gri/Pages/default.aspx (Accessed: 28 April 2020)

Hanifan, G. L., Sharma, A. E. and Mehta, P. (2012). 'Accenture – Why a sustainable supply chain is good business'. Available at: https://www.accenture.com/t20150522t061611_w_/ph-en/_acnmedia/accenture/conversion-assets/outlook/documents/1/accenture-outlook-why-sustainable-supply-chain-is-good-business.pdf (Accessed: 28 April 2020)

Intel (2019). 'Supply Chain Responsibility At Intel' Available at https://www.intel.co.uk/content/www/uk/en/corporate-responsibility/supply-chain.html (Accessed: 9 August 2020)

Köksal, D., Strähle, J., Müller M. and Freise, M. (2017). 'Social sustainable supply chain management in the textile and apparel industry – A literature review'. *Sustainability 2017*, 9, 100. Available at: https://www.mdpi.com/2071-1050/9/1/100 (Accessed: 28 April 2020)

Kotler, P. (2011). 'Reinventing Marketing to Manage the Environmental Imperative'. Available at: http://www.mindful-consumption.org/images/articles/reinventing-marketing.pdf (Accessed: 28 April 2020)

Lieb, K.J. and Lieb, R.C. (2010). 'Environmental sustainability in the third-party logistics (3PL) industry'. *International Journal of Physical Distribution & Logistics Management*, Vol. 40, No. 7, pp. 524–33. Available at: https://www.researchgate.net/publication/239294215_Environmental_sustainability_in_the_third-party_logistics_3PL_industry (Accessed: 28 April 2020)

Lin, X., Ho, C. M. and Shen, G. Q. (2017). 'Who should take the responsibility? Stakeholders' power over social responsibility issues in construction projects'. *Journal of Cleaner Production, Vol. 154* (2017), pp. 318–29. Available at: https://www.sciencedirect.com/science/article/pii/S0959652617307035 (Accessed: 28 April 2020)

López-Gamero, M. D., Molina-Azorín, J. F. and Claver-Cortés, E. (2010). 'The potential of environmental regulation to change managerial perception, environmental management, competitiveness and financial performance', *Journal of Cleaner Production*, Vol. 18, pp. 963–974.

Marchet, G., Melacini, M. and Perotti, S. (2014). 'Environmental sustainability in logistics and freight transportation: A literature review and research agenda'. *Journal of Manufacturing Technology Management*, Vol., 25, No. 6, pp. 775–811

McPherson, S. (2019). 'Corporate Responsibility: What To Expect In 2019'. Forbes. Available at: https://www.forbes.com/sites/susanmcpherson/2019/01/14/corporate-responsibility-what-to-expect-in-2019/#10d0696c690f (Accessed: 9 August 2020)

Oliveira, P. and Sullivan, A. (2015). 'Sustainability and its Impact on Brand Value'. Interbrand. Available at: https://www.interbrand.com/wp-content/uploads/2015/10/3.-Sustainabilityand-its-impact-in-BV.pdf (Accessed: 28 April 2020).

Patel, V. J. (2020). 'Rivian, Amazon Provide New Details on Upcoming Electric Vans'. Available at: https://www.futurecar.com/3771/Rivian-Amazon-Provide-New-Details-on-Upcoming-Electric-Vans (Accessed: 28 April 2020).

Peloza, J., Falkenberg, L. (2009). 'The role of collaboration in achieving corporate social responsibility objectives'. *California Management Review*, 51, 95–113

Piecyk, M. I. and Björklund, M. (2015). 'Logistics service providers and corporate social responsibility: Sustainability reporting in the logistics industry'. *International Journal of Physical Distribution & Logistics Management, Vol. 45, No. 5*, pp. 459–85

Pinterest (2019). 'Pinterest 100'. Available at: https://www.pinterest100.com/en-us/ (Accessed: 28 April 2020)

Porter, M. E. and Kramer, M. R. (2011), 'Creating Shared Value', *Harvard Business Review*, Vol. 89, No. 1, 2011, pp. 2–17

Sadler, D. and Lloyd, S. (2009), 'Neo-liberalising corporate social responsibility: A political economy of corporate citizenship', *Geoforum*, Vol. 40 No. 4, pp. 613–622

Simpson, D., Power, D., Samson, D. (2007) Greening the automotive supply chain: a relationship perspective. *International Journal of Operations & Production Management*, Vol. 27, No. 1, pp. 28–48

Starbucks (2020). 'Empowered to Live Well'. Available at: https://www.starbucks.com/careers/working-at-starbucks/benefits-and-perks (Accessed: 28 April 2020)

Tetrapak (2020). 'Welcome to planet positive'. Available at: https://www.tetrapak. com/sustainability/planet-positive (Accessed: 28 April 2020)

The Global LAMP Index® (2010). Available at: https://www.lampindex.com/the-global-lamp-index (Accessed: 28 April 2020)

United Nations Climate Change (2020). 'What is the Paris Agreement?'. Available at: https://unfccc.int/process-and-meetings/the-paris-agreement/what-is-the-paris-agreement (Accessed: 28 April 2020)

United Nations Global Compact (2020). 'Supply Chain Sustainability: The Business Case'. Available at: https://www.unglobalcompact.org/what-is-gc/our-work/supply-chain/business-case (Accessed: 28 April 2020)

Villena, V. H. and Gioia, D.A. (2020). 'A More Sustainable Supply Chain'. *Harvard Business Review*, March–April 2020 Issue. Available at: https://hbr. org/2020/03/a-more-sustainable-supply-chain (Accessed 28 April 2020)

Watts, J. (2018). 'We have 12 years to limit climate change catastrophe, warns UN'. *Guardian*. Available at: https://www.theguardian.com/environment/2018/oct/08/global-warming-must-not-exceed-15c-warns-landmark-un-report (Accessed: 28 April 2020)

Wave of Innovation and Growth. *Harvard Business Review* (January/February).

Wind, J. and Frederick, J. (1972). 'A General Model for Understanding Organizational Buying Behavior'. *Journal of Marketing*, 36 (2), pp.12–19. Available at: https://www.jstor.org/stable/1250972?seq=1 (Accessed: 28 April 2020)

Xia, Y., Tang, T. L-P. (2011). 'Sustainability in Supply Chain Management: Suggestions for the auto industry'. *Management Decision*, Vol. 49, No. 4, pp. 495–512

Yu, T., Liang, X., Shen, G. Q. and Shi Wang, G. (2019). 'An optimization model for managing stakeholder conflicts in urban redevelopment projects in China'. *Journal of Cleaner Production*, Vol. 212, 1 March 2019, pp. 537–47. Available at: https://www.sciencedirect.com/science/article/pii/S0959652618337739 (Accessed: 28 April 2020)

CHAPTER FIVE

Beyond Corporate Social Responsibility

5.0 Chapter introduction

What better way to start a chapter on 'Beyond Corporate Social Responsibility' than diving in a little deeper to find out what we already know about it. In our opening chapter we introduced the concept of corporate social responsibility – but as marketers, often commissioned with communicating the values and sustainable pursuits of the organization, are we clear on what it actually means from a practical perspective? If the honest answer is 'no', then you're not alone. According to a bespoke study of UK and US citizens, only one in three people are aware of CSR and what it means (Stankovic, 2019). And further, the level of understanding differs depending upon demographics. When considering going 'Beyond Corporate Social Responsibility' then, it's only prudent to start off by getting some clarity on exactly what CSR is, where it came from and what it means for organizations.

Therefore, in this chapter we'll briefly cover its heritage and focus, facts and stats, considering what organizations can be doing in an idealistic world, versus the reality of what they're actually doing. We'll touch on external forces, such as the rise of the conscious consumer and the part consumers and employees play in forcing organizations to wake up to the reality of belief-driven consumerism, as well as looking at case studies from organizations that are coming together as a 'movement' for real change, and the practicalities of taking a stance and making a commitment to go beyond the often described 'tick box' CSR activities and to actually change what being a responsible business represents.

Our objective for this chapter is that you come away fully educated about CSR and what companies are doing to go beyond it, so that, from a brand and marketing perspective, you can question current frameworks or activities, understand the pitfalls and be inspired by those organizations that are truly moving beyond CSR, to bring about change for the better within your own activity and organizations.

5.1 Where are we?

The history of CSR and responsible business could effectively be traced back 5,000 years to Ancient Mesopotamia, where in around 1700 BC, King Hammurabi introduced a code that meant that builders, innkeepers or farmers were put to death if their negligence caused the death of, or major inconvenience to, local citizens. History is filled with stories about the failure of businesses contributing sufficiently to society, and complaints and schemes, some 'self-managed', to better manage the profit and people balance. The term 'Corporate Social Responsibility' (CSR) is officially attributed as being coined by American economist Howard Bowen in his 1953 publication *Social Responsibilities of the Businessman* (ThomasNet. com, 2019). The publication largely focused on the simple endeavour of businesses giving back to the very societies that afforded them to drive revenues and profit. However, it wasn't until the 1970s that the concept of the social contract between businesses and society was introduced by the Committee for Economic Development. This was based on the idea that companies function and exist because of public consent and therefore have an obligation to contribute to the needs of society. CSR continued to evolve throughout the 1980s and 90s, marking the beginning of widespread global approval and adoption of CSR, including models and frameworks aligned with strategic business planning to assess impact and outcomes of CSR programmes.

5.2 What is CSR?

'The focus of corporate social responsibility is to boost shareholder trust and increase long-term profits in a sustainable and ethical way by taking ownership of corporate decisions and improving them' (www. thegivingmachine.co.uk).

From a business perspective, CSR is now generally understood as a 'framework' or series of largely self-regulated initiatives that a company engages with or implements in order to achieve a balance of economic, environmental and social imperatives (aligned with the triple bottom line approach – profit, people, planet) whilst at the same time addressing the needs of shareholders and stakeholders. Although the overriding message is relatively simple – do good business and be responsible whilst driving profit for shareholders – the reality is that CSR is complex and vast, so that without any formal compliance and steady, audited guidance, it leaves the concept rather rudderless and open to interpretation.

Within your own organization, CSR may be a strategic driving force, embedded within strategy and culture and aligned with organizational objectives, supported by rigorous programmes and initiatives rolled out as part of your operating framework. Or, indeed, it may be less of a strategic endeavour, perhaps seen as something that you have to do, evoking the occasional eyeball rolling around the boardroom with the CSR box being ticked with a token gesture of an annual charitable donation. We love the analogy from Prof. Dr Thomas Beshorne, director of the Institute for Business Ethics at the University of St Gallen, in his attempt to explain CSR in a 10-minute YouTube video: 'CSR is a bit like teenage sex, most say they are doing it, but they aren't. And those that are doing it, are doing it badly' (Beschorne, 2019).

Regardless of the stance within your own organization, companies are seemingly starting to care more about corporate social responsibility. It's difficult to find exact figures that reveal how many organizations actually have a CSR mandate in place and are practically implementing activities, and the impact that creates, but one piece of global research showcases that amongst the largest 250 companies in the world in 2015, 92 per cent produced a CSR report informing shareholders and the public about the organization's activities, seeing a 64 per cent increase in activity reported since 2005. Further, Fortune Global 500 firms spend around $20 billion a year on CSR activities (Bartels and King, 2015).

5.3 The practicalities and why companies really need to get on board now

Corporate social responsibility is complex and can show up in many forms. Common examples include:

- reducing carbon footprints;
- improving labour policies;
- participating in Fairtrade;
- charitable giving;
- volunteering in the community;
- corporate policies that benefit the environment;
- social and environmentally conscious investments.

CSR encourages companies to evaluate their business practices and plans to focus on becoming more ethical and conscious of their impact, which is not only good for society and the environment but is also proven to be good for brand and profits, too, which leads us to conscious consumers, the bottom line and employee engagement.

The rise of the conscious consumer

As we've touched on, as consumers have become more connected digitally, so too have they become more educated and empowered when it comes to considering the environmental, social and political impact of their purchasing habits. According to a study by Walnut Omnibus (Oligschlaeger, 2019), the conscious consumer is here to stay and the trend is on the rise, with 75 per cent of the public consciously modifying their behaviour when it comes to consumer items – and being prepared to pay more for eco-friendly and sustainable products. And in another study, by GlobalWebIndex, two-thirds of consumers think it's important to contribute to the community they live in, buying into brands that partner with causes or charities being seen as a simple way for conscious consumers to feel like they're contributing and giving back (Stankovic, 2019).

For example, TOMS, the sustainable footwear organization, pledged to donate a free pair of shoes to a child in need whenever a pair was sold. This resulted in more than 60 million pairs of shoes being donated. In April 2020, amidst the global Covid-19 pandemic, TOMS donated one-third of their net profits to the TOMS Covid-19 Global Giving Fund to support partners on the frontline of the global health crisis (www.toms.co.uk).

The GlobalWebIndex research further showcases that:

- 1 in 10 consumers are loyal to their favourite brands because they know the company makes charitable donations;
- 68 per cent of online consumers in the US and UK would or might stop using a brand because of poor or misleading CSR;
- 84 per cent say a poor environmental track record would or might cause them to stop buying from a brand;
- nearly half (43 per cent) are willing to pay a premium for socially conscious or environmentally friendly brands.

What's interesting is that whilst the younger demographic (16–24 year olds) are generally less aware of the term CSR and what it stands for, they are far from ignorant when it comes to what corporate social responsibility stands for – and they are the age demographic that make up the 43 per cent most likely to want the brands they buy from to produce eco-friendly products and support charities, compared to only 31 per cent of 55–64 year olds. Furthermore, whilst price has traditionally been the main influencer in determining purchase decisions, their research data suggests that generally consumers are not only willing to buy more frequently from brands with a strong CSR message, but that they will also pay more for their products, and this is growing, rising from 49 per cent in 2011 to 57 per cent in 2019.

In a further study, 78 per cent of Gen Zers were more likely to buy a product or service from a company that gives back to society; 56 per cent are willing to pay more for a product or service from a company that gives back; and 69 per cent believe brands should stand up for what they believe in, even if it's controversial. Further, 67 per cent have stopped purchasing or would consider stopping purchasing (27 per cent) from a company if it stood for something or behaved in a way that didn't align with their values (Ferguson, M., 2018). These findings are further echoed in Brandwatch's 'Global Consumer Trends 2020' report, which revealed that 18–24 year olds are more likely than any other age group to choose 'approach to sustainability' when talking about reasons they'd choose to buy from a brand (Brandwatch, 2020).

The key takeaway from the various research findings is that consumers are generally more aware, educated and concerned about what they purchase and the reputation and values of the organizations they're purchasing from.

CSR and the bottom line

The Project ROI study, commissioned by the Campbell Soup Company and Verizon (Barney, R., 2020) set out to uncover the return on investment to the bottom line of CSR practices. Whilst the study found that the highest drivers of ROI for any company is providing high-quality products and services, they also found that effective CSR practices boosted business performance, delivering a higher ROI than if a company with the same products did not engage with CSR. The report also found that taking a long-term approach to CSR returned the most financial benefits, increasing the market value of a company by 4–6 per cent and over a 15-year period increasing shareholder value by approximately $1.28 billion.

CSR and employee engagement

As well as driving ROI, the study also found that engaging in meaningful CSR could avoid revenue losses of up to 7 per cent of a company's market value – and importantly reduce employee turnover rate by a significant 50 per cent, determining that when CSR is practised in a company, employees are more engaged and more committed to work productively.

By 2025, millennials will make up three-quarters of the workforce, with research stating that 64 per cent of this generation of workers won't take a job at a company that doesn't have strong social responsibility practices in place (Coleman, A., 2019). Further, and important for future employee engagement, 83 per cent of Gen Zers see a company's purpose as a core consideration in where to work – and they won't take companies on their word alone, with 75 per cent of these true technology natives doing research to see if a company is really walking the talk (Porter Novelli/Cone, 2019). Importantly, their study further indicates that firms should not use CSR initiatives as merely another tool to benefit their HR strategy. Workers care about the genuine use of prosocial incentives and may react negatively to firms using social initiatives to increase productivity or profits.

5.4 Things that need to be acknowledged as not perfect

Trust plays its part in responsible marketing

Today, as consumers, we have more choice than ever when it comes to which brands we spend our money with. It's a theme we keep returning to as trust and transparency are a significant component of building brand loyalty, and when it comes to cause-related campaigns and brands being seen to take a stand, it appears that we are becoming increasingly cynical and are acutely aware of false purpose.

There have been a number brands that have paid the price and felt the backlash for jumping on the value-based, cause-related marketing bandwagon and 'woke-washing' (a term that describes a driving sentiment to improve the world but that doesn't take real action). For example, in 2019, Cadbury launched a Unity Bar for Indian Independence Day – a blend of dark, milk and white chocolate – and used the launch of the bar to make a point about celebrating diversity. However, it didn't go well and there was an unprecedented level of unrest and vitriol towards the brand on social media, with people upset that Cadbury had embarked on an opportunistic marketing campaign by jumping on a sensitive subject (Ritson, M., 2019).

The lesson from a marketing perspective is to tread very carefully and ensure that your purpose is fully baked into brand values and that you are authentic with any cause-related marketing activities – and also have a clean bill of health should consumers decide to do their research (which, as we've outlined previously, we know they do). A report from GlobalWebIndex (Stankovic, 2019) highlights the factors that alienate people most from a brand:

- poor environment track record (84 per cent);
- unsustainable packaging (83 per cent);

- poor compliance record (82 per cent);
- irresponsible sourcing of materials (82 per cent);
- poor human rights track record (82 per cent).

The report goes on to outline the top 10 industries cited as being in need of better CSR policies:

1) energy
2) pharmaceutical
3) food
4) manufacturing
5) transport
6) fashion
7) automotive
8) financial
9) construction
10) Internet

What's interesting is that, as we've highlighted previously, fashion is one of the largest contributors to harmful industries – with water pollution, toxic chemical use, plastic packaging and textile waste being major issues – yet it's down the list at position six with only 43 per cent of US and UK Internet users believing that the fashion industry should hold itself more accountable for having a better CSR policy.

Beyond CSR and the B Corp movement

'We are building a global economy that uses business as a force for good' (https://bcorporation.net).

When we talk about brands taking a stand, an increasing number of consciously driven organizations are removing the ambiguity aligned with CSR and taking matters into their own hands by joining the global movement known as 'B Corporations'. Founded in 2006, certified B Corporations are businesses dedicated to and, importantly, held accountable for, balancing purpose with profit and using business as a force for good.

There are three key components of B Corp certification:

1) Verified performance – assessing overall positive impact of the company.

2) Legal accountability – companies are legally required to consider the impact of their decisions on their workers, customers, suppliers, communities and the environment, amending their legal governing documents to consider purpose with profit, committing you to consider stakeholder impact for the long term by building it into your company's legal structure.

3) Public transparency – all B Corporations undergo a 'B Impact Assessment', a rigorous assessment that evaluates how your company's operations and business model impacts your workers, customers, community and the environment. And as champions of transparency, each company's B Impact Report is available to all via the central website (https://bcorporation.net).

Gaining accreditation is far from a 'one and done' tick-box assessment. B Corporations have to recertify every three years, and certifying as a B Corporation goes beyond product- or service-level certification. B Corporation Certification is the only certification that measures a company's entire social and environmental performance, from supply chain and input materials through to charitable giving and employee benefits. The certification proves that a business is continuously meeting the highest standards of verified performance and committing to 'The B Corporation Declaration of Interdependence'.

The B Corporation Declaration of Interdependence

We envision a global economy that uses business as a force for good.

This economy is comprised of a new type of corporation – the B Corporation – which is purpose-driven and creates benefit for all stakeholders, not just shareholders.

As B Corporations and leaders of this emerging economy, we believe:

- That we must be the change we seek in the world.
- That all business ought to be conducted as if people and place mattered.
- That, through their products, practices, and profits, businesses should aspire to do no harm and benefit all.
- To do so requires that we act with the understanding that we are each dependent upon another and thus responsible for each other and future generations.

BCorporation.net

At the time of writing, there are 3,285 accredited B Corps around the world, across 150 industries, spanning 71 countries. Any for-profit organization can become a B Corp, and there are tiered accreditations tailored to the size and profitability of an organization – from start-ups to large multi-billion revenue-generating corporations. B Corps include a range of organizations, a small sample including: Ben & Jerrys, Patagonia, Arbonne, Natura, The Body Shop, Teapigs, Vita Coco and Cook Trading.

Accreditation isn't for the faint-hearted – there are more than 100 different criteria and the bar keeps rising year on year. Accreditation is administered by the not-for-profit B Lab, which operates a global network of accreditors (that themselves are B Corporations). Their role is to support those going through accreditation, facilitate the assessment and ensure standards are met and adhered to. There are more than 70,000 organizations that have taken the B Impact Assessment – it's a free and useful assessment that your organization can use to run some situation analysis in relation to purpose and profit. You can take the assessment here: https://bimpactassessment. net. You'll also find case studies and assessment scores on the website. It's worth noting that on a scale of 0–200, the average assessment score for a B Corporation is 80 – and that even dedicated pioneer Patagonia only has a score of 107!

To find out more about B Lab and B Corporations first-hand, we spoke to James Perry, current co-chairman and former CEO of Cook Trading Ltd (a certified B Corp), who is also the co-founder of the UK's B Lab.

James told us:

Being a B Corp starts with intent. B Corps are a very strong community built on sharing best practice, supportive relationships and trust. There's a collective deeper idea of what business stands for. As a B Corp you're part of a global movement. Traditionally, the purpose of business and the supporting legal structure is to generate as much profit as possible for shareholders. However, as a B Corp, you're operating within a different paradigm – it's about driving profitable solutions whilst considering how you can do that and at the same time, do good for people and planet.

To become a B Corp you have to truly want to be in service of people and planet as it means making some sacrifices. Doing things the right way may cost you a bit more and can be hard work – so you really have to want to do them. At Cook, we took decisions to pay our employees the living wage and implemented energy supply systems which meant some considerable financial investment – but didn't cost the earth.

For those organisations where there may be a desire for the accreditation, but the genuine commitment and intent is missing, within such a strong and like-minded community, it's quickly evident. As a global movement we're all championing the credibility of the B Corp status. Whilst re-certification is a formal process, the community is pretty much self-policing: those that aren't fully invested or are invested for the wrong reasons are quickly identified and they don't remain in the community.

5.5 B Corp case study – S'well

We also interviewed, Sarah Kauss, founder and executive chairwoman of reusable insulated products brand S'well (swell.com). S'well recently received B Corp accreditation (2019), and so we were keen to understand why she had chosen to pursue this route.

1) Where does CSR fit into S'well generally?
'It, like design, is a part of our DNA. Since day one, I've worked to ensure S'well was not only in the business of creating beautiful products that perform, but also in the business of giving back. We create products, build programmes and work with people that are focused on positively changing the world.'

2) How does B Corp accreditation impact your business – is it helping you to have a clear framework for CSR and keeping you accountable?
'Being a B Corp has helped us benchmark our success, create a roadmap for the future and evolve our commitment to responsible business strategically. We appreciate having a respected third-party resource and community to help guide us as we continue to build a business built on sustainability and social impact.'

3) Why did you want to achieve B Corp status?

'When I founded S'well in 2010, I had one mission: reduce the use of single-use plastic bottles while helping communities in need. Love for the planet and its people has driven our actions since day one, attracting purpose-driven team members and guiding the way we do business. S'well's B Corp Certification reaffirms our commitment to being a leader in sustainable living through higher levels of verification tied to environmental and social performance, transparency and accountability. We're using our learnings from this incredible process and the amazing B Corp network to evolve the way we approach responsible business for the future and look forward to sharing more updates with you as they happen.'

5.6 Chapter summary

From a marketing sustainability perspective, when it comes to CSR there are a number of practical aspects for you to consider. With regard to brand reputation and owning the customer journey, marketing is usually championing these areas – and within this chapter we've highlighted how brand reputation, conscious consumerism and also employee engagement is impacted by an organization's CSR efforts. As we've demonstrated throughout this chapter, there are a number of positive CSR benefits for organizations:

- brand reputation and image;
- customer loyalty;
- employee engagement and satisfaction;
- financial bottom line impact.

Brands and organizations have encountered significant backlash, often exacerbated by the reach of social media, when seemingly cause-related initiatives aren't delivered authentically. We've evidenced the positive impact to the bottom line that can be derived when organizations take a stand and align with the more conscious values of their audiences. We've also shared insights into movements such as B Corps that are taking the ambiguity away from CSR and creating clear and accountable frameworks and targets that commit organizations to take action and stand by their brand promise and the triple bottom line.

Marketing today isn't simply about talking about organizational purpose and values, it's about evidencing impact and understanding what's important to your customers, and aligning with their purpose and values too. When it comes to responsible marketing, throughout this entire book we challenge you to consider how you can take practical steps in relation to: packaging, plastic, energy, the climate, waste, partnerships and supply chains. Each aspect is part of the economic, social and environmental umbrella of CSR.

5.7 Action points to consider

Corporate social responsibility is something that you may already be ahead of the game on, and your cause-related marketing activities may be exactly where you need them to be. If not, here are some practical aspects for you to question and consider:

No.	Action	Considerations	Next Step
1	Assume corporate social responsibility.	How can cause-related marketing initiatives fit into your CSR plan? And if they're in there already, are they authentic?	Commit to taking the lead to drive two cause-related marketing initiatives that align with purpose and audiences.
2	Be aware of conscious consumers.	Do you understand the purpose and values of your audiences?	If not, perhaps you could develop a survey and undertake some consumer research to better understand their views around sustainability and issues that are close to their heart – so that you can learn more about what they're basing their purchasing decisions and choices upon.
3	Aim for employee engagement.	An internal marketing initiative – could you lead and champion an initiative with your HR department to better understand the needs of employees? How do they feel about the organization's CSR efforts? How diverse is the workplace? Are employees kept up to date and aware of the CSR work the organization embarks on?	Run an internal audit to identify any 'gaps' and develop a structured action plan to improve activities or initiate communications.

No.	Action	Considerations	Next Step
4	Do a B Impact Assessment.	Take the B Impact Assessment – whilst you may not be considering B Corp accreditation, the assessment will give you a benchmark and stimulate thinking around what's possible for your organization. It will also help you to better understand any potential gaping holes.	Complete the B Impact Assessment at https://bimpactassessment.net/ and see how your business compares.
5	Work with other companies.	How can you take inspiration from B Corp companies?	Review the case studies or look for organizations similar to yours. What ideas and best practice can you implement?

And we'll close the chapter with some wise words from business and management academic Henry Mintzberg: 'Successful corporate social responsibility initiatives will never match or remedy the effects of corporate social irresponsibility.'

5.8 Chapter 5 references

Barney, R., (2020). 'Project ROI – Project ROI: Defining the Competitive and Financial Advantages of Corporate Responsibility and Sustainability'. Babson College. Available at: Good360.org (Accessed: April 2020)

Bartels, W. and King, A. (2015). 'The KPMG Survey of Corporate Social Responsibility Reporting 2015'. KPMG. Available at: https://home.kpmg/content/dam/kpmg/pdf/2015/12/KPMG-survey-of-CR-reporting-2015.pdf (Accessed: 29 June 2020)

Brandwatch. 'Global Consumer Trends 2020'. Available at: https://www.brandwatch.com/reports/consumer-trends-for-2020/ (Accessed: 29 June 2020)

Certified B Corporation – https://bcorporation.net/ (Accessed: 29 June 2020)

Coleman, A. (2019). 'Should business be paying more attention to CSR?' *Telegraph*, 8 October 2019. Available at: https://www.telegraph.co.uk/business/ready-and-enabled/why-corporate-social-responsibility-is-important/ (Accessed: 29 June 2020)

Ferguson, M. (2018). 'How Gen Z Are Leading Brands to Listen and Act'. Available at: https://medium.com/dosomethingstrategic/how-gen-z-are-leading-brands-to-listen-and-act-2c05e341255d (Accessed: 29 June 2020)

Mintzberg, H. (2017). 'Be the Change. The Future is Here, Why BDC believes in social entrepreneurs'. Available at: https://bthechange.com/the-future-is-here-why-bdc-believes-in-social-entrepreneurs-1973ab86168a (Accessed: 29 June 2020)

Oligschlaeger, A. (2019). 'Rise of the Conscious Consumer'. Available at: https://www.walnutunlimited.com/rise-of-the-conscious-consumer (Accessed: 14 January 2019)

Porter Novelli/Cone (2019). 'Undivided – Gen Z Purpose Study'. Available at: https://www.conecomm.com/research-blog/cone-gen-z-purpose-study (Accessed: 29 June 2020)

Prof. Dr. Beschorner, T. 'What is CSR' (video), University of St. Gillan. Available at: https://youtu.be/E0NkGtNU_9w (Accessed: 29 June 2020)

Ritson, M. (2019). 'Cadbury's brand purpose is just "woke-washing"'. *Marketing Week*. Available at: https://www.marketingweek.com/mark-ritson-cadbury-brand-purpose-woke-washing/ (Accessed: 29 June 2020)

Stankovic, K. (2019). 'Do consumers actually care about Corporate Social Responsibility?', GlobalWebIndex. Available at: https://blog.globalwebindex.com/chart-of-the-week/corporate-social-responsibility/ (Accessed: 29 June 2020)

The Giving Machine.com (www.thegivingmachine.co.uk). Corporate Social Responsibility – A Simple Guide. https://www.thegivingmachine.co.uk/corporate-social-responsibility-simple-guide/ (Accessed: 29 June 2020)

ThomasNet.com, (2019). 'A Brief History of Corporate Social Responsibility (CSR)'. Available at: https://www.thomasnet.com/insights/history-of-corporate-social-responsibility/ (Accessed: 29 June 2020)

Toms (www.toms.co.uk). (Accessed: 26 April 2020)

CHAPTER SIX

Reducing Waste in The Workplace

6.0 Chapter introduction

It is (thankfully!) increasingly widely accepted that reducing waste is one key component of conserving the earth's resources and trying to protect against even more serious issues in the future.

Many business leaders and more and more of their customers are conscious of the impact to the planet purely created through how we live our lives, and are to an increasing extent focusing efforts on the reduction of landfill waste with more recycling, food composting and the use of reusable rather than single-use items. But what of reducing waste in the workplace? It is perhaps fair to say that many companies have yet to apply the same standards to their day-to-day offices and marketing practice.

Whilst it is hard to imagine that many companies in the 2020s are activity choosing *not* to put their energy into workplace waste reduction, it is also not yet a strong boardroom topic – and despite its obvious benefits, reducing waste is often mired with traditional business-case thinking and a focus on outdated methods of assessing return on investment (ROI) because it's perceived that in many cases employing waste reduction doesn't seem to directly produce revenue or lead to short-term cost saving. However, as we've suggested, we believe this issue needs to be owned by marketing teams, who are better equipped to explain how undertaking a waste management programme can in fact be a source of competitive advantage and cost reduction in the long term.

6.1 Where are we?

This chapter will explore ideas for how companies can practically begin to address the issue of waste in their specific marketing activity, but also how to rethink the wider context of the office environment and also areas of waste produced as a consequence of business activity.

According to Rod Tonna-Barthet, CEO of KYOCERA Document Solutions UK: 'Paper is arguably one of the most visible environmental impacts in the office environment and our research suggests that the average office worker uses 45 pieces of paper every day, much of which goes to waste' (Tonna-Barthet, 2019).

Let's be honest, for many of the companies we work for, and work with, managing this type of office waste is not that much a priority, is it? The reasons for this are interesting in themselves and it's perhaps a combination of 'turning a blind eye' and a lack of understanding about the material impact their business is making on the environment. In our experience, this is often just a factor of ignorance about what the alternatives are. It is perhaps then understandable that it feels even more inconvenient to establish a specific programme of work in this area. However, don't be discouraged – read on! Even if your business is not *quite* ready to establish a managed piece of work to help develop more environmentally appropriate measures, there are multiple simple and massively effective ways your company can reduce waste that are not too painful to implement, are greatly impactful to the environment and, helpfully, can both make, and save, your company money.

Let's focus on an immediate area that is likely to pique interest in your company – the need to better manage costs. Great news: strategies that reduce waste can really help with this. However, we need to acknowledge that a lack of progress on reducing waste is often due to ignorance about where to begin. For example, a recent report from Iron Mountain ('Strategies To Reduce Waste In Marketing

Collateral', 2019) revealed that 42 per cent of companies surveyed in regulated industries simply don't know where to start in terms of reducing waste.

Targets – or lack thereof

Another issue for business (and an issue repeated a lot throughout this book) is the lack of clear targets for reducing waste – how does a company know what it is aiming to do?

In 2018, the European Commission backtracked on their previous ambitious target set of legislative promises on reducing waste and recycling – including the phasing out of using landfill for recyclable rubbish and a commitment to cut food waste by 30 per cent by 2025.

And it is not just Europe that is struggling with this issue; the US arguably has its own struggles with recycling. The US is 25th in global recycling rankings, according to a 2017 report (Gray, 2017). The report also notes that the European countries contained in the report typically recycle 30 per cent of their plastic waste, whilst the US only recycles 9 per cent, of which a large part is electronic or e-waste – an increasingly pernicious issue, as we'll cover later in this chapter.

Time for a circular rethink

Waste experts are increasingly lobbying for waste to be treated as a resource (Balch, 2015) rather than through the traditional linear 'make-use-dispose model' on which our society is built and that needs to be removed from most companies' way of working. Instead, it is key to adopt 'circular' practices, whereby the elements of recycling and reuse are also woven into our businesses and wider economic systems. For starters, this switch requires a massive overhaul of how waste is conceived. Even the word is loaded: 'waste isn't actually wasted material,' says Marcus Gover, director at the UK advocacy group WRAP, 'it's a valuable commodity. And the first companies that need to recognize that are the waste (or should that be value?) management companies'. By 2025, waste disposers 'won't be burying or burning people's rubbish as they do today', states Gover. These companies will merge into what he terms the 'reprocessing industry', where their central role is not to dump stuff but to return 'valuable resources to manufacturers'. This is an exciting proposition, which of course requires a similar rethink by the designers and manufacturers too. 'The goods of today,' Gover says, 'need to be seen as the raw materials of tomorrow'. When that happens, products will begin to be made with a view to lasting longer and to being easier to repair and ultimately dismantle. Philips' easy-to-disassemble light bulb provides an illustrative case in point.

Waste food segregation and composting

Target 12.3 of the SDG states: 'By 2030, halve per capita global food waste at the retail and consumer levels and reduce food losses along production and supply chains, including post-harvest losses'. In accordance with this goal, a major change that companies can look at practically is their internal management of food. According to the Food and Agriculture Organization of the United Nations (2013) the global volume of food wastage was estimated at 1.6 billion tonnes of primary product equivalents, with food wastage's carbon footprint estimated at 3.3 billion tonnes of carbon dioxide equivalent of greenhouse gases released into the atmosphere per year. Unfortunately, this is due to the fact that a low percentage of all food wastage is composted; much of it ends up in landfills, and represents a large part of municipal solid waste.

This therefore represents a key issue, about which business should be informed by concrete guidance from government on how companies could, and should, approach waste management – for example the UK government's 2018 food and drink material hierarchy:

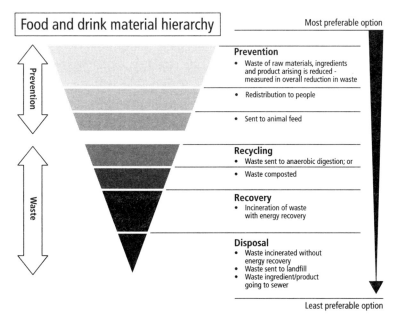

Figure 2 (https://jg-environmental.com/waste-management-case-study/kingsley-print-printing-waste/)

Increased company responsibility and measurement

As consumers' attitudes to waste change, it is also time for fast-moving consumer goods (FMCG) manufacturers, consumer products brands and retailers to address the need to sell recyclable packaging. According to Conrad MacKerron, director of the corporate social responsibility programme at the As You Sow Foundation, less than 14 per cent of plastic packaging is currently recycled in the US, noting: 'Businesses responsible for those sales need to step up and take a strong measure of responsibility for financing collection and recycling of post-consumer packaging' (Balch, 2015).

It is clear that there are many sources of waste, and we'll discuss plastic and indeed packaging in more detail in later chapters. For now, let's explore some sources of potential waste in terms of what you, and your company office environment, are likely to be producing, to help us develop a new mindset about this issue. This is likely to necessitate your own company taking a much more holistic approach to measuring 'what good looks like'. According to research by PwC (PwC, 2018), more than 93 per cent of CEOs surveyed said that measuring both their financial and non-financial performance would enable them to better identify and manage their risks, as until now, it's been hard to quantify and monetize social and environmental impacts, leaving them stranded outside traditional accounting and ROI decisions.

6.2 Why do companies need to do something about this now?

The growing global environmental change movement is increasingly highlighting how opportunities to help the planet can also present real tangible business benefits. By embracing more sustainable practices that offer a low carbon footprint, businesses can reduce waste and save on cost. Throughout this book, we discuss many macro-level strategies and opportunities, but there is a huge opportunity for companies to make significant changes in their general day-to-day office practice too. Whilst marketing and business increasingly turns digital, it is essential to recognize that from a very practical perspective there are still multiple ways to reduce waste in your workplace. Let's explore some examples and why your company needs to do something about this now.

Going as close to paperless as possible

Whilst it is clear that recycling is essential, a greater impact will come from actually using less – or no – paper in the first place. One of the biggest culprits for this is the use of paper for 'one-off' meetings, such as monthly senior management team meetings or board meetings, for which huge packs of reports (paper) are produced, and often never used again, only to sit (pointlessly) in a filing cabinet. Simply distributing such documents digitally would make a significant difference and with the onset of commonly available programs, such as Google Docs, Dropbox and OneDrive, and multiple inexpensive services that allow teams to sync and share files, such as Trello, Slack and ToDoist, there are no longer any excuses for a company not to use digital distribution of documents rather than printed documents. Encourage team members to store key manuals, policies and other bulky documents online – for example, don't print out employee handbooks when you don't need to, just share them online via an intranet or simply PDF digital copies.

If you really (really) **must** print

We do, however, acknowledge that sometimes printing is necessary. Despite the best efforts of several companies, putting a 'think before you print' message at the bottom of your emails is not always enough (but please do that all the same!). Mandating printing double-sided can immediately save up to 50 per cent on paper use and costs, as can reducing colour printing as it generally uses more ink. Really simple changes to your word processing software of choice to reduce margin settings so that your printer uses less paper can also be highly effective.

It is amazing how many companies still do not insist that all confidential documents are shredded and unwanted paper recycled rather than discarded. A simple remedy to this can be to position a paper recycling point next to every printer and photocopier (or even fax machine if you still have one), so that your team can deposit unwanted paper in them at the source of a lot of the problems. Also, going back to the points raised in our supply chain chapter, ensure that you are buying paper from companies that can evidence that they are looking to minimize their environmental impact, including buying only chlorine-free paper with a high percentage of recycled or recyclable content. Think also about buying paper made from other sustainable sources – for example, hemp, bamboo or organic cotton – and actively seek out retailers that use these recyclable materials as well as more sustainable shipping and packaging methods. You should also aim to reuse the boxes in which your paper and other shipments are transported, rather than immediately discarding them.

Reuse stationery

As well as paper for printing, there are multiple ways to ensure that the receptacles it goes in are as environmentally sound as possible. Do documents need to be retained in that dusty filing cabinet? Check if you have a legal requirement to do so. If you do need to keep things, try to reuse old file folders and binders and provide sustainable stickers so employees can write over and reuse them. As well as switching employees to using black-and-white printing, investigate whether you can buy recycled toner and ink where possible, as single-use cartridges are made from both plastic and metal and greatly contribute to office waste being sent to landfill.

Upgrade your kitchen

A large factor in encouraging people to recycle in an office environment is making it more convenient for them. A major place for wastage and missed opportunities is in the office kitchen. A practical, but all-too-often missed, way to address this is to provide separate food and recyclables bins, and a general rubbish bin for anything that really can't be recycled.

The same applies to the canteen. You should also encourage staff to opt to buy food that comes in recyclable packaging rather than Styrofoam containers. Are they doing the latter out of pure laziness? Or, potentially is there also a lack of understanding of the pressing need to make sure food packaging is truly compostable or recyclable? Do you signpost this issue? Do you help educate your staff on this point?

As we'll explore in other chapters, properly cleaning food packaging brings its own difficulty in terms of recyclability, but in general, encouraging team members by placing signs above the various bins and clarifying what goes where seems like a sensible first step. If you want to take it to another level, consider providing more segregated recycling opportunities – for plastic, glass and paper.

Another really effective way to reduce waste is to provide reusable dishes, silverware and glasses for use by team members as well as any office guests. Try to avoid providing single-use paper plates, Styrofoam, plastic cups or plastic utensils. As well as saving money on these items, you'll also find they are much nicer to use and, win-win, are far more sustainable.

Another option is to promote and facilitate ways for your team to bring in their own food and drink from home if they wish to do so – providing energy-efficient ways to store and heat it up and then places where they can wash the containers they used to transport it, rather than having to rely on takeaway packaged food and drink.

As we outline in Chapter 7, takeaway cups are not as easy to recycle as people have previously thought, due to the heatproof and leakproof mixture of paper and plastic in their inner lining. There are only a small number of specialist plants in the UK that are able to process disposable used cups, and as a result, rather shockingly, more than 99.75 per cent don't get recycled (BBC News, 2018). Connected to this, look to buy condiments in bulk, opting for refillable dispensers and avoiding the use of multiple sachets for items such as sugar and cream.

Provide employees (and clients!) with reusable containers

You could take the above a step further, and surprise and delight employees at the same time, by providing staff with their own reusable water bottle and coffee/tea receptacle – fully branded; be proud of taking this step. Whilst there is an initial associated cost, ultimately you'll save on plastic water bottles, promote wellness, and get free advertising when staff carry it outside the office – marketing at its best! And, importantly, you're making a stand on leading by example when it comes to practising sustainability. In conjunction with this, instal a filtered water tap or place pitchers of water in the office fridge so that employees can fill up their reusable bottles easily and resist the urge to buy bottled water. You can see, then, that stamping out single-use plastic is pretty simple to achieve and, as you'll read in the next chapter, of critical importance.

Gift sustainably

In many cultures and companies it is customary to give gifts during key cultural and religious periods, and often this constitutes printed material and physical items that, whilst a token of appreciation, are often immediately disregarded. Think twice before defaulting to the same tired and true methods, and instead look at options of planting a tree as a gift, or making a donation to a charity.

Please also consider how much you produce for events, and how you clean up redundant materials and marketing collateral. For example, if adequate recycling facilities are not provided by event organizers, can you instead make use of better facilities at your home, office or warehouse? If you can, take your material with you and dispose of it responsibly, if it really can't be reused. Remember the three Rs: reduce, reuse, recycle.

6.3 Things that need to be acknowledged as not perfect

We hope that some of the previous suggestions resonate with you, and that you can see there are a number of significant and really rather simple opportunities you can explore to make improvements.

However, there is a counterpoint to these practical suggestions that is the real elephant in this proverbial room: as marketers, our activities do produce a large quantity of the 'stuff' that is contributing to this major global issue.

Reducing unnecessary travel and transportation

Despite the advances in technology in terms of video conferencing, there are still inevitably reasons to travel and use transportation in any modern business. Face-to-face meetings are still necessary on occasion, as is people working together in an office environment. However, this does not mean that you cannot look to make this more sustainable. Introducing policies such as encouraging people to work from home if they do not need to be in the office, and walking/running or biking or using more environmentally friendly public transportation to travel to and from work – can all make a significant contribution to offsetting environmental impact. Of course, by encouraging employees to walk or bike to work, it is also sensible to offer showers and private changing areas at your office, if that is possible. If you do instal showers, or even if you can just update your existing toilets and sinks, look at installing technology that can conserve electricity by reducing your water heater's output (i.e. low-flow faucets and toilets, and perhaps even renewable energy solutions).

When business travel is absolutely necessary, try to encourage employees to use public transport or efficient vehicles such as fully electric or hybrid cars. Reducing the use of more carbon-emitting transport options such as flying is also key to environmental impact, so do try to use video conferencing whenever possible. The implications for this due to the unprecedented growth of video conferencing necessitated by the Covid-19 pandemic will also develop in the coming years, with several global companies such as Twitter already announcing that employees will be able to work from home even after the pandemic restrictions come to an end. This in turn is likely to lead to a reduction in travel and have other unexpected consequences.

There is also a growing need to think outside of the box in terms of encouraging better eco practices among your workforce – you can't always just rely on the best intentions of your team members. For example, consider offering some form of incentive or bonus to your 'green commuters' if they do not use an inefficient car to travel to work, or at least carpool where possible. You could also champion supporting alternative working schedules outside of the traditional 9-to-5 commute.

Prior to the Covid-19 pandemic, the growing prevalence of the likes of WeWork and shared office spaces was helping to break down traditional ways of working, and post-pandemic, businesses do increasingly need to rethink the traditional notion of employees having their 'own' space, not least because working in shared environments has the benefit of informal networks and unexpected collaborations between companies emerging. Furthermore, whilst we'd encourage more companies to consider this model of downsizing and office space sharing, especially if you have a distributed or mobile workforce that means the office is rarely fully occupied, you could also consider allocating office space based on a schedule. As a further incentive, by reducing their office footprint companies can also save on other waste-generating aspects, such as the need for office furniture and equipment, as well as seeing a reduction in the use of utilities.

NB: of course, all of the above will need to be re-evaluated in the light of Covid-19's impact on the workforce (Deloitte, 2020), but the theory still stands.

Smarter use of office equipment

Even if you are able to reduce the use of office space by your workforce, there are many hidden sources of waste inherent in keeping an office operational. It must be recognized that the manufacturing and the short life span of some office equipment can also contribute greatly to future landfill waste. Consider ways that old or unwanted office equipment can be recycled – could employees use it themselves in their home environments to create their own flexible working spaces, for example? The attraction of brand-new furniture is understandable, but it does not need to be the default position – buying used or refurbished furniture and office equipment such as printers or photocopiers from other companies and offices can result in significant savings in terms of both cost and environmental impact. Also consider longer-term investments and seek to buy more high-quality equipment, which has the potential to last and not become obsolete. There are also a growing number of organizations that rent furniture to offices. This allows furniture to be used multiple times and significantly reduces waste. Businesses can add to, reduce and even regularly refresh the look and feel of their office spaces without adding to landfill.

Reducing the use of utilities

We must, of course, recognize that running an office sustainably can be difficult – it will require heat, electricity and water. However, what might seem relatively minor changes to air conditioning, lighting and fixtures can make a huge difference in your energy consumption (saving the environment and bills!). Try to manage and monitor your office environment as much as possible – check and adjust your thermostat levels, switch to dimmable, auto-sensing or energy efficient light bulbs where you can, and explore whether you can switch to a more green energy company using sustainable or other alternative energy sources. It is always good to take advantage of natural lighting wherever possible, so make sure nothing is obscuring windows – it is amazing what repositioning some desks and old filing cabinets can do to let in more natural light.

There is also time outside of normal office hours when considerable reductions in waste can be made. Although devices can sit in a 'stand by' mode when not in use, many still need to be unplugged to be fully turned off. You should therefore encourage employees to shut down and unplug copiers, printers, vending machines and other equipment when they leave the office every evening – and don't forget that the last one to leave turns out the lights!

Addressing your e-waste

Technology is the backbone of the global economy and there is no point in hiding from that. For this reason, reducing our consumption in this area is an extremely tricky issue, but it is one that must be addressed because the world has a significant, and escalating, e-waste problem (Gladstone, 2020). As computers, consoles, smartphones, TVs, printers and a host of household items hit recycling and landfill sites, they present a health hazard thanks to the use of lead, chromium, cadmium and other materials in their ageing circuitry.

In several major countries a contributing factor to this issue is the outdated (or non-existent) nature of e-waste recycling laws. For example, in the US, approximately only 25 states (plus Washington, DC) have legislation in place that actively addresses e-waste recycling, according to Jason Linnell, head of the National Center for Electronics Recycling (NCER) ('E-Waste State of the Union: Recycling Facts, Figures and the Future', 2020).

However, according to the Global E-waste Statistics Partnership, through their information portal www.globalewaste.org – an open source portal that visualizes e-waste data and statistics globally, by region and by country – e-waste presents an opportunity worth more than $62.5 billion per year, with the potential for creating millions of new jobs worldwide (United Nations University, 2019).

There are, however, a number of practical ways you can minimize your impact right now. Many companies fail to recycle their e-waste, yet old smartphones, computers, monitors, printers and other equipment can often be recycled in some way, and do not need to go straight to landfill. You should also try to invest in high-quality, energy-efficient items when you have to purchase IT equipment, which will not become obsolete too quickly. Equally, try not to automatically upgrade resources every time the latest phone or laptop is released, and if you do, make sure you have a route to recycling – either offering the old one as a hand-me-down or for sale, or to be recycled.

When it comes to using the devices, there can also be hidden energy inefficiencies. Adjusting – or ideally banishing – screen savers and enforcing a policy for people to switch off their PCs when in meetings (and definitely when they leave the building) can greatly streamline your company's overall computer energy efficiency.

Rethinking printed marketing collateral

Although the prevalence of traditional print marketing has diminished significantly as a result of more and more digital activity, many companies still produce print material in significant volumes. Due to the rapidly changing business and consumer environment, the accusation that much of this material is 'outdated' the moment it is produced can be seen as valid and important. As such, requiring print to hold long-term value is essential. By doing so, businesses can save significant time and resources – both in terms of procurement and production in print marketing materials.

If you do have to print, consider your options. Many printing companies now compete on how their services ensure efficient print operations and minimize waste, with the savings (hopefully!) then being passed on to the client. However, few companies view optimization of print from a waste reduction in production basis, rather looking at it as a pure cost-cutting exercise; perversely, printing in higher volumes sometimes produces efficiencies in cost, but can lead to overprinting and more waste. We are all aware of boxes full of now-redundant print material sitting in cupboards, under desks and in warehouses for this very reason. Conversely, some print media can be reused and recycled very effectively, as will be the case if you are reading books such as this one, having borrowed it from a colleague!

According to North Carolina State University ('How Your Business Can Cut Costs by Reducing Waste', 2017), another simple way for businesses to reduce waste is by keeping direct mailing lists current. A lack of high-quality targeting is commonly a contributory factor to producing wasted print collateral. Ensuring there are processes in place to routinely remove redundant information (such as incorrect addresses, long-departed business contacts etc), can help refine campaigns, reduce the amount being printed, save costs, and provide an improved sense of a campaign's true value. A use of strong campaign performance analytics to reduce overspend on print materials is often overlooked.

6.4 Case study – PwC – Waste Reduction

Leading professional services firm PwC describes its purpose as to 'build trust in society and solve important problems. It is this focus which informs the services we provide and the decisions we make'.

The company's strategy is focused on being innovative, responsible and, as a progressive employer, focused on developing a diverse and agile workforce, attracting – and empowering – outstanding people. As it seeks to lead by example, it also is determined to be technology enabled, deliver exceptional value to its clients and invest in sustainable growth ('About Us', 2020) in order to make a positive impact on society.

Building trust and tackling waste

Everything PwC does is based on developing trust – from its work with clients, how it runs core operations, to supply chain and community engagement activities, everything is aligned to its purpose. It has four key focus areas for outcomes related to the UN Sustainable Development Goals ('Our Purpose', 2020)

- Working with purpose
- Empowering people and communities
- Becoming a low carbon and circular business
- Being a fair and trusted business

PwC is also taking action in terms of waste, paying more attention than ever to the lifecycle of raw materials used in its business, with a strategy to 'decouple material consumption from business growth and move towards a circular economy' ('Reducing our waste and material consumption', 2020).

PwC has maintained its achievement of zero waste to landfill for all the 'hub' and food waste generated in its offices since 2012. Any materials not able to be recovered are sent to generate energy through incineration.

PwC is not stopping there; it also has an active programme to reduce its consumption of key consumables – by 2017 it had reduced paper consumption by 64 per cent and water by 40 per cent compared to what is describes as its 'baseline' year of 2007. By 2022 the company has set targets to reduce its consumption of paper by 80 per cent and water by 50 per cent, reduce its overall waste volumes by 75 per cent (compared to 2007) and to recycle 80 per cent of its operational waste – eliminating incineration wherever possible, in spite of the increase in its global headcount

Practical office waste management

On its website, PwC cites initiatives such as a clear-out of old archived files as helping to increase the volume of paper it recycled, boosting recycling to 90 per cent in 2019. Recognizing there is work to do in reducing the remaining 10 per cent not currently reused or recycled, it has implemented a programme of engaging its stakeholders to identify future solutions.

PwC has also noted that it implemented a 'Going Circular' strategy through promoting collaboration to find and pioneer better solutions via a combination of waste management, employee awareness and engagement with suppliers.

PwC utilizes its TIMM (Total Impact Measurement & Management) framework to effectively measure its change programme and help it value the impacts of a business in three ways:

1) Direct impacts: from a business's own activities.
2) Indirect impacts: recognizing that a business has responsibility for some of the impacts of organizations in its supply chain – impacts associated with the manufacture of goods consumed by the business, for example.
3) Induced impacts: the effects of spending by a business's employees, or suppliers' employees, in the wider economy.

It is clear that PwC are developing a long-term waste and material consumption strategy that adopts the principles of the 'circular economy' we have discussed at length – reducing, reusing, recycling and transitioning to circular solutions in its office and beyond.

6.5 Chapter summary

In this chapter we have discussed the need to adopt a target-led approach, but also recognized that change can, and arguably should, begin in the environment closest to you – your own workplace. Waste management has an inextricable link to developing a contemporary corporate responsibility strategy in your business. Case studies from companies such as PwC clearly show that actively developing your company's waste and material consumption strategy can greatly assist the performance of your company.

As this chapter has demonstrated, to truly begin to reduce waste in the workplace, every company's leadership team needs to progressively adopt the principles of a 'circular economy', where is it not enough to just try to produce products in a more environmentally friendly way, but rather the whole chain of use of materials within a company needs to be looked at end to end.

There is a clear opportunity for marketing professionals to lead the charge internally in terms of signposting and encouraging ways team members can actively reduce, reuse and recycle as part of a highly practical programme of work to transition your company to circular solutions to waste reduction. As highlighted, a great deal of waste management is based on employee awareness and encouragement to change behaviour, as is supplier engagement with reducing harmful materials and approaches. There are clearly countless ways to reduce waste in your workplace. We'd really encourage you to try as many of these suggestions as possible. We hope you will find it surprisingly easy to implement, and you will also begin to see a real reduction in costs over time – and positive feedback and engagement from your colleagues.

Coming up with and owning your business's office waste management strategy is a key way in which you can lead in embedding sustainability in day-to-day activity on your journey, and another example of how you can use sustainability as a source of competitive advantage. Managing and reducing waste across the globe is a tough issue to handle. Whilst many of you will be creating things for a living and be responsible for marketing products and services that involve production of things that are single- or limited use, we hope it is clear from some of the micro and macro considerations in this chapter that you can make a difference and reduce the waste.

Keep going – it all REALLY counts!

6.6 Action points to consider

Managing waste can be a daunting task; however, hopefully some of the practical guidance in this chapter has given you some ideas. The following actions are suggested to help get you get underway on this journey:

No.	Action	Considerations	Next Step
1	Walk around your office and make some notes on what you see being used on a daily basis.	Where is waste being created that could be avoided?	Write down 10 suggestions your company can implement in the next 30 days.
2	What is this waste costing your company?	Try to estimate the monthly costs of the items you've identified.	Write a mini business case for what making some changes looks like.
3	Make it a boardroom discussion.	It is amazing how seldom the 'office environment' is referred to at board level (maybe because the senior team often don't face the same challenges as team members do!).	Ask to show senior management a simple presentation on what you've found, and what you are going to drive in terms of change. There's no need to make it a big 'ask' – more of an FYI!
4	How sustainable is your marketing practice?	What initiatives do you have planned or underway that are going to create waste?	Write down ways you could improve or really reduce the amount of waste you are producing.
5	How can you mitigate the inevitable ways you are creating waste?	How can you avoid creating more and e-waste?	Come up with three practical ideas for how you can avoid sending more e-waste from your office to landfill this year. Can you recycle old computers and office furniture in some proactive way (i.e. donating it to charity/schools etc)?

In Chapter 7, we will now go on to analyse how to begin the task of eliminating plastic waste, and in Chapter 8 we will tackle other ways to reduce the overall carbon footprint created by your business's activities. In Chapter 10, we'll revisit waste again in relation to packaging. In the meantime, rest assured that with action there are plenty of ways your company can be more sustainable in its approach to waste. Just remember that as a responsible marketer, you need to pay attention to your immediate environment in order to be as consistent in your approach as possible.

6.7 Chapter 6 references

Balch, O. (2015). 'The future of waste: five things to look for by 2025'. *Guardian.* Available at: https://www.theguardian.com/sustainable-business/2015/feb/23/future-of-waste-five-things-look-2025 (Accessed: 28 April 2020)

BBC (2018). 'Plastic recycling: Why are 99.75% of coffee cups not recycled?' Available at: https://www.bbc.co.uk/news/science-environment-43739043 (Accessed: 28 April 2020)

Deloitte (2020). 'COVID-19's impact on the workforce'. Available at: https://www2.deloitte.com/uk/en/pages/human-capital/articles/covid-19-impact-on-the-workforce-insight-for-hr-teams.html (Accessed: 28 April 2020)

Department for Environment, Food & Rural Affairs (2018). 'Statutory guidance. Food and drink waste hierarchy: deal with surplus and waste'. Available at: https://www.gov.uk/government/publications/food-and-drink-waste-hierarchy-deal-with-surplus-and-waste/food-and-drink-waste-hierarchy-deal-with-surplus-and-waste (Accessed: 28 April 2020)

Federal Electronics Challenge (2013). 'The Benefits of Automatic Duplexing'. Available at: https://www.epa.gov/sites/production/files/2013-09/documents/fec_automatic_duplexing.pdf (Accessed: 28 April 2020)

Food and Agriculture Organization of the United Nations (2020). 'Food wastage footprint'. Available at: http://www.fao.org/3/i3347e/i3347e.pdf (Accessed: 28 April 2020)

Food and Agriculture Organization of the United Nations (2020). 'Food wastage: Key facts and figures'. Available at: http://www.fao.org/news/story/en/item/196402/icode/ (Accessed: 28 April 2020)

Food and Agriculture Organization of the United Nations (2020). 'Indicator 12.3.1 – Global Food Loss and Waste'. Available at: http://www.fao.org/sustainable-development-goals/indicators/12.3.1/en/ (Accessed: 28 April 2020)

Gladstone, N. (2020). 'The United States has a colossal e-waste problem. This is why'. Available at: https://www.digitaltrends.com/cool-tech/e-waste-recycling-united-states/ (Accessed: 28 April 2020)

Gray, A. (2017). 'Germany recycles more than any other country'. Available at: https://www.weforum.org/agenda/2017/12/germany-recycles-more-than-any-other-country/ (Accessed: 28 April 2020)

Iron Mountain (2019). 'Strategies To Reduce Waste In Marketing Collateral'. Available at: https://www.ironmountain.com/resources/general-articles/s/strategies-to-reduce-waste-in-marketing-collateral (Accessed: 28 April 2020)

Kosior, E. (2020). 'Reducing food waste takes innovation and a change in mindset'. Available at: https://www.newfoodmagazine.com/article/109462/food-waste/ (Accessed: 28 April 2020)

ISCG (2016). '10 ways to reduce waste in the workplace'. Available at: https://www.iscginc.com/blog/2016/4/18/10-ways-to-reduce-waste-in-the-workplace (Accessed: 28 April 2020)

Investment Recovery Association (2020). 'E-Waste State of the Union: Recycling Facts, Figures and the Future'. Available at: https://invrecovery.org/e-waste-state-of-the-union-recycling-facts-figures-and-the-future/ (Accessed: 28 April 2020)

IT Brief (2019). 'Culture changes are key when taking on sustainability – KYOCERA'. Available at: https://itbrief.com.au/story/culture-changes-are-key-when-taking-on-sustainability-kyocera (Accessed: 28 April 2020)

North Carolina State University (2017). 'How Your Business Can Cut Costs by Reducing Waste'. Available at: https://content.ces.ncsu.edu/how-your-business-can-cut-costs-by-reducing-wastes (Accessed: 28 April 2020)

PwC (2020). 'Reducing our waste and material consumption'. Available at: https://www.pwc.co.uk/who-we-are/our-purpose/low-carbon-circular-business/waste.html (Accessed: 9 August 2020)

PwC (2020). 'About Us'. Available at: https://www.pwc.co.uk/who-we-are.html (Accessed: 9 August 2020)

PwC (2020). 'Our Purpose'. Available at: https://www.pwc.co.uk/who-we-are/our-purpose.html (Accessed: 9 August 2020)

Tonna-Barthet, R. (2019). *The Recycler*. 'Kyocera UK calls for culture changes for sustainability'. Available at: https://www.therecycler.com/posts/kyocera-uk-calls-for-culture-changes-for-sustainability/ (Accessed: 28 April 2020)

United Nations University (2019). 'Global E-waste Statistics Partnership Launches Web Portal to Help Address Global E-waste Challenge'. Available at: https://unu.edu/media-relations/releases/global-ewaste-statistics-partnership-launches-web-portal.html (Accessed: 28 April 2020)

CHAPTER SEVEN

Plastic: Reduce, Reuse, Recycle

7.0 Chapter introduction

The problems with and surrounding plastic continue to grow, and since it became a high-profile topic the level of misunderstanding has increased considerably. Misinformation is rife and messaging is unclear. More questions are being asked than answered. What is bad plastic and is all plastic bad? What makes up a plastic? How do I reduce my plastic consumption and if I recycle then, surely, I am doing my bit – right?

The original meaning of the word plastic meant 'pliable and easily shaped' (*History and Future of Plastics,* 2020). Plastic has been around since 1907, when Leo Baekeland invented Bakelite, which was the first fully synthetic plastic. However, the production of plastic and the products it was used in grew rapidly during World War II. Concerns about the material, its usage and disposal aren't new – in fact, they emerged in the 1960s and have continued ever since. However, it was David Attenborough's *Blue Planet II* that dramatically shone the spotlight on plastic in 2017 when he showed the world the damage that mass production and careless disposal of plastic was having on oceans and how it was impacting the reefs and animals that lived there. But it goes further than the ocean: the land, air and seas are all being heavily impacted by plastic and the damage to the environment is considerable.

Throughout this chapter we are going to look at production, usage and disposal, and try to give a clearer picture of plastic so that you can make better-informed decisions. We also aim to help responsible marketers really understand how they are contributing to the problem and, more importantly, how they can become a bigger part of the solution. Plastic is everyone's problem and everyone's responsibility. In researching this book, we found how large parts of the plastic lifecycle are totally misunderstood, misleading and, most of all, efforts to tackle the issue are failing, and it's these factors that are greatly impacting our ability to effect positive change.

7.1 Where are we?

The plastic problem is beyond measure. As we moved into 2020, the latest facts and figures were staggering. In 2018, 359 million tonnes of plastic ('Plastics – the Facts', 2019), were produced globally, and demand actually went up by 3.5 per cent ('The Future of Petrochemicals', 2018) despite the world waking up to the impact plastic was having on the environment. The study also showed that 39.9 per cent of all plastic produced ('Plastics – the Facts', 2019) was used in packaging (more on this in Chapter 10).

When it comes to the disposal of plastics, it is important to make the point that given the way in which different plastics are made and their vast range of uses, production levels and disposal levels will never be the same or even close to the same. However, there is no doubt that given that nearly 40 per cent of all plastic produced is for packaging (nearly 143 million tonnes), the disposal figures are poor. In the EU, only 12 per cent or 17.8 million tonnes of plastic packaging was collected as waste in 2018. Of that, 7.4 million tonnes was recycled and 7 million tonnes used in energy recovery, which left 3.4 million tonnes that went to landfill. Now, whilst marketers themselves cannot directly make the changes required to improve a country's recycling infrastructure, the way in which they market their products and the packaging they use could be far more transparent, so that consumers know if the products they send to recycling can actually be recycled. We'll talk more about this later.

Marketing has played a part in creating the plastic problem through driving increased consumer demand for products that come in plastic packaging. However, on the flip side marketing has also raised awareness of the plastic problem through high-profile campaigns, such as Greenpeace's 'Dead Whale' (www.greenpeace.org) and Surfrider Foundation's 'What goes into the Ocean goes into you' (www.surfrider. org), and Sky's 'Ocean Rescue' campaign (www.skyoceanrescue.com). These campaigns have made the growing problem very real, but it is how they are followed up and used to inform decision-makers and change behaviours that will determine their real impact and success. Throughout 2019, we saw plastic move on to the high-priority lists of governments that looked to new laws, businesses that started making numerous pledges and working towards ways of reducing their packaging, and consumers who questioned more deeply their purchasing decisions and how they disposed of plastic. If we are to paint a fully rounded picture on plastic and provide clarity and understanding then we first need to separate the good, the bad and the single-use.

The good

Not all plastic is bad. In fact, there are plastics that are needed and have a positive impact on the environment. Pipes, for example, were once made of lead, and that resulted in lead poisoning. They went on to be replaced by pipes made from steel, which rusted over time, which not only made them unreliable and costly to repair, but the rust contaminated the water supply. Plastic pipes, however, are efficient and robust. Their manufacturing process requires less energy and so is better for the environment. They provide a safe transportation system for water and need replacing and repairing far less, plus when they are replaced, they can be recycled. Plastic pipes conform to key international standards ISO 14025, ISO 14040 and ISO 14044. Assessment found that 'the environmental impact of plastic pipe systems from cradle to grave in building services and pressure applications including soil and waste, hot and cold water and fresh water supply across all environmental criteria was much lower than non-plastic alternatives like cast iron and copper and in sewage similar to non-plastic alternatives (concrete)' (Heathcote C, 2020). Plastics used in transport such as planes, trains and cars are more durable, making them safer. Plastic is lighter, which makes them more fuel-efficient and therefore reduces emissions. Finally, plastic has revolutionized the healthcare industry due to its versatile nature. Amongst the many examples, it has been instrumental in improving sterility and safety and has improved prosthetics and joint replacements.

The bad

Plastic packaging is a major contributor to the increasing levels of waste being put into the environment, causing untold damage. Global demand for food and the ease and speed with which food is produced, packaged and transported across countries continues to increase year on year. Consumers want choice and access to foods from all over the world in an instant. With this come numerous environmental impacts and the plastic packaging our food is contained in is one of them. However, whether we agree or not, there *is* a need for food to be packaged in a way that keeps it safe for consumption and plastic currently meets that need. Plastic food packaging plays an important role in protecting against contamination and the spread of disease. It also preserves food for longer, reducing waste and the serious issue associated with food waste.

As we'll explore in greater detail in Chapter 10, alternatives to plastic, such as plant-based packaging, are being produced but they require investment for testing and to enable the upscaling of production to a level that equals plastic in terms of quantity and affordability on a mass scale.

The single-use

Single-use plastic is ugly and unnecessary. Plastic bags, straws, cutlery, cups, water bottles, cotton buds – the list of examples goes on and on (and on). And yet there are sustainable alternatives to all these things if you think about it. The pointless nature of these items, which we not only use just once but also usually for just a matter of minutes before disposing of them, has led to a multitude of problems that have put countries and the environment in crisis.

It is these items that generally end up in landfill due to the mix of materials used to make them, the different colours used to 'differentiate' (or market them) and then there's their different shapes and sizes. Most recycling centres do not have the technology to pick out such small items and to develop this facility is not seen as cost-effective. And, with the rate at which plastic waste continues to increase, there also isn't the capacity to recycle it all and so it ends up being incinerated, causing air pollution, or else is buried or dumped, shipped overseas to be 'recycled' (read buried or dumped), and left to wash into rivers and oceans. Developed countries used to send huge volumes of plastic packaging that could not be recycled in country to China. In fact, until 1 January 2018, China was the world's biggest importer of recycled materials. However, the World Trade Organization (WTO) and China's Ministry of Environmental Protection then announced that they would no longer be taking imports of mixed paper, post-consumer plastics and vanadium slag due to the polluted condition of the waste that was being sent. This, however, has only shifted the waste problem to other countries that are willing to continue to receive the waste. If the current production and waste management trends continue, roughly 12,000 metric tonnes of plastic waste will be in landfills or in the natural environment by 2050 (Geyer et al, 2017). This is unsustainable on every level and needs to stop.

7.2 Why do companies need to do something about this now?

As discussed in Chapter 3, business is being seen as the catalyst for change. Public focus and awareness has never been so strong, and it will take a combined effort to effect change. The current levels of plastic being produced and already in the environment are not sustainable and if change is going to happen then it needs to come from innovation, regulation and societal change.

Innovation

Innovation can come in many forms and there are currently numerous organizations that are creating alternative packaging solutions made from sustainable, natural and renewable sources. For example, Notpla ('Edible and biodegradable. The alternative to plastic', 2020) innovates using brown seaweed, and have successfully created packaging for beverages and sauces that is truly biodegradable and is even fit for human consumption. We'll discuss innovative packaging solutions in more depth later in the book, but needless to say there is no shortage of more sustainable options.

As well as alternative packaging, we are also seeing promising innovations coming from using non-recyclable plastic, which would otherwise go to landfill. Examples include Scottish company MacRebur, which developed and patented a way to use waste plastic in roads, alongside asphalt producer Pat Munro. Qube, an India-based start-up, has developed a brick made entirely of plastic waste.

And then there are companies looking at how 3D printing can use non-recyclable plastic, further helping to reduce our waste problem. Construction in particular is an industry that can benefit from these innovations and by investing in them build a more sustainable future. Another industry, fashion, is also investing in the reuse of non-recyclable plastics. Probably most well-known are big brands such as Adidas, which started making footwear from ocean plastic. In 2020, Adidas announced it would launch new fabrics made from recycled polyester and marine plastic waste, expanding its product lines.

The benefits of the circular economy are therefore clear and innovations such as those discussed demonstrate that we can reduce our dependency on virgin plastic, which in turn reduces demand, production and waste.

Furthermore, it's not just innovation coming from the redesign of products and reuse of plastic that is driving companies to do something now. We are seeing more apps that aim to help consumers make more sustainable choices. For instance, Giki is an app that shows a range of health and sustainable information for products on sale in UK supermarkets. Giki say one of the purposes of their app is to 'encourage consumers to put pressure on brands to be more transparent' (www. gikibadges.com). Another example is Eugène (Casady, 2016) – an app that allows users to scan products and then tells you how you can recycle them. Sky Ocean Ventures is supporting Eugène, alongside other innovators. It is notable that Sky has an impact investment fund of £25 million (Sky Ocean Rescue, 2020) to help companies accelerate their ideas and bring about faster change. Large brands such as Sky and Unilever are therefore supporting innovation, by working with, investing and acquiring brands with strong sustainable credentials or propositions. At the same time, they are divesting from non-sustainable brands, showing that innovation is surely a key driver in the war on plastic.

Supporting regulations and infrastructure

Progress is slower when it comes to regulations, though this is not a reason not to do something now. There will come a point when organizations have no choice but to change what they do or how they are doing it. We discussed an example of this – earlier – with China announcing they would no longer be taking the world's non-recyclable materials. This has created both challenges and opportunities across the world for different organizations and countries. Another more recent example involves the 'European Strategy for Plastics in a Circular Economy', which came about in January 2018. This strategy is aimed at transforming the way plastic products are designed, used, produced and recycled in the EU. In 2019, the EU Parliament approved a new law banning the production and availability of single-use plastic items such as plates, cutlery and straws from July 2021. In addition, they have also imposed targets on recycling for countries and rules on the percentage of recycled plastic that the producers must use in their products.

These regulations are being put in place to strengthen the infrastructure to drive business to operate more sustainably. Unfortunately, there is still resistance to such regulation, despite the facts and figures that show the negative impact plastic has on the environment. Indeed, some organizations are using marketing to get around regulation, relabelling single-use plastic cutlery and plates as 'reusable'. This is a way of trying to reposition the product away from being classified as single-use and placing the accountability on the consumer to wash the products and reuse them. The labelling, classification and messaging that comes with plastic products places the spotlight firmly on marketing and the requirement that it looks at what it is doing and how it too can change and innovate to improve. Sadly, lack of transparency in messaging is a tactic being used by businesses to delay or avoid investing in sustainable innovation, whether that be redesigning the products they already have or looking at alternative solutions. This is something we will discuss in more detail.

Fundamental societal change

In order to reduce plastic pollution, we need to reduce the amount of plastic produced and used. Research shows that we are seeing changes in society driven by a number of different factors. Regulation and global initiatives such as the Paris Agreement and, more specifically to this chapter, the New Plastics Economy (www.newplasticseconomy. org) – set up by the Ellen MacArthur Foundation in collaboration with the UN Environment Programme (UNEP) – are providing society with ongoing facts and knowledge on plastic issues. Working with government, NGOs, business, academics and investors, the New Plastics Economy strives to 'endorse the common vision of a circular economy for plastic, where plastic never becomes waste' ('The New Plastic Economy Global Commitment 2019 Progress Report').

Innovation, as we have discussed, demonstrates to consumers that there are alternative, more sustainable solutions. High-profile awareness campaigns and the amplification of these alongside a growing voice across social media platforms is also adding to growing societal interest, and changes in behaviours are now showing through; how products are packaged can determine our purchase decisions. Research by the GlobalWebIndex in 2019 on 'Sustainable Packaging Unwrapped' (GlobalWebIndex, 2019) stated that: '42 per cent of respondents say "products that use recycled/sustainable materials are important in their day-to-day shopping"', and '53 per cent say they have reduced the amount of plastic they use in the past 12 months'. However, the same research also shows that price and brands they trust are still the highest considerations when it comes to purchase decisions, but should a brand be seen to be environmentally unfriendly, then '61 per cent say they would be likely to switch to a more environmentally friendly brand'. The results, whilst not conclusive, reflect that consumers are thinking more about sustainability, but there is still work to be done.

One development is a growing trend towards zero-waste stores – stores that supply loose produce, such as pulses, pasta, rice, grains, cereals, dried fruit, nuts and many other things. This concept has been growing and with it the range of items, which now include cleaning products and toiletries (Howell, 2019). As well as these independent stores, supermarkets such as Marks & Spencer and Sainsbury's have also launched refill incentives, the latter announcing in 2020 that: they would 'trial Ecover refill stations for washing-up liquid and laundry detergent. This gives shoppers the chance to fill up their empty cleaning bottles in stores, instead of purchasing a new plastic one' (Walden, 2020).

This is all a step in the right direction. If society is going to truly embrace a more sustainable plastic circular economy, all organizations need to do more to drive behaviours towards reusing packaging or no packaging at all.

7.3 Things that need to be acknowledged as not perfect

The GlobalWebIndex packaging research showed that the top four things consumers want is:

1) packaging that is recyclable (64 per cent);
2) packaging that is reusable (53 per cent);
3) no overpackaging (46 per cent);
4) biodegradable and compostable packaging (39 per cent).

It also revealed that consumers remain price conscious, and that sustainability versus price varies by age. The younger demographic

(16–24 years) are willing to pay more for sustainable products. This presents a significant challenge for brands to overcome and this is where marketing plays a significant role in providing consumers with reasons why they should engage. Marketing also needs to be clearer, more authentic and provide the complete picture. Terms being used when marketing plastic packaging, such as 'bioplastic', 'biodegradable' and 'compostable', are leading to even more confusion, with some consumers thinking they are more environmentally friendly. Biodegradable plastics are actually a contaminant in plastic recycling facilities and have to be separated out, driving up recycling costs. Alternative packaging to plastic can carry other environmental impacts, such as requiring more energy in the production process, or it could be that it cannot be reused as many times as the plastic version. The current landscape is awash with labelling that is totally misleading, storytelling that is inconsistent or incomplete, and too much responsibility is being placed on the consumer.

Reduce and reuse

Reduce and reuse must come first in the fight against plastic, whether it's packaging or the product itself. Consumption unfortunately has reached such levels that consumers expect an abundance of choice and availability, and being more sustainable will inevitably result in less choice. Consumers say they want packaging and products that are reusable, but intentions and actions can be very different. Just look at how we consume bottled water!

Despite being one of the most polluting products in the world, single-use bottled water consumption continues to grow. A million plastic bottles are bought around the world every minute and that number will jump another 20 per cent by 2021. And yet tap water (in countries where it's drinkable) in a reusable water bottle is undoubtedly the most sustainable and cheapest way to drink and transport water on an individual level. By just changing this one behaviour, the reduction in single-use plastic waste would be enormous. Yet figures show that despite the wide range of reusable water bottles available, on average in the UK a person uses 156 single-use plastic water bottles a year (Green Cities, 2018). Half a litre of water costs on average 30p, which equates to £46 per year (Water UK, 2020). Even premium reusable water bottles cost less than £20. If price is still the driving factor in the majority of consumer purchase decisions then why isn't everyone switching to reusable water bottles? And why isn't empowerment marketing being used to drive this critical behavioural change?

The answer: ease, convenience, cost and marketing. Bottled water is positioned as a 'healthier' option versus other drinks, with major drinks brands all heavily marketing their water products as consumers shift away from soft drinks containing high levels of sugar. Another reason for multiple purchases are the warnings on single-use bottles that state they should not be refilled for health reasons. However, most single-use water bottles are made from polyethylene terephthalate (PET), which is approved by multiple associations and authorities for both single and repeated use. PET has been tested extensively and to date there is no actual evidence of migration of toxic amounts of chemicals from the plastic to the contents (Bumgardner, 2020).

So, in a world where there are so many conflicting messages, how do we change behaviours built up around ease and convenience and move towards a more sustainable way of living? Empowerment marketing is about delivering highly effective, authentic messages that give consumers the information and opportunity to make choices and take actions. When it comes to sustainable marketing, sustainably doesn't always work as or need to be the lead message; it is more important to show consumers that their choice has a positive impact. People like to know that what they are doing is making a difference and can deliver change.

A great example of an organization doing this is One Water (www. onewater.org). As well as creating different packaging formats for their water, they provide facts on what makes up their packaging and how to recycle it. To further strengthen their consumer purchase drivers, their 'Instant Hero' campaign (Mortimer, 2014) focused on making their consumers the hero, stating that by switching to One Water consumers are directly helping to fund clean water projects in Africa. This means that those consumers who still want to purchase 'packaged' water can do so knowing that they are giving back to important societal issues whilst still making their convenience purchases. The key is to ensure that consumers are aware of the organizations that have sustainability at the heart of their business, which is easier said than done when the amount of choice and noise are at an all-time high.

Recycle

Recycling has been around for a long time and as shown by the GlobalWebIndex research cited earlier, consumers want to do it. It is a behaviour that most people have adopted, and it enables them to feel like they are making a difference and having a positive impact. Labelling products as recyclable is therefore a positive marketing tactic, despite the fact that many of the items in reality are being incinerated or end up in landfill. We discussed earlier in the chapter how the recycling infrastructure cannot support the volumes coming through, that smaller items cannot be picked out and coloured plastics cannot be recycled with clear plastics. If we look at the labelling of items such as coffee cups, sandwiches and other convenience food packaging, they are generally marketed as recyclable. And, in theory, as separate components, this may be true. However, the reality is that packaging or products made using mixed materials simply cannot be recycled.

So, how do you increase recycling rates for a product that can't be recycled? Disposable coffee cups are made of paper and a waterproof plastic lining, so unless these two components are separated, which cannot be done at most standard recycling facilities (but can easily be done by the consumer of course), they go to landfill. In response to this, Costa removed the recyclable label from its cups in 2016, though many other disposable cups still show it, which is giving consumers the wrong message. Also in 2016, Costa set up its initiative 'You enjoy it. We recycle it' (Corbin, 2016), whereby the company works with an independent waste management company and pays waste collectors for every tonne of coffee cups collected, in order to fund the right infrastructure. They decided that by encouraging customers to bring their takeaway cups back to Costa they can reduce the amount that go to landfill – and of course the whole issue is avoided if people simply bring their own cups with them, a consumer action that is incentivized by a discount at Costa and many other coffee shops and cafes.

New research released by YouGov at the end of 2019 ('YouGov Results Fieldwork 19th–20th September, 2019') revealed that 'just 8 per cent of people strongly believe that recycling labelling on products is clear' and 'only 12 per cent of them trust recycling labelling on products'. The On-Pack Recycling Label (OPRL) group launched its new recycling label rules in January 2020, moving the majority of packaging to a binary labelling system of 'recycle' or 'don't recycle'. Coffee cups will be given a specialist label to increase awareness and support in-store collections. These changes will make it clearer to consumers what they can and cannot recycle, although accountability sits with all parts of the stakeholder chain. Yet organizations need to stop passing on the responsibility and become part of the solution. At this time when change is occurring continually, marketers need to be more aware and understand the rules that could impact them and their products. By being more aware they can potentially use these changes and regulations to change their product's packaging or change their messaging. This will drive business growth within their markets whilst building a more valuable relationship with their customers. Recycling, however, is not the solution; it should be the last resort. We need to first reduce and reuse.

7.4 Case study – Ethique – reduce, reuse, recycle

Reducing our reliance and use of plastic is an absolute must. There needs to be a change in organizational approach, a review of the infrastructures that support how we dispose and recycle plastic and a change in habits and social factors.

One company that is doing just this is Ethique, a zero-waste beauty and lifestyle brand whose products are solid bars that are activated with water. According to the company, their scheme #giveupthebottle has so far 'prevented over 9 million bottles, jars & tubes from being made and disposed of. By 2025, we aim to have hit 50 million' (www. ethique.com). Their approach is to not only make sustainable, ethical products that their customers love, but also to make a point of raising awareness of the plastic problem and educate their consumers about the choices they are making. Through providing information on their website on the issues their product aims to solve, the reasons why consumers should buy their products becomes much more powerful:

Paying for water is a total waste:
An average bottle of shampoo or body wash can be made up of 80% water. Conditioner is even higher – about 95%. So basically, you're paying for a big ol' plastic bottle of water. That seems pretty unnecessary when there's water in your shower already, right?

Our bars are concentrated, so a conditioner bar is equivalent to five bottles (or 1.7L) of liquid conditioner, usually lasting 6–8 months. Using one conditioner bar, instead of the equivalent 5 bottles, saves up to 5L of water. A lot of precious water is used to make each plastic bottle, not to mention the carbon produced mining and manufacturing them!

We don't need any nasty ingredients:
We only use 100% naturally-derived ingredients and they are all biodegradable. No parabens, petroleum by-products, palm oil (and its derivatives), synthetic fragrances, formaldehyde donors or other nasty ingredients you often find in plastic bottles of shampoo, conditioner and moisturiser.

When you #giveupthebottle you're stopping plastic from clogging the ocean, and avoiding those harsh chemicals.

Reproduced by kind permission of Ethique. More information can be found at www.ethique.com

Behavioural change is key to rescuing our plastic consumption and if we can change that behaviour at the start of the purchase journey instead of at the point we have purchased, used and are about to dispose then all the better.

Ethique explain their packaging in a clear, meaningful and relatable way:

Compostable packaging is beautiful and works perfectly:
We ship our bars all over the world so they need to be packaged in something. We use cardboard with soy inks and no plastics or laminates, so they're completely compostable at home. Even our in-shower containers are plastic-free. Made from bamboo fibres and cornstarch, they can go straight in your home compost.

No plastic, no laminate, no chlorine
Our packaging goes to the very heart of what Ethique stands for. Our solid bars are designed to do away with water, and with it, the plastic bottles.

But just swapping out plastic for paper isn't good enough – paper production can come with a raft of other environmental concerns too. When designing our packaging, we took all those factors into account, to make it as earth-friendly as possible:

No landfills needed
Our packaging, shipping boxes and padding are free from laminates and plastic (including our packing tape), which means they can go straight into the home compost and will disappear in a matter of months.

Made in NZ from renewable forests
No rainforests were harmed in the making of these boxes. They're made in NZ from PEFC-certified paper stock from sustainably sourced forestry.

Chlorine and acid free
It takes water to make paper, so when the wastewater gets pumped out, we want to make sure it's as clean as possible. Even trace chlorine in water can pollute waterways and make fish sick.

Plastic-free in-shower storage containers
You heard that right. We've stuck to our no-landfill guns, even when it came to creating something you'll keep for a long time.

Whilst there are lots of ways to store our bars, our in-shower containers are specially designed for the purpose. We hope you never throw them away, but if you do, they can go straight into your compost – they're made with those renewable superstars, bamboo and corn.

Reproduced by kind permission of Ethique. More information can be found at www.ethique.com

The company's approach to messaging is open and informative. Furthermore, Ethique is also not simply passing the responsibility down to the consumer. They have designed their proposition to meet their purpose: they inform and educate their consumers in a non-patronizing way and enable informed decisions to be made, which allow consumers to give back to society and the environment. We have discussed the use of social marketing as an effective way to change behaviours, but if society cannot relate to the message or it is unclear (sometimes even misleading) then it will never have the desired impact. Ethique uses simple language and provides examples that give context and meaning at every stage of the customer journey. Most importantly, they give a reason to not just buy but to change your behaviour from buying plastic bottled products to solid products:

Why pay for water?
Our bars are concentrated, you add the water, not us. An average shampoo or bodywash can be made up of up to 80% water. Conditioner is even higher, at up to 95%. It doesn't make sense to pay for water, package it in plastic bottles and use harsh chemicals to preserve it, when there is water in your shower already.

When you #giveupthebottle and move into solid products you are not only giving up plastic, but also saving water.

(Ethique 2020 #giveupthebottle)

7.5 Chapter summary

In this chapter we have discussed the fact that not all plastic is bad. In fact, plastic as a material is highly beneficial and is needed in key industries and products, not least medical equipment. However, the level of plastic waste coming from areas such as food packaging that is either not necessary or cannot be recycled due to colour or type, and single-use plastics for which there are sustainable alternatives, needs addressing more urgently than ever. Plastic is an area where, as we have discussed, there are high levels of misinformation, but opportunity and change is also happening. We are seeing governments working to bring in new laws and new regulations concerning plastic, ranging from outright bans to plastic packaging taxes that encourage greater use of recycled plastic. Organizations and marketers are being presented with an opportunity to innovate, change direction and influence behaviours. Supermarkets are moving to more loose produce instead of packaged foods and are looking at more sustainable refill models within their business. Exciting innovations are being worked on by start-ups and supported by larger organizations. Recycling labelling is being made clearer and consumer understanding is starting to grow, not just in terms of recycling but in the need to reuse and repair first. It's early days, however, and there is still a lot more to do; recycling infrastructures need to be improved across the world. Agreed methodologies on how initiatives are measured and centralized reporting methods need to be agreed. This would go some way to reduce greenwashing – a term that means: 'to make people believe that your company is doing more to protect the environment than it really is' (Cambridge Dictionary 2020). Labelling products as 'organic' or 'eco-friendly' are not proof points that can be substantiated with insight and fact; they are just nice to have, and can be extremely misleading.

One of the biggest areas of change needs to be the stories that sit behind the products. Marketers can take consumers on a journey and never has it been more important to deliver all parts of a story when the subject is so complex and there's so much mistrust in the world. Consumers are more aware and open to change – the focus on the problem is well documented – but unless they have all the information across all areas then change will be slow or not widely adopted. It is not enough to inform them about one part of the story. The manufacture, the reason to buy, the usage and the disposal should all be marketed effectively, since all parts of the process impact the environment. Explaining things such as using fewer different types of plastics and designing simpler products could instantly improve recycling rates. Increasing messaging and driving demand towards food that's sourced locally or in country, which reduces waste and the need for plastic packaging due to the shorter distance the food needs to travel, are all reasons to engage and effect change but are not necessarily clear to consumers. Marketing needs to consider the broader message and story when it comes to plastic in order to influence the right behaviour. The objective can no longer be solely based on the sales of product. Do we want consumers to reduce, reuse or recycle? This is often not made clear enough. Pulling together all the complex pieces of the journey in a way that educates and informs is where the opportunities lie, and those organizations that get this right will be the ones that benefit.

7.6 Action points to consider

No.	Action	Considerations	Next Step
1	Consider the whole journey from manufacture to disposal and beyond.	Consumers do not sit and think about the entire journey. They rely on what they read and see. What do you want them to know and how can you be more transparent?	Map out each part of the journey and how you intend to tell the story in a way that doesn't complicate the matter. Use your knowledge to educate your customers too. Provide reason and context behind why you are doing what you are doing so they too can make informed decisions.
2	Understand the regulations that are in place and coming in the future.	What changes are coming? Do they/ will they impact your products? Is your messaging in line or will it require change?	Plan ahead. Don't wait for the rules to take effect. How can you use these to innovate how you do things or inform on your marketing communications to stay ahead of your competitors and evolve your sustainable development?
3	Consider your use of plastic.	Identify any areas of your products and services that may be using plastic that is not necessary or cannot be recycled.	What sustainable alternatives could you introduce to reduce or remove these entirely?
4	Review your recycling labelling on your products and services.	Consider how you can make the recycling options on your packaging clearer?	What ways can you use to encourage your consumer to also reuse and repair?
5	What exciting innovations could you develop with other partners?	What start-ups and other partner companies could you work with to produce innovative new ideas?	What companies could help you solve a problem with your products and services?

7.7 Chapter 7 references

Bumgardner, W. (2020). 'Can I Reuse My Plastic Water Bottles?'. Available at: https://www.verywellfit.com/can-i-reuse-my-bottled-water-bottle-3435422 (Accessed: 1 March 2020)

Cambridge Dictionary (2020). Available at: https://dictionary.cambridge.org/us/dictionary/english/greenwash (Accessed: 26 May 2020)

Casady, T. (2016). 'Scan your garbage's barcode, and this smart code will tell you to recycle or trash it'. Available at: https://www.digitaltrends.com/home/uzer-eugene-smart-trash-can/ (Accessed: 29 February 2020)

Corbin, Tony (2016). 'Costa and Starbucks launch in-store recycling schemes'. Available at: https://www.packagingnews.co.uk/news/markets/foodservice/costa-and-starbucks-launch-in-store-recycling-schemes-29-11-2016 (Accessed: 29 February 2020)

Costa Coffee (2020). 'You enjoy it. We recycle it'. Available at: https://www.costa.co.uk/responsibility/our-cups/ (Accessed: 1 March 2020)

EDN Staff (2018). Green Cities 'Fact Sheet, Single Use Plastic'. Available at: https://www.earthday.org/fact-sheet-single-use-plastics/ (Accessed: 1 March 2020)

Ethique (2020). #giveupthebottle. Available at: https://ethique.com/pages/give-up-the-bottle (Accessed: 28 May 2020)

Ethique (2020). www.ethique.com (Accessed 29 May 2020)

Geyer, R., Jambeck, J.R. and Lavender, K. (2017). 'Production, use, and fate of all plastics ever made', *Science Advances*, 19 July 2017: Vol. 3, no. 7, e1700782 DOI: 10.1126/sciadv.1700782. Available at: https://www.researchgate.net/publication/318567844_Production_use_and_fate_of_all_plastics_ever_made (Accessed: 15 February 2020)

Greenpeace (www.greenpeace.org). 'Dead Whale' (Accessed: 13 February 2020)

Heathcote, C. (2020). 'How green is plastic pipe?' Available at: https://blog.wavin.co.uk/how-green-is-plastic-pipe/ (Accessed: 15 February 2020)

History and Future of Plastics (2020). Available at: https://www.sciencehistory.org/the-history-and-future-of-plastics (Accessed: 11 February 2020)

Howell, M. (2019). 'Britain's best zero-waste shops and where to find them'. *Telegraph* Available at: https://www.telegraph.co.uk/food-and-drink/news/britains-best-zero-waste-shops-find/ (Accessed: 29 February 2020)

IEA (2018). 'The Future of Petrochemicals'. Available at: https://www.iea.org/reports/the-future-of-petrochemicals (Accessed: 15 February 2020)

Mortimer, Natalie (2014). 'One Water champions everyday "heroes" in new campaign'. Available at: https://www.thedrum.com/news/2014/06/16/one-water-champions-everyday-heroes-new-campaign (Accessed: 15 February 2020)

New Plastic Economy Initiative Partnership (2019). 'The New Plastics Economy Global Commitment 2019 Progress Report'. Available at: https://www.newplasticseconomy.org/assets/doc/Global-Commitment-2019-Progress-Report.pdf (Accessed: 29 February 2020)

Notpla (2020). 'Edible and biodegradable. The alternative to plastic.' Available at: https://www.notpla.com/products-2/ (Accessed: 15 February 2020)

Plastics – the Facts 2019 (2020). Available at: https://www.plasticseurope.org/application/files/9715/7129/9584/FINAL_web_version_Plastics_the_facts2019_14102019.pdf (Accessed: 12 February 2020)

Plastics Europe (2019). 'Plastics, The Facts 2019'. Available at: https://www.plasticseurope.org/application/files/9715/7129/9584/FINAL_web_version_Plastics_the_facts2019_14102019.pdf (Accessed: 29 February 2020)

Refill Oxford (2019). 'The Facts'. Available at: https://www.refilloxford.org/facts (Accessed: 1 March 2020)

Science History Institute (2020). 'Science Matters: The Case of Plastics'. Available at: https://www.sciencehistory.org/the-history-and-future-of-plastics (Accessed: 15 February 2020)

Sky Ocean Rescue (2020). 'About us'. Available at: https://www.skyoceanrescue.com/about (Accessed: 29 February 2020)

Sky Ocean Rescue (www.skyoceanrescue.com) (Accessed: 13 February 2020)

Surfrider (www.surfrider.org) 'What goes into the Ocean goes into you' (Accessed: 13 February 2020)

Walden, L. (2020). 'M&S and Sainsbury's launch in-store refill stations'. *House Beautiful.* Available at: https://www.housebeautiful.com/uk/lifestyle/eco/a31183913/supermarket-refill-stations/ (Accessed: 1 March 2020)

Water UK (2020). 'National Refill Day'. Available at: https://www.water.org.uk/ news-item/national-refill-day/ (Accessed: 1 March 2020)

YouGov (2019). 'YouGov Results Fieldwork 19th–20th September, 2019'. Available at: https://d25d2506sfb94s.cloudfront.net/cumulus_uploads/ document/kex3hc1tu8/YouGov – Recycling more extended results.pdf (Accessed: 29 February 2020)

CHAPTER EIGHT

Climate Change and the Carbon Challenge

8.0 Chapter introduction

Climate change is the biggest challenge we, as a collective human race, face. When trying to understand it and how an organization or individual can have a positive impact, it's hard to not to get lost and be overwhelmed by the sheer size and complexity of the problem. Add to that the fact that climate change is not within our individual control and it almost seems an impossible challenge.

However, as we address climate change it is important that we all take responsibility and educate ourselves. A YouGov study (Smith, 2019) of 30,000 people across 28 countries, showed that: 'most expect climate change to have a large or moderate impact on their lives', but they also believe it is not too late to stop it, if we take radical action. According to the study, attitudes towards climate change between Eastern and Western countries differed, in so much as concern amongst those from Eastern countries was far greater. Awareness and understanding of the challenges and opportunities is vital as actions in relation to climate change can vary from country to country, business to business and all the way down to an individual level. We have access to the science, the data and the insights that show what is happening to the planet. Whether it is an in-depth piece of research or a Google search, we can all access information and gain more knowledge and understanding.

Climate change is a broad and complex topic that could never be covered in a single chapter of a book. For our purposes, this chapter will focus on specifically where business has a role and can make an impact and how responsible marketers, through the sharing of stories and fuelling of new ideas, can provide a clearer understanding across industries and society of what businesses are currently doing and could be doing to address climate change and drive behaviours that generate positive results. We will discuss how climate change goes beyond just selling green products, how social marketing plays a key role and how to navigate your way through the murky waters of carbon offsetting. We will highlight the importance of transparency and open communication, providing examples where this has and hasn't worked, and what more can be done by both the government and business to support a global challenge that affects everyone and everything.

8.1 Where are we?

Big headlines, big consequences

Visibility and awareness of the term 'climate change' has grown rapidly over the last five years, but are the details that sit under what the scientists are saying really understood and are we going far enough to ensure that actions being taken are having a positive impact? United Nations 'Sustainable Development Goal 13' (UN SDG13, 2019), which states: 'Take urgent action to combat climate change and its impacts', is very clear about where we are now. 'Increasing greenhouse gas emissions are driving climate change. In 2017, greenhouse gas concentrations reached new highs. Moving towards 2030 emission objectives compatible with the 2°C [3.6°F] and 1.5°C [2.7°F] pathways requires a peak to be achieved as soon as possible, followed by rapid reductions.' Hard-hitting facts such as reports from observations from the Mauna Loa Observatory in Hawaii show that: 'carbon dioxide levels today are higher than at any point in at least the past 800,000 years, leading to rising global temperatures' ('Trends in Atmospheric Carbon Dioxide', 2019). 'May 2019 saw the highest recorded peak in atmospheric carbon dioxide in 61 years of observation'. 'The Global Climate Report – January 2020' reported that: 'the global land and ocean surface temperature for January 2020 was the highest in the 141-year record.'

One of the most significant headlines came in 2018 following the IPCC special report 'Summary for Policymakers, 2018' on the impacts of global warming. The report stated that: 'global warming is likely to reach 1.5°C [2.7°F] between 2030 and 2052 if it continues to increase at the current rate' (IPCC, 2018). What all reports and bodies are saying, in no uncertain terms, is that we have little time to limit global warming to a maximum of 1.5°C (2.7°F) in order to avoid climate breakdown.

Ongoing rises in temperatures have a number of different effects on the planet. From an environmental impact, it leads to unpredictable weather systems such as increased hurricanes and typhoons. Oceans get warmer and ice melts, and melting ice causes sea levels to rise. Rising sea levels cause flooding, flooding damages coastal habitats, which in turn can lead to the death of fish, birds and plants. From a societal standpoint, it will impact the availability of fresh water, food and energy, with a bigger impact being felt in the poorer and developing countries across the world. When you change how the planet works, you move into the clutches of a vicious cycle with damning consequences.

Cause and complexity

So what is causing the increase in carbon dioxide levels? Well, we know that the majority of sources are caused by human activity, such as manufacturing cement and steel and burning fossil fuels for energy.

Non-renewable fuels, which include coal, oil and natural gas, supply about 80 per cent of the world's energy, and 20 countries are responsible for at least three-quarters of the world's greenhouse gas emissions (Nunez, 2019). Clearing forests and ploughing soils emits carbon dioxide into the air. Agriculture is the leading cause of deforestation: one and a half acres of forest is cut down every second, that is the equivalent to 20 football fields every minute (Rinkesh, 2020). Add to that the other gases that heat the planet, coming from industrial sites and landfills, and the earth's atmosphere continues to warm at a rate that is not sustainable.

And it's not just industrial and agricultural activity that keeps increasing the levels of carbon dioxide. Behaviourally, consumerism is a key contributor. Take travelling, for example. People travel more now than ever before; whether it is for business or pleasure, affordable flight prices and the increase of routes and availability have made travelling more accessible. The ever-growing use of planes, trains and other types of transport adds to the climate change problem – so much so that the global aviation industry produces around 2 per cent of all human-induced carbon dioxide emissions. Aviation is responsible for 12 per cent of carbon dioxide emissions from all transport sources, compared to 74 per cent from road transport ('ATAG Facts and Figures', 2020).

Another example is fashion, an industry that we have referenced throughout this book, and for good reason. Its impact on the environment is damaging on multiple levels, and climate change is no exception. A report produced by the European Parliament in 2019 highlighted the extent of the impact the fashion industry and our consumption habits had on climate change. The report stated that: 'The amount of clothes bought in the EU per person has increased by 40 per cent in just a few decades, driven by a fall in prices and the increased speed with which fashion is delivered to consumers.' It went on to report that: 'Clothing accounts for between 2 per cent and 10 per cent of the environmental impact of consumption' (Šajn, 2019). The fashion industry contributes specifically to climate change at every stage of the clothing lifecycle, starting with the materials. Cotton requires high levels of agricultural resources from land, water and pesticides whilst synthetic fabrics, such as polyester and nylon, are made from fossil fuels. Then there is the mass manufacturing of the clothes, which emits high levels of carbon dioxide into the atmosphere, followed by their transportation and distribution around the world, which emits yet more. At the end of the lifecycle, the majority of clothes are discarded with: '85 per cent of all textiles ultimately ending up in a landfill or incinerated' ('Drawdown Framework', 2020). And, if you look at the role of marketing, fashion is a prime example of where it has played a part in driving overconsumption, using low prices, increased product cycles and free shipping and returns as a means to increase demand. It is no secret that the industry is one of the most unsustainable in the world today, and marketing is in part responsible for that.

When you take the examples above and try to break down the complexity and size of the issue, combatting climate change seems like an impossible challenge, especially when the impact is sometimes neither visible nor entirely within our control. Yet the understanding of what needs to happen at a broader level is out there. Organizations such as Project Drawdown (https://drawdown.org) – a not-for-profit organization founded in 2014 by a group of climate scientists and the world's leading resource for climate solutions – provides ongoing information and research to support all parts of the global stakeholder chain. They have published detailed plans and timelines of what needs to be done to change the path we are on and move towards positive change. The 'Drawdown Framework' states that all parts of the climate equation need to happen, including: 'stopping the sources of greenhouse gas pollution, supporting and enhancing the sinks of carbon dioxide found in nature, and helping society achieve broader 'transformations'. They also provide solutions by source and area of action.

There are solutions, and change is already happening in some countries, industries and organizations, but it is not happening at the pace or scale required. Whether it be through businesses or a single individual's action, the solutions and the 'why' need to be communicated more effectively. Ultimately, businesses need to lead the charge, working closely with government, policymakers and NGOs, but it doesn't stop there. Unless the wider population understands the impact their actions have, climate change will always feel too big and too far away for anyone to really invest in for the long term.

8.2 Why do companies need to do something about this now?

The reasons are clearly set out. First, the damage to the environment in some cases will be irreversible, changing the landscape and its inhabitants forever. Second, the damage to the global economy, predicted by the WWF's 'Global Futures' report (2020), reveals the crushing impact to global economies, industry and trade. The headline results state that: 'a 0.67 per cent fall in global GDP every year by 2050 under a business as usual [BAU] scenario'. The effect will be huge: 'the cumulative impact from 2011 to 2050, discounted to 2011 terms, is a loss of US$9.87 trillion under BAU'. They also predict: 'global price hikes for key commodities such as timber (+8 per cent), cotton (+6 per cent), oil seeds (+4 per cent) and fruit and vegetables (+3 per cent).'

Awareness of the impact of climate change is high and society is more open to behavioural change. A YouGov study of more than 9,000 consumers across the USA, UK, Italy, Canada, Spain, the Netherlands and Sweden highlighted that a majority (66 per cent) of consumers confirm that: 'they would feel more positive about companies that can demonstrate they are making efforts to reduce the carbon footprint of their products' (YouGov, 2019). Our chapters on the importance of leadership and stakeholder engagement refer to the fact that never has there been more of a need for all parts of society to come together in a global effort to drive change, and that companies are under increasing pressure from consumers, shareholders and employees to demonstrate that they are serious about sustainability. If we combine all of this, it is clear why companies need to do something now: they have no choice.

United Nations and the climate agreements

At the very top of the climate change stakeholder chain is the United Nations. As stated at the start of this chapter, the United Nations Sustainable Development Goal (SDG) 13 (2020) is to: 'Take urgent action to combat climate change and its impacts.' If we look more specifically at the objectives of SDG 13 there are areas in which marketing can be a direct catalyst for change. As well as focusing on the integration of climate change measures into national policies, the objectives within SDG13 also mention the 'improvement of education and awareness-raising'. Marketing is a key function for communication, raising awareness and educating society, as highlighted in the chapter on plastic and packaging, and we'll discuss a little later in this chapter exactly why marketers need to go beyond the broadcasting of information when it comes to sustainable development. For, if we are to succeed and meet climate change targets, then we require a number of different strategies to work together on a long-term basis.

This need for global agreement and a unified approach as the only way to fight climate change is well known and there have been numerous conventions and agreements over the years. The United Nations Framework Convention on Climate Change (UNFCCC), which is responsible for supporting the global response to the threat of climate change, came into being in 1992 at the Rio Earth Summit. New negotiations saw the strengthening of the global response in 1995 and the Kyoto Protocol was adopted in 1997, but only entered into force some years later, in 2005. Following the Kyoto Protocol, the most recent and probably most publicized agreement is the 2015 Paris Agreement, which includes 189 countries. The agreement commits governments to submit their plans to cut emissions and to work together and independently to: 'keep global temperatures well below 2°C [3.6°F] above pre-industrial times and to pursue efforts to limit them further to 1.5°C [2.7°F].' Unfortunately, despite the agreement, global carbon emissions: 'increased 1.7 per cent in 2017 and a further 2.7 per cent in 2018; it has been estimated that the rate of increase in 2019 will be among the highest on record. The last four years have been the hottest on record, with 2019 on track to make it five' ('Climate change report card: These countries are reaching targets', 2019). There is still a lot of work to be done and this brings us down to the next layer in this global stakeholder chain: governments.

Governments

Governments' role in climate change is to lead the international effort and be responsible for the development of plans, 'nationally determined contributions' (NDCs), and ensure their countries invest in the right projects and actions in line with NDCs to deliver on climate targets. The Paris Agreement, unlike previous agreements, makes tracking and public reporting mandatory, with developed countries legally required to report their greenhouse gas emissions on an annual basis. This means that essentially those countries that aren't on track will be publicly named and shamed. Strict policies need to be implemented and rolled out internally within governmental departments and externally across businesses and society. Investment in areas such as renewable energy, reduction in fossil fuel investment, restoration and preservation of forests and the reduction of carbon emissions from transportation systems are just some of the projects that need to be addressed and actioned. The governments need to be open and transparent and also be held to account if they are not falling in line with its targets.

Extrapolating and analysing all the data, and understanding the variety of relevant bodies and targets, is a bit of a minefield, to say the least. The Climate Action Tracker (www.climateactiontracker.org) is an independent scientific analysis that measures government action against the Paris Agreement targets, tracking and reporting which countries are on and, more importantly, off target. A practical and valuable source of data, it gives a clear view on where we are globally as a collective in our progress in tackling climate change.

Business

Regardless of size, industry or geographical location, every business should have a sustainable strategy that addresses climate change. The challenges are broad and there are multiple areas that need to be addressed. Organizations need to work with governments to understand the regulatory landscape they will be operating in and invest and innovate in new technologies and ways of working to ensure progress is made and carbon emissions are reduced. Whilst the need to work in line with the Paris Agreement is key, it should not stop industries looking independently at innovative ways of incorporating areas such as implementation of renewable energy, new sources of product, more efficient manufacturing and supply chains, internal travel and transportation methods, and ways to minimize waste, instead of using only recyclable materials. Unilever's 'Sustainable Living Plan' has three main goals in which sit multiple strands. Their goal is: 'by 2030 to halve the environmental footprint of the making and use of our products as we grow our business' ('Our

Sustainable Living Report Hub', 2020). They are focusing on reducing greenhouse gases in a number of areas, from manufacturing, transport and refrigeration to energy consumption in their offices and reducing employee travel.

The carbon footprint of sites and buildings in which organizations operate is also a key factor in reducing an organization's carbon footprint, no matter how big or small. It is important that the strategy you develop is focused both internally and externally. Microsoft has started to invest in building sustainable business campuses and data centres, running them on 100 per cent carbon-free electricity. Microsoft states that it will: 'continue to keep our house in order and improve it, while increasingly addressing sustainability challenges around the globe by engaging our strongest assets as a company – our employees and our technologies'. ('We're increasing our carbon fee', 2019) However, those organizations that are making progress in their targets to reduce carbon emissions and become carbon neutral also need to ensure that their employees understand and live by the values they set.

So, how can marketers take this complex topic and market it effectively? The challenges that sit firmly at the heart of the issue are manifold. There are multiple different actions that can be taken, each action has multiple pathways to and within it, and there is currently no unified way to calculate and measure actions globally. Add to that, the positive impact on climate change isn't visible to most, it's a long-term strategy with no fixed end point and not all elements are in any single person's, organization's or country's control. It's difficult to market something you cannot directly see or control.

Marketing climate change cannot therefore be done through a single approach; it requires a combination of approaches. Social marketing (not to be confused with social media marketing), is one such area that should be considered. Social marketing is the 'systematic application of marketing concepts and techniques to achieve specific behavioural goals relevant to the social good' (Lazer and Kelley, 1973). Social marketing is used in healthcare to encourage societal behaviours such as giving up smoking and eating a healthy diet, for example the NHS '5 a day' campaign, which encourages people to eat at least five portions of fruit or vegetables a day. Social marketing is not about selling products or services; it is rather all about making people aware of the reasons they need to change behaviours.

Used effectively, strong social marketing goes beyond the campaign, it will be based on insight and fact, it runs for a sustained period, it alerts and informs, and it is also often repeated or 'always on'. Behind it sit support and tools that help to effect behavioural changes and encourage people to maintain change. Many social marketing campaigns are done in partnership with another organization. This sustained approach over a period of time, continuously educating and promoting the benefits of behavioural change and new ways of thinking, can be an extremely powerful tool. Social marketing in relation to the environment is frequently used by NGOs, something we will discuss in more detail in Chapter 11. Social marketing in relation to business and climate change is slightly different as organizations generally want to sell products and services.

Social marketing can be used by brands to communicate their values. By having a relationship with a specific brand that has a strong purpose and ensures that all parts of its business have a positive impact on the environment, consumers get the best of both worlds. The value exchange is one that can increase loyalty to the brand and enhance its reputation whilst giving the customer something they want and making them feel like they have supported the environment as part of their purchasing decision. Climate change cannot happen on its own; both sides of the value exchange need to play their part for the outcome to become a reality. However, organizations need to be clear on the benefits, and transparency is of the upmost importance.

An example of this is Yorkshire Tea and their Yorkshire Tree campaign (Yorkshire Tree, 2020), in which they pledged to 'plant a million new trees over five years in the UK and Kenya'. They have planted millions of trees over the years and saved large areas of rainforest, which is critical in mitigating climate change. Yorkshire Tea want to sell their tea, they are open about the fact that their tea bags and their packaging use wood, yet they are committed to ensuring that the wood comes from select forests that commit to plant new trees as others are chopped down and used. Once educated, this gives an additional reason for the consumer to buy their particular tea when they are considering which brand to purchase. In an FMCG market where consumers purchase constantly and often with little consideration beyond price and quality, social marketing can provide a broader reason, whilst at the same time educating and raising awareness generally.

However, whilst brands work hard on their sustainable development plans, they need to be mindful of their role in the stakeholder chain. Their influence is strong and when they prioritize product sales above hitting their sustainable targets this can deliver a message that's far more damaging. The subject of sourcing sustainable palm oil, for instance, is complex and one many brands are failing to meet their pledges on. The WWF Palm Oil Buyers Scorecard January 2020 (www.palmoilscorecard. panda) reported a long list of organizations that failed to meet their targets. Some simply moved those targets out, and not for the first time. Organizations that invest both internally and externally in sustainable climate change strategies have to ensure they are prepared to meet their targets and have the evidence to support their claims. Their power to influence and change societal behaviours is strong, so if they are seen to fail in these and simply keep moving the timeframes, then what message is that giving? The answer: it undermines the seriousness of climate change and runs the risk of resetting behaviours. If society thinks it is OK to miss targets because that's what big business is doing, what incentive do we have to change our behaviours?

8.3 Things that need to be acknowledged as not perfect

Net zero, carbon neutral

Meeting targets and objectives requires a combined effort, so why is the progress so slow? Why are governments, organizations and society not meeting the targets being set? One issue, and one we touch on throughout this book, is the need to improve the consistency of models, measures and messaging. The terms that sit within the frameworks that organizations are working to and making claims on differ vastly. A paper published by the Science Based Target Initiative (SBTi) explained that: 'the various approaches to climate neutrality differentiate in at least four aspects: 1) the time frame of the target, 2) the scope of the activities included in the target, 3) the climate impacts from those activities and 4) the climate mitigation approach used by companies to meet their targets' (Pineda and Faria, 2019). The variation leads to confusion across all parts of the stakeholder chain and what and how actions are being measured is not consistent across the board, resulting in the messages being mixed, unclear or, worse, incorrect and therefore pointless. There's a lot to consider and as Mark Lapping, CEO of Aquapak, states in his interview with us in Chapter 10: 'You need an "ology" just to work your way around it all.'

Whilst the headlines make for impressive reading – 'Aim for 1 Billion Passengers to Fly on Sustainable Fuel Flights by 2025' (IATA press release 2020); 'Microsoft will be carbon negative by 2030' (Smith, 2020); and 'BP sets ambition for net zero by 2050, fundamentally changing organization to deliver' (BP press release, 2020) – the race to the bottom is not based on a consistent foundation that can be measured or compared. In other words, there is no central reference point. Organizations therefore need to ensure that they are providing the insight and basis on which their claims are being made. They need to work with the right partners, legislation and certifications, but most importantly they need to work together so society has a central point of reference and can trust that what is being worked towards is actually a genuine target.

Navigating carbon offsetting

Carbon offsetting is a term that is well marketed, and is one of the ways to achieve sustainable climate change targets. Carbon offset schemes allow individuals and companies to invest in environmental projects so they can neutralize or offset their own carbon footprints. The objective is to produce less waste and use more renewable energy in order to meet the 'net zero', 'carbon neutral', 'climate neutral' targets.

There are two parts to carbon offsetting. First, the compliance market, which is mandatory for industrial polluters such as power plants. Second, the voluntary side, which allows companies and individuals to invest in projects. Some environmentalists doubt the effectiveness of offsetting and others argue it is just passing the problem from one place to another. Still others argue that some organizations use it as a means to put off addressing what they should be doing to be more sustainable. The fact remains that unless you address your own carbon footprint, offsetting is essentially pointless; it's only when the two things are done together that they can have a real impact.

Investing in offset fund projects is tricky; there are multiple global projects grouped under broader headings such as 'restoration of forests' or 'investment in energy efficient projects' that focus on the reduction of fossil fuels being used, and both businesses and individuals can choose to participate in carbon offsetting. The authenticity of the project you invest in needs to be well researched prior to investment. This complicated journey isn't only difficult for users to navigate, but for businesses that want to communicate what they are doing, the message can be difficult to articulate and in reality the practice can be open to both positive and negative outcomes.

A famous example of this is when the band Coldplay released its second hit album, *A Rush of Blood to the Head*. The band said it would offset part of the environmental damage caused by its production by planting 10,000 mango trees in southern India. However, those plants never grew due to the arid conditions (Dhillon and Harnden, 2006). Good intention – but lack of execution and, importantly, accountability.

Certifiers and providers

It is important to ensure a project is credible. There are many offset certifiers, such as Plan Vivo Foundation, SCS Global Services, Verra and Gold Standard, the list goes on. Gold Standard is one of the most well-known certifiers, a not-for-profit organization formed by the WWF and other NGOs that ensures the credibility and integrity of environmental projects. They propose a: 'standard that sets requirements to design projects for maximum positive impact in climate and development – and to measure and report outcomes in the most credible and efficient way' (Gold Standard, 2019).

Then there are providers – organizations that enable businesses and individuals to take part in offsetting schemes, although in 2017, Gold Standard made it possible to purchase carbon credits online directly from them. Reputable providers will only offer projects that have been certified. MyClimate, EcoAct, Cool Effect and NativeEnergy are all examples of providers that offer a range of services to both individuals and organizations. For organizations, providers will work out your carbon footprint; it is worth noting that there are many different 'carbon calculators' available, so the choice of provider and how reputable they are is important. Following your carbon calculation, the provider then selects projects that best align to your business, charging an amount based on their own greenhouse gas price per tonne. EasyJet work with providers EcoAct and First Climate to offset their carbon footprint through the purchasing of carbon credits that fund various projects. In addition, there has been investment in more eco-friendly planes, ensuring flights are at full capacity wherever possible and reducing fuel usage. EasyJet state: 'Since November 2019, 9 million customers have taken net-zero carbon flights' (EasyJet, 2019).

As we researched this book, it became very clear that it is vital to do your homework before you embark on a carbon offset investment due to the many variables. Equally, marketing your actions is also highly complicated due to the many different ways in which it can be interpreted. Be mindful of greenwashing, and avoid headline grabbing with unbelievably large numbers or dates set too far in the future. Ensure all actions can be translated into financial impact and visible business outcomes.

Carbon labelling

Like many other labels we see on products, such as the ingredients, nutritional and recycling information, carbon labelling will tell consumers the environmental impact the product has on the planet. This approach, alongside the other labels, is to enable consumers to make more informed decisions. With the understanding and awareness of climate change being higher today than it has ever been, it's an effective way to market the sustainability of products. A YouGov study for climate change labelling revealed that: 'more than half of respondents (52 per cent) agreed that they do not generally think about the carbon footprint of a product before buying it. Additionally, two-thirds (67 per cent) of consumers support the idea of a recognisable carbon label to demonstrate that products have been made with a commitment to measuring and reducing their carbon footprint' (Carbon Trust, 2019).

Quorn recently announced claims to be: 'the first meat-free food manufacturer to achieve third-party certification of its carbon footprint figures – via the Carbon Trust – which is being integrated into its own food labelling' (Smithers, 2020). By being provided with clear information, consumers can make choices that help them to reduce their own carbon footprints. However, as with everything that is carbon related (or so it seems), the issue of consistency is again a factor to be aware of and one that could put brands into a questionable situation and leave them open to criticism. For example, Tesco launched carbon labelling in 2007 only to drop it in 2012 due to the amount of work involved across the range of complex supply chains. In addition, the lack of action by other retailers to follow suit meant carbon labelling didn't get the attention it needed.

Ecolabelling as a whole has come under criticism. When visible on packaging, it is meant to act as a symbol consumers can trust. Its purpose is to make the product or service stand out and act as key differentiator in the market. When it comes to purchasing decisions, the value exchange with the customer is as we mentioned earlier in the chapter: they get a product they want whilst having a positive impact on the environment. However, as discussed in relation to recycling, labelling – and, as we'll touch on later, packaging – is open to misinterpretation and misuse by brands, especially if there are multiple labels, terms, symbols and certifications. At the point of researching this topic, the Ecolabel Index, the largest global directory of ecolabels' website, showed they were tracking: '458 ecolabels in 199 countries, and 25 industry sectors' (www.ecolabelindex.com).

When it comes to labelling or making claims linked to the environment, businesses need to be cautious as they can run the risk of being accused of greenwashing. Ryanair, for instance, was accused of greenwashing in February 2020 when it claimed in a marketing campaign that it had the lowest carbon emissions of any major airline in Europe. The Advertising Standards Agency subsequently banned the ad as Ryanair could not substantiate its claim (Sweney, 2020).

Yet labels *are* an effective device when used in the right way. The *British Medical Journal*, however, has gone one step further, proposing: 'a low cost, scalable intervention to facilitate change in individuals' and society's views and behaviour: with warning labels at points of purchase of fossil energy or services dependent on large amounts of fossil fuel, for example at petrol stations, on energy bills, and on airline tickets' (Ho, 2020). This is taking labelling and using it as part of a broader social marketing approach. They are not using a label as a symbol to sell a product but rather to inform consumers that products such as petrol and flying have negative impacts on the environment. The purpose of these labels is to inform and give consumers the power to make more informed decisions. Through this, they will either reduce frequency of or deter purchase, or over time look for alternatives that are better for the environment. Such an example would be someone who went on to make the decision to switch from a petrol car to an electric one.

8.4 Case study – Patagonia

We have discussed how the fashion industry contributes specifically to climate change at every stage of the clothing lifecycle. This includes the impact on agricultural resources, from land, water and pesticides, to the use of fossil fuels and the mass manufacturing of the clothes, which emit high levels of carbon dioxide into the atmosphere.

Patagonia is a clothing company, an activist organization and a B Corp that is dedicated to meeting the highest standards of social and environmental performance, transparency and accountability. The company is clear in its approach that only a combined effort across all areas of this highly complex challenge will make an impact and reduce the effect of climate change: 'we are enmeshed in carbon emissions: making polyester thread from oil, weaving fabric on machines run on fossil fuels, dyeing fabrics with chemical dyes and waterproofing jackets, sewing shirts in factories, transporting pants from one country to another or from one city to another, shipping clothes in plastic mailbags to the people who order them, driving to work.' ('How We're Reducing Our Carbon Footprint', 2020)

Their target is to eliminate or mitigate all their carbon emissions by 2025, based on a four-part process.

As discussed in this chapter, you must first understand your organization's own impact and carbon emissions. Until organizations can reduce their own carbon emissions, areas such as offsetting are simply moving the problem somewhere else, limiting a reduction overall.

Patagonia's approach was:

1. Measure Our Impact.

A third-party validated system is in place to measure our impacts so we can make informed decisions and track our progress.

In 2017, we underwent a comprehensive greenhouse gas audit – an inventory of our company's emissions, from extraction of raw materials to material creation to delivery of products to customers. We drew upon energy bills, transportation reports and life-cycle analysis of different materials, then had our analysis verified by a third party, just as scientists submit their research for peer review.

By gaining this vital understanding and identifying the points within your organization that you need to dedicate your focus to you can begin to look at how you approach these areas to deliver real change. This level of understanding is also key to the information you flow through your organization providing reason and knowledge behind your purpose. Patagonia identified exactly where they needed to focus to reduce their damage to the environment.

2. Reduce Our Impact.
Avoid the need for energy where we can, improve efficiency where we can't.

Materials and Technology
Discovering that nearly 86 per cent of our total carbon emissions as a company come from the creation of the materials we use in our products has galvanized our staff to incorporate recycled materials wherever possible and support circular economies at every opportunity.

Quality and Worn Wear®
The longer our products last, the less impact they have, so creating products of superior quality is one of the most ecological things we can do. 'Extending the life of clothing by an extra nine months of active use would reduce carbon, waste and water footprints by around 20–30%.' Therefore, creating durable products is one of our highest priorities and is the foundation of the 'Ironclad Guarantee' on our products.

Shipping Products
Our products are shipped all over the place. To reduce our shipping footprint, we analyze our shipping routes to minimize distances traveled, switch to less energy intensive modes of transportation (i.e. ocean freight over air) and increase 'drop shipping' where products ship directly from factory to regional distribution centers. In Summer 2018, we added a new distribution center in Pennsylvania, which significantly reduces the carbon intensity of shipping products to customers on the East Coast of the U.S.

Our Supply Chain Task Force
We created our Chemical and Environmental Impacts Program (CEIP). This global team manages environmental impacts in our

global manufacturing supply chain from the textile mills to the subcontractors of our sewing factories.

Patagonia Buildings
We currently have over 75 Patagonia operated stores across the globe, seven regional headquarters and two distribution centers. When opening new locations, we've long prioritized the use of existing buildings over new ones and have developed a set of sustainable building principles to guide their development. These include low-impact construction techniques, energy efficiency and renewable energy, passive heating/cooling, reclaimed materials and low-VOC paints.

Sustainable Commuting
In 2010, we launched our Drive-Less Program to encourage employees to avoid single-occupant vehicle commuting. Each year Patagonia rewards employees who carpool, ride a bike, skateboard or take public transportation by reimbursing them $2 per trip, and up to $500 per year.

3. Convert to Renewable Energy.
Move away from fossil fuels to cleaner, renewable energy sources for everything we do.
   Owned and Operated Locations and Supply Chain and Non-Connected Investments.

4. Capture Carbon.
Invest and test ways to remove warming gases from the atmosphere (i.e. carbon insetting sequestration programmes). Think of these efforts as the difference between stopping the mess, and cleaning it up.

(Patagonia, 'The Climate Crisis', 2020)

Patagonia are a benchmark organization that many others can learn from when it comes to reviewing, understanding and reducing the impact business has on climate change. Their open and inclusive approach includes all stakeholders and looks at every element of their supply chain. They understand what they need to do and why and they ensure their message is clear.

8.5 Chapter summary

Throughout this chapter we have explained that it is clear that climate change is a topic so broad and so complex that only a global effort will change the direction in which the world is heading. We have discussed how governments need to deliver on their commitments to the Paris Agreement and act as the lead in their respective countries, reporting on their progress and adjusting targets as required by the agreement. We have also looked at how organizations need to work with governments, as well as innovating and leading the way, investing in new technologies and ways of working to ensure progress. Stories of success should be shared with a view to creating best practice and fuelling new ideas across industries, which can escalate the pace of change. With everyone working towards a common purpose, there is even more of a need for complete transparency.

Marketing's role in educating and informing society on climate change is important both in terms of the need to raise awareness but also to change behaviours on a mass scale. No single individual can effect the collective change that is required, so investment in long-term social marketing campaigns built upon fact and supported with solutions is critical to the continuous education required to change long-term behaviour patterns.

As highlighted when considering the complex world of carbon offsetting, first note that internal targets are as important as external ones. Start with getting acquainted with your own carbon footprint and implement a sustainable plan of action to reduce them before looking at ways to offset. Investigate all areas of this complex process and use only credible providers that offer only certified projects. It is only through this approach that emissions will reduce overall as opposed to simply being moved around, and investment will go to those projects that can really make a difference.

Always minimize the risk of accusations of 'greenwashing' by undertaking genuinely useful activities. Reputation is critical when it comes to the environment, and all parts of the stakeholder chain, from investors through to consumers, are now more aware and looking at how businesses operate. Organizations need to use their influence and reach to support meeting our global targets.

The coronavirus pandemic that took hold in 2020 had a devastating impact on society and the economy. The impact it had on climate change as restricted movement and social distancing became the norm was extraordinary. Global lockdowns in the early part of the year reduced manufacturing, and the aviation industry saw entire fleets of planes grounded. Whilst it remains to be seen if these collective pauses taught us anything about the damage we are doing to our environment, what can't happen is for climate change to fall to the bottom of the world's agenda. The clock is still running down, and vaccines aren't an option against what is happening to our planet.

8.6 Action points to consider

No.	Action	Considerations	Next Step
1	Review the commitments of the Paris Agreement in the context of your own company.	Develop your own method of reporting on your progress towards achieving the targets.	Consider how you might set more ambitious targets than are suggested by the agreement.
2	Consider how your organization could work with government to innovate and lead the way.	Investigate if any government support is available to help invest in new technologies that can support your sustainability strategy.	Consider if your ways of working are set up to ensure continued progress towards your objectives.
3	Share your progress.	Consider what stories of success you have that could be shared, with a view to creating best practice and fuelling new ideas.	How could you provide even greater transparency on your progress?
4	Articulate your company's carbon offsetting commitment.	Start with gaining a clear understanding of your own carbon footprint and implement a plan of action to reduce it.	In what way can you offset your carbon emissions? What certified projects or organizations could you partner with to further reduce your emissions?
5	How has the coronavirus pandemic changed your strategy?	Consider how the coronavirus has affected your carbon emissions.	Have there been any unintended improvements as a result of coronavirus? For example, less travel – how could this be developed further?

8.7 Chapter 8 references

ATAG (2020). 'Facts & Figures'. Available at: https://www.atag.org/facts-figures.
html (Accessed: 28 March 2020)

Big Room Inc. (2020). 'Ecolabel Index (2020)'. Available at: http://www.
ecolabelindex.com/ (Accessed: 28 March 2020)

BP press release (2020). 'BP sets ambition for net zero by 2050, fundamentally
changing organization to deliver'. Available at: https://www.bp.com/en/
global/corporate/news-and-insights/press-releases/bernard-looney-
announces-new-ambition-for-bp.html (Accessed: 14 March 2020)

Cambridge Dictionary (2019). 'Greenwash'. Available at: https://dictionary.
cambridge.org/dictionary/english/greenwash (Accessed: 28 March 2020)

Carbon Trust (2019). 'Research reveals consumer demand for climate change
labelling'. Available at: https://www.carbontrust.com/news-and-events/news/
research-reveals-consumer-demand-for-climate-change-labelling (Accessed:
1 April 2020)

Dhillon, A. and Harnden T. (2006). 'How Coldplay's green hopes died in the
arid soil of India'. Available at: https://www.telegraph.co.uk/news/worldnews/
asia/india/1517031/How-Coldplays-green-hopes-died-in-the-arid-soil-of-
India.html (Accessed: 14 March 2020)

Earth System Research Laboratories, Global Monitoring Laboratory (2019).
'Trends in Atmospheric Carbon Dioxide'. Available at: https://www.esrl.noaa.
gov/gmd/ccgg/trends/ (Accessed: 13 March 2020)

EasyJet (2019). 'Leading the industry on sustainable travel'. Available at: https://
www.easyjet.com/en/sustainability (Accessed: 28 March 2020)

Gold Standard (2019). 'A higher standard for climate security and sustainable
development'. Available at: https://www.goldstandard.org/impact-
quantification/gold-standard-global-goals (Accessed: 28 March 2020)

Ho, S. (2020). 'High-Carbon Products Should Have Smoking-Style Health
Warnings, Experts Say'. Available at: https://www.greenqueen.com.hk/high-
carbon-products-should-have-smoking-style-health-warnings-experts-say/
(Accessed: 28 March 2020)

IATA Press Release (2020). 'Aim for 1 Billion Passengers to Fly on Sustainable
Fuel Flights by 2025'. Available at: https://www.iata.org/en/pressroom/
pr/2018-02-26-01/ (Accessed: 28 March 2020)

IPCC, World Meteorological Organization, Geneva, Switzerland (2018).
'Summary for Policymakers.' In: 'Global Warming of 1.5°C. An IPCC Special

Report on the impacts of global warming of 1.5°C above pre-industrial levels and related global greenhouse gas emission pathways, in the context of strengthening the global response to the threat of climate change, sustainable development, and efforts to eradicate poverty'. Available at: https://www.ipcc.ch/sr15/chapter/spm/ (Accessed: 13 March 2020)

Lazer and Kelley (1973). 'Social Marketing Works' (2020) Available at: https://www.thensmc.com/sites/default/files/Social_marketing_works_NHS.pdf (Accessed: 15 March 2020)

Microsoft blog (2019). 'We're increasing our carbon fee'. Available at: https://blogs.microsoft.com/on-the-issues/2019/04/15/were-increasing-our-carbon-fee-as-we-double-down-on-sustainability/ (Accessed: 29 March 2020)

National Geographic (2019). 'Climate change report card: These countries are reaching targets'. Available at: https://www.nationalgeographic.co.uk/environment-and-conservation/2019/09/climate-change-report-card-these-countries-are-reaching (Accessed: 29 March 2020)

NOAA National Centers for Environmental Information (2020). 'State of the Climate: Global Climate Report for February 2020', Available at: https://www.ncdc.noaa.gov/sotc/global/2020 (Accessed: 19 May 2020)

NOAA National Centers for Environmental Information (2020). 'State of the Climate: Global Climate Report for January 2020'. Available at: https://www.ncdc.noaa.gov/sotc/global/202001. (Accessed: 13 March 2020)

Nunez, C. (2019). 'What Are Fossil Fuels?'. Available at: https://www.nationalgeographic.com/environment/energy/reference/fossil-fuels/ (Accessed: 28 March 2020)

Patagonia (2020). 'The Climate Crisis'. Available at: https://eu.patagonia.com/gb/en/climate-crisis (Accessed: 28 May 2020)

Patagonia (2020). 'How We're Reducing Our Carbon Footprint'. Available at: https://www.patagonia.com/stories/how-were-reducing-our-carbon-footprint/story-74099.html (Accessed: 28 May 2020)

Pineda, A. C. and Faria, P. (2019). 'Towards A Science-Based Approach To Climate Neutrality In The Corporate Sector'. Science Based Targets. Available at: https://sciencebasedtargets.org/wp-content/uploads/2019/10/Towards-a-science-based-approach-to-climate-neutrality-in-the-corporate-sector-Draft-for-comments.pdf (Accessed: 28 March 2020)

Project Drawdown (2020). 'Drawdown Framework'. Available at: https://bigthink.com/politics-current-affairs/is-fashion-bad-for-the-environment?rebelltitem=4#rebelltitem4 (Accessed: 29 March 2020)

Report of the Secretary-General UN (2019). 'Sustainable Development Goal 13' Available at: https://sustainabledevelopment.un.org/sdg13 (Accessed: 13 March 2020)

Report of the Secretary-General UN (2019). 'Sustainable Development Goal 13'. Available at: https://sustainabledevelopment.un.org/sdg13 (Accessed: 29 March 2020)

Rinkesh (2020). '51 Breathtaking Facts About Deforestation'. Available at: https://www.conserve-energy-future.com/various-deforestation-facts.php (Accessed: 28 March 2020)

Šajn, Nikolina (2019). 'Environmental impact of the textile and clothing industry'. Available at: https://www.europarl.europa.eu/RegData/etudes/BRIE/2019/633143/EPRS_BRI(2019)633143_EN.pdf (Accessed: 28 March 2020)

Smith, B. (2020). 'Microsoft will be carbon negative by 2030'. Available at: https://blogs.microsoft.com/blog/2020/01/16/microsoft-will-be-carbon-negative-by-2030/ (Accessed: 28 March 2020)

Smith, M. (2019). 'International poll: most expect to feel impact of climate change, many think it will make us extinct'. Available at: https://yougov.co.uk/topics/science/articles-reports/2019/09/15/international-poll-most-expect-feel-impact-climate (Accessed: 13 March 2020)

Smithers, R. (2020). 'Quorn to be first major brand to introduce carbon labelling'. The *Guardian*. Available at: https://www.theguardian.com/environment/2020/jan/09/quorn-to-be-first-major-brand-to-introduce-carbon-labelling (Accessed: 1 April 2020)

Sweney, M. (2020). 'Ryanair accused of greenwash over carbon emissions claim'. The *Guardian*. Available at: https://www.theguardian.com/business/2020/feb/05/ryanair-accused-of-greenwash-over-carbon-emissions-claim (Accessed: 29 March 2020)

Unilever (2020). 'Our Sustainable Living Report Hub'. Available at: https://www.unilever.com/sustainable-living/our-sustainable-living-report-hub/ (Accessed: 29 March 2020)

WWF (2020). 'Palm Oil Buyers' Scorecard January 2020'. Available at: https://d2ouvy59p0dg6k.cloudfront.net/downloads/wwf_palm_oil_scorecard_2020.pdf (Accessed: 28 March 2020)

WWF (2020). 'Global Futures: Modelling the global economic impacts of environmental change to support policy-making'. Available at: https://www.wwf.org.uk/sites/default/files/2020-02/Global_Futures_Technical_Report.pdf (Accessed: 29 March 2020)

Yorkshire Tea (2020). 'Yorkshire Tree Campaign'. Available at: https://www.yorkshiretea.co.uk/yorkshire-tree (Accessed: 29 March 2020)

CHAPTER NINE

Sustainable Energy

9.0 Chapter introduction

In a world rich in natural resources – sun, sea, wind and air – it's no surprise that the pursuit of capitalizing on these natural resources to provide an alternative energy solution to the more destructive fossil fuels has been on the agenda for a number of years.

Clean energy, green energy, renewable energy, sustainable energy – regardless of what we call it, aligned with climate change targets and initiatives, investment and interest in challenging the norms of energy provision has grown significantly over the past decade. And yet, whilst there's a growing interest, this approach is most certainly not mainstream. Fossil fuels, in the form of oil, petrol, diesel, gas and coal, dominate our energy provisions, and aligned with this, have created some of the wealthiest and most powerful organizations in the world.

As well as becoming a throwaway society, we've also become a society driven by convenience – the convenience of simply flicking a switch to light, heat and fuel our homes and businesses, to hop into our cars, trains or buses to commute each day to work or school, or to fly from country to country. It means that as a collective happily driven by convenience, we rarely stop to consider the impact of fossil fuel use or the alternatives. Whilst price wars have raged amongst the main energy providers, and we occasionally bear the brunt of rising energy costs, the reality is that competition in the energy sector is now fierce. When locked into 'annual contracts' it can be challenging to switch to alternative, greener solutions at exactly the time you want to; however, regulators have made switching suppliers, including renewable providers, far easier than ever before.

As we will evidence throughout this chapter, energy is like many of the topics relating to sustainability – highly complex – yet appetite from government, industry and consumers is shifting as the reality of our dependency on these 'dirty' and finite resources comes home to roost. Our focus in this chapter then is to illuminate the alternative energy solutions and educate you about where we currently find ourselves, what's to come and, critically, what it means for climate change, business and you, the responsible marketer.

9.1 Where are we?

It's useful to start at the very beginning, well, pre the Industrial Revolution, a time when most of the heating and lighting resources we used were mainly based around renewable solutions. Animals were used to plough fields and turn mills, wind and water powered mills to grind wheat, we burned wood and other plant materials – materials we today call biomass – and the shipping trade, fuelled by the wind, had been in operation for centuries.

Whilst there's lots of evidence that fossil fuels have been used to fuel many endeavours throughout ancient history, the mass exploitation and commercialisation, fuelling the birth of powerful associated mega-industries, began in the late eighteenth century. It's reported that regardless of the abundance of supply, even during the Industrial Revolution, thinkers of the day forecast a time when we'd run out of these finite resources, referred to as 'peak coal' or 'peak oil'. For this reason, in the mid-nineteenth century preparation for a post-coal world began, with interest in solar technology being pursued as a longer-term solution (Mason, 2019).

In the 1950s, the reality of our ever-growing population, together with environmental pressure and industrial concern about the finite supply of fossil fuels drove a surge towards renewables. This was accelerated by air pollution concerns, highlighted by the death and devastation during the worst air pollution incident to date: the 1952 London Smog Disaster, a four-day smog that resulted in 12,000 deaths and more than 100,000 people becoming ill (Potenza, 2017). As a result of the disaster, the Clean Air Act 1956 was passed. This focused on reducing smoke pollution, increasing the use of electricity and gas, and reducing the use of solid fuels. A decade later, in 1968, the Clean Air Act 1956 initiated the development of tall chimneys for burning coal, liquid or gaseous fuels across Europe and the US, the basic principle being the higher the chimneys, the better the dispersal of air pollution (www.air-quality.org.uk). Since that time, initiatives such as the Paris Agreement have championed countries around the world to continue to transition towards low-carbon, renewable energy to mitigate air pollution and align with and support climate change objectives.

Returning to the SDGs, goal number 7 is to: 'Ensure access to affordable, reliable, sustainable and modern energy for all' (UN, 2020). Energy is effectively essential in everything we do – from fuelling our homes to cooking the food we eat, general food production, our day-to-day working lives and economic growth, commuting, schooling, technological developments and innovation, travel and healthcare – so as a collective, when it comes to climate change and improved air quality, and therefore improved quality of life, it's in all of our interests to seek cleaner, more sustainable energy solutions.

A report on the progress of SDG Goal 7 in 2019, however, doesn't paint a positive or as progressive picture as is required, as summarized below:

- The global electrification rate rose to reach 89 per cent in 2017. However, some 840 million people around the world are still without access to electricity – with 50 per cent found in sub-Saharan Africa.

- Access to clean cooking fuels and technologies reached 61 per cent in 2017. However, close to 3 billion people still rely primarily on inefficient cooking systems and are exposed to dangerous levels of air pollution.
- The level of renewable energy consumption has increased from 16.6 per cent in 2010 to 17.5 per cent in 2016. Much faster change is required to meet the set climate goals. ('Sustainable Development Goals Knowledge Platform', 2019)

The reality is that whilst renewable energy is gaining more of a foothold, finite fossil fuels continue to dominate supply. The World Energy Council has been monitoring and ranking 128 countries on their ability to provide sustainable energy since the 1920s, and in 2010 introduced their World Energy Trilemma Index – a framework to track progress across three dimensions. For the past decade, the annual index has been measuring: '1) Energy Security [a country's capacity to meet current and future energy demand reliably], 2) Energy Equity [a country's ability to provide universal access to affordable, fairly priced and abundant energy for domestic and commercial use] and 3) Energy and Sustainability [the country's progress towards mitigating and avoiding environmental harm and climate change]' ('2019 World Energy Trilemma Index Report').

The report outlines that European countries feature prominently within the environmental sustainability dimension, with many EU members ranking amongst the top 10: 1) Switzerland; 2) Sweden; 3) Denmark; 4) United Kingdom; 5) Finland; 6) France; 7) Austria; 8) Luxembourg; 9) Germany; 10) New Zealand. It's encouraging to learn from the report that Denmark has increased its share of wind generation to more than 50 per cent and has increased its share of biofuels to more than 20 per cent – overall reducing fossil-fuelled electricity generation from 83 per cent in 2000 to just 27 per cent in 2017.

Meanwhile, China's rapid expansion over the past few decades has largely been fuelled by coal and to this day China remains a significant polluter. However, since the Chinese government implemented its Renewable Energy Law in 2006, the country has seriously progressed towards renewables. It, however, is also still at position 72 out of the 128 world rankings. However, there is clearly a shift in focus, as China is the only country that remains in the top 10 improvers over the period 2008 to 2019, reporting steady growth of its sustainability score. China is reported to be the biggest sovereign investor in clean energy and low-carbon sources including solar, wind, nuclear and biomass, with a 'Five Year Plan' including 'Green Growth' as one of its key objectives aiming to reduce emissions, pollution and support a shift to green energy.

By contrast, Kazakhstan, Nepal and India are countries whose energy sustainability index has dropped. Kazakhstan's domestic electricity consumption has doubled over the past two decades and that growth has largely been met by fossil fuels, thus reducing the diversity of its energy system and depressing the country's sustainability score. Not surprisingly, countries rich in fossil fuels tend to exhibit a long-term negative trend when it comes to their sustainability scores. The GCC (Gulf Cooperation Council), including Middle Eastern countries – Saudi Arabia, Kuwait, the United Arab Emirates, Qatar, Bahrain and Oman – have the lowest share of renewables compared to all other regions in the world. Also, countries such as Nigeria, Congo, Gabon (again fossil fuel-rich countries) are less able to focus resources on renewable energy due to economic and political instability and even corruption around policy implementation. So, whilst it's encouraging that there's global recognition that more needs to be done to move towards sustainable energy solutions, and progress is happening, challenges and appetite differ from country to country.

The International Renewable Energy Agency (IRENA) is an intergovernmental organization serving as the global central platform and centre of excellence for renewable energy policy, resource and knowledge. They provide a number of services related to reviewing progress of renewable energy around the world, mapping capacity and cost studies. They have a mandate to encourage and support governments to adopt enabling policies, and provide practical advice to accelerate renewable energy implementation and share knowledge and technology transfer to provide clean, sustainable energy for the world's growing population.

Their 'Renewable Capacity Statistics 2020 Report' (Camero, 2019) showcases that, globally, renewable energy sources have continued to dominate new additions to the world's power generation mix throughout 2019, with renewable capacity reaching 2,537 gigawatts (GW) globally by the end of 2019, up 176GW from the previous year. Wind and solar power accounted for 90 per cent of the world's newly added renewable capacity. Renewables represented 72 per cent of total capacity additions in 2019. However, their 'Global Renewables Outlook 2020 Report' discusses the very real gap between aspiration and the reality of countries tackling climate change as 'remaining as significant as ever, despite mounting evidence of the harm that climate change is causing.' Global energy-related carbon dioxide emissions have risen by 1 per cent per year over the last decade. And whilst efforts to switch to greener energies is happening, the distribution of that effort, as highlighted by the 'World Energy Trilemma Index Report', is uneven. Fossil fuels continue to dominate energy dependence and impact high levels of air, water and soil pollution. This is clearly significant: the World Health Organization reports that air pollution causes 7 million premature deaths per year (Majid, 2018).

Table 1 Renewables in the world's current energy mix

Renewable energy share (TFEC)*	Historical progress: 2015–18	Where we are heading: 2030–50	Where we need to be: 2030–50
	9.5–10.5%	17–25%	28–66%

*Total final energy consumption (TFEC)

As can be seen in Table 1, where we're heading, whilst positive, falls far short of where we need to be to meet SDG targets. According to the IRENA report, renewables must grow four times faster and the decade 2020–30 must be a decade of action.

9.2 Why do companies need to do something about this now?

As outlined previously, some countries are being more proactive than others when it comes to embracing renewable energies and as Table 1 outlines, we've got quite a bit of ground to make up if we are to hit desired targets. And if the fundamental challenges of air pollution aren't enough to urge companies into action, there are a number of other motivating factors.

All is not as it seems

When it comes to baselines, some studies are pointing towards the fact that things are worse than we originally thought, and that the oil and gas industry has had a far worse impact on the climate than previously believed. Indeed, one study implies that human emissions from fossil methane have been underestimated by up to 40 per cent (Watts, 2020). When it comes to key climate change culprits, methane – a colourless, odourless gas that many plants naturally share into the atmosphere – has a greenhouse effect that is approximately 80 times more potent than carbon dioxide over a 20-year period and, according to the UN Environment Programme, it is responsible for at least 25 per cent of global heating (unenvironment.org). The study's findings propose that the share of 'naturally released' fossil methane has been significantly overestimated, illuminating that human activities are 25–40 per cent more responsible for fossil methane in the atmosphere than originally thought. This aligns with an earlier study in the magazine *Science*

(Alvarex, et al. 2018), which revealed methane emissions from US oil and gas plants to be 60 per cent higher than had been reported to the Environmental Protection Agency.

As fossil fuel mining pockets become more difficult to find, new extraction methods, such as fracking (hydraulic fracturing) – which involves drilling down into the earth before rock is fractured by pressurized liquid made up of water, sand and chemicals, to enable natural gas and petrol to flow more freely – is also adding to global methane emissions. And as Dave Reay, executive director of the Edinburgh Centre for Carbon Innovation states: 'If the study is right, gas, coal and oil extraction and distribution around the world are responsible for almost half of all human-induced methane emissions. Add to that all the carbon dioxide that is then emitted when fossil fuels are burned, and you need look no further for the seat of the climate emergency fire' (Science Media Centre, February 2020). This is a very good reason for organizations to take a faster shift towards renewable energy.

Impact of global pandemic

Amidst the grip of the first wave of the coronavirus pandemic, on 7 April 2020, global carbon dioxide emissions plummeted to levels not seen since 2006 – suggesting that the coronavirus pandemic might have led to the largest reduction in CO_2 ever recorded. However, most of the world had stopped travelling, eating out and going about their usual consumerism and work. And whilst this behaviour was 'unprecedented' and an unmatched experiment, 80 per cent of emissions were untouched – showcasing just how much of a reduction in consumption is required if we are to meet the necessary reductions that the United Nations have said are necessary over the next decade (Storrow, B. 2020).

From an overall impact on energy, the International Energy Agency (IEA) predicts a 6 per cent drop in global energy demand, which is seven times as much as it was after the 2008 global financial crisis. However, they also showcase that demand for renewable energy is predicted to grow 1 per cent this year, with demand for renewable electricity, particularly via hydropower, expected to grow by 5 per cent. And in April 2020, amidst the pandemic, the IEA and the Danish government hosted a high-level ministerial roundtable discussion on making clean energy a key part of the global economic recovery programme, recognizing that renewable energy and energy efficiency are key in the fight against climate change and at the same time can provide significant job potential and economic turnaround (IEA, April 2020).

It's more cost-efficient

Figures contained in the latest IRENA 'Renewable Power Generation Costs Report' showcase that the cost of renewable energy has reduced over the past year, to the point where almost every source of green energy can now compete on cost with oil, coal and gas-fired power plants (Dudley, May 2019).

To give you some detail, hydroelectric power is currently the cheapest source of renewable energy, at an average of $0.05 per kilowatt hour (kWh), but the average cost of developing new power plants based on onshore wind, solar photovoltaic (PV), biomass or geothermal energy is now usually below $0.10/kWh. This is closely followed by offshore wind, which costs about $0.13/kWh. The figures are global averages and don't take into consideration the cost of project development, which can vary significantly. For example, the cost of producing electricity from a biomass energy plant can range from $0.05/kWh to a high of almost $0.25/kWh.

The key takeaway is that all these cleaner, renewable fuel types are now able to compete with fossil fuels such as oil and gas. IRENA state that these trends are likely to continue over the next decade, particularly for solar and wind power technologies, stating that more than 75 per cent of the onshore wind and 80 per cent of the solar PV capacity due to be commissioned next year will produce power at lower prices than the cheapest new coal, oil or natural gas options. And note to reader: these cost findings were reported in 2019, before the impact of the global pandemic, and so the situation for renewable power costs is likely to be even more favourable.

As well as government bodies and global initiatives, there are other organizations championing the cost-effectiveness of renewable energy solutions. Project Drawdown (https://drawdown.org), which we talked about earlier, is on a mission to help the world reach 'drawdown', the point in the future where levels of greenhouse gases in the atmosphere stop climbing and start to steadily decline. Their message about electricity production is that we need to move away from fossil fuels as quickly as possible and instead explore the vast range of cost-effective alternative solutions. They offer 100 practical solutions, from small-scale to centralized large-scale projects, including harnessing the power of the sun, kinetic energy, the movement of wind and water, alternative heat sources such as geothermal and nuclear, and other innovative and highly practical solutions, some of which we'll explore a little later in this chapter.

Consumers and publishers are becoming more conscious

In January 2020, in a move to reduce the company's carbon footprint and align with their increased reporting on climate emergency, the *Guardian* became the first major global news organization to declare an outright ban on taking money from any business primarily involved in extracting fossil fuels, including many of the world's largest polluters. Their statement was: 'We believe many brands will agree with our stand and might be persuaded to choose to work with us more as a result. The future of advertising lies in building trust with consumers and demonstrating a real commitment to values and purpose' (Waterson, January 2020).

Whilst welcomed by environmental groups such as Greenpeace, it will be interesting to see from a marketing perspective if and how other brands follow suit. Mark Ritson, marketing professor and columnist for *Marketing Week*, calls for marketers to take a similar stand and 'end big oil brands' strategy of distracting the world from the harm they are doing' (Ritson, January 2020). As we've stated in previous chapters, consumers are increasingly voting with their feet and aligning with organizations and activities that offer greener solutions and match their own values. However, in order for consumers to understand the stance of the organization, communications need to be shared so as to educate the consumer and motivate them to make change. One study showcases the power of social influence as one of the most effective ways to motivate positive pro-environmental consumer behaviour. Telling online shoppers that other people were buying eco-friendly products led to a 65 per cent increase in consumers making at least one sustainable purchase. Telling university students that other commuters were swapping their mode of commuting from air-polluting cars to bicycles led to five times as many people switching to sustainable transport compared with those who were simply given information about alternatives. Further, in the same study, it was revealed that a major predictor of whether people will instal solar panels or not is whether or not their neighbours have done so. When an advocate shared *why* they had installed residential solar panels, 63 per cent more people followed suit than when the advocate had not actually installed panels. This is useful evidence that marketers should optimize communications and persuasion tactics by ensuring they're simply telling audiences about the shifts customers or influencers in their audience's sphere are taking (White et al 2019).

Energy security

Energy security is potentially something we as consumers don't really think about too much when it comes to the greater need for renewable energy. As cited earlier, energy security is one of the three aspects measured on the World Energy Trilemma Index and refers to the stability of energy provision. The reality is that being dependent on other countries for energy supply is fine when everything is peaceful and nations are trusted, but when those relationships sour, the threat of energy supplies being cut or price hikes can totally destabilize economies. It's predicted that energy security will become even more of a threat as fossil fuels continue to dwindle. Oil prices have a knock-on effect for the economy and when pricing becomes erratic so does global harmony; where demands outstrip supply, it could lead to global conflict. Therefore, reducing dependency on the few major territories that produce the most energy in order to create a wider array of more dispersed renewable and localized energy centres, enabling countries to be as energy self-sufficient as possible, is a way to counter these foreseeable and very serious challenges.

Technology, innovation and opportunity

Advances in technology and innovation are creating a broader range of sustainable energy solutions for people and organizations. Domestic and commercial waste, from food production, to general waste and even human waste, whilst not new, have become viable means of alternative, greener, renewable power sources. Increasingly, buses and vehicles are powered by waste products. One Colorado city, Grand Junction, is processing its human waste into renewable natural gas (biomethane) to run its vehicles (Sevcenko, 2016). Fish factories are producing biodiesel from the tonnes of fish innards, scales and bones that are not suitable for the food market, yet are full of fat (energy). In developing countries, using the waste from farmed products, as in the case of incinerating the stems and leaves (biomass) from mustard plants, is providing electricity to thousands of rural homes, with the ash then acting as fertilizer and being ploughed back into the fields. Another example is the creation of biofuel from olives. Production of olive oil creates four times its weight in waste, but the Phenolive Project (http://phenolive.eu) turns that waste into electricity and heat.

Wood remains a key source of energy in many parts of the world, and as we'll explore a little later, can lead to harmful deforestation. In countries such as Kenya or Cambodia, coconut shells are providing a sustainable alternative to traditional wood charcoal. What's more, coconut charcoal burns longer, costs less and doesn't require the felling of trees. It also provides a solution to the management of coconut waste.

When it comes to harnessing wind power, Moya Power is an energy generation system that makes use of a lightweight flexible sheet that's been developed to harvest low-grade wind energy and turn it into electricity. It's effectively a curtain-like structure that can be installed into existing infrastructures without the need for destructive land clearing, unlike comparable large wind turbines. The product can also be used in the ceilings of metro/tube stations and other internal structures where wind power can be captured (www.moyapower.com). Another way of harnessing solar power is via our miles and miles of roads. The Netherlands already has a 70m (230ft) long solar bike path, and France is now following in the same track. The country plans to install 1,000km (6,215 miles) of specially designed photovoltaic solar panelling on its roads over the next five years, with the aim of expanding its renewable energy capacity (Ruiz, 2018). Another innovative area that's being researched further is the farming of microalgae, whereby large microalgae farms would transform sunlight and carbon dioxide into bioethanol.

9.3 Things that need to be acknowledged as not perfect

As outlined in the case study on the next page, biofuels have considerable potential to provide a more ecological sustainable solution than existing fossil fuel energy supplies. As a renewable energy resource, biofuel is big business. It's reported that by 2022, the biofuel marketplace will reach $218.7 billion (Kennedy, 2018). However, whilst biofuels are positioned as renewable energy resources, not all biofuels come with a sustainable footprint.

Transport accounts for 28 per cent of energy-related greenhouse gas emissions (EEA.Europa.eu, 2019) and due to the steady growth of cars in the developing world, levels of emissions are increasing faster than ever. Burning biofuels in cars then seems like the perfect solution, assuming that bio-based crops don't emit carbon. Brazil established its biofuel programme almost 40 years ago, with almost all cars burning some element of biofuel. In 2005, the US established its first national renewable fuel standard under the Energy Policy Act, calling for 7.5 billion gallons of biofuels to be used annually by 2012. In 2008, the European Union established the Renewable Energy Directive, requiring EU countries to meet the target of 10 per cent of renewable energy in transport by 2020.

However, over the past decade, a number of challenges have arisen. Farmers were incentivized to start growing crops for fuel instead of food, which drove up food prices and changed land use – change that experts say is causing more carbon emissions as farmers focus on clearing forests, releasing locked-up carbon into the atmosphere. A study commissioned by the European Commission in 2016 made public for the first time the sources of biodiesel in Europe. The study concluded that the EU's renewable laws had probably increased carbon emissions since their inception in 2009, with emission increases happening not only when forests are cleared, but also when land used to grow food is switched to the growing of crops for the more profitable biofuel. Of all the biofuels, palm oil has the highest associated level of greenhouse gas emissions and, worryingly, three times the emissions level of fossil diesel. Despite all the negative press around palm oil and deforestation, a vast amount of it is still used, and in 2016 45 per cent of palm oil used in Europe ended up in the tanks of cars – the equivalent to four Olympic-sized swimming pools of palm oil every day (Jobert, 2016). In June 2019, EU lawmakers agreed to limit the amounts of crop-based biofuels that can be used to meet EU renewable targets. However, they declined to issue an outright ban on palm and soybean oil and in the US and Brazil policies are encouraging a higher use of biofuels.

It should be remembered, though, that not all biofuels are bad. Environmental groups are therefore continuing to push for the eradication of subsidies on food-based fuels, but at the same time put policies into place to incentivize the development of advanced and more truly sustainable biofuels (Keating, 2019).

Another key challenge is transparent reporting. Many accidents associated with energy and fuel go underreported. For example, a blowout at a natural gas well in Ohio in 2018 is reported to have discharged more harmful methane over a three-week period than the collective oil and gas industries of France, Norway and the Netherlands in an entire year (Watts, 2020). And of course, whilst currently environmentalists and climate change champions are positive about the impact on air pollution due to the current global pandemic, what's not clear is whether the fossil fuel industry will bounce back with a vengeance afterwards, offering bargain basement oil prices, in an act of desperation amidst a struggling recovering economy, distracting the much-needed longer-term planning and transition towards long-standing, cleaner, greener energy.

9.4 Case study – Stena Bulk and GoodFuels

GoodFuels, a pioneer in sustainable biofuels, partnered with Stena Bulk to trial a sustainable marine biofuel using the vessel *Stena*

Immortal, which ran on 100 per cent biofuel during a 10-day sea trial. The trial was successful, and subsequently offers the shipping industry a credible near-zero carbon alternative for ocean-going tanker vessels typically powered by heavy fuel oil (HFO) and very-low sulphur fuel oil (VLSFO). The fuel that GoodFuels launched in 2018 reduces greenhouse gas emissions by 83 per cent and substantially reduces sulphur dioxide air pollution emissions. Maritime transport emits around 940 million tonnes of carbon dioxide annually and is responsible for approximately 2.5 per cent of greenhouse gas emissions, so this recent trial is a positive step towards renewable energy use in the shipping sector (Goodfuels.com).

9.5 Chapter summary

Some experts have predicted the year in which we will reach the peak of global fossil fuel use, referred to as the 'coal and oil peak', as being 2023. However, recent news articles, some of which we've cited in this chapter, are reporting that the global pandemic has brought the 'peak' earlier – advising us that now is the perfect time for change. Regardless of whether it's now, in three years' time or later still in this next decade, we hope that the information you've gleaned from within this chapter inspires you to do something about either innovating around greener, renewable energy solutions or at least questioning current practice and looking at ways that you can switch to greener, more sustainable suppliers.

From a marketing perspective, we've given you plenty to think about. If you have already opted for renewable energy solutions within your organization or aligned renewables to your brand values, is it a story that you share with your team, customers and wider audiences – or is it merely a statement that's lost within your annual report? From a messaging perspective, if it's truly something the organization has embraced (no greenwashing, thank you), then there's opportunity to build your responsible energy position into your brand values and actively share what you're doing in this significant and important area. You should also showcase the impact of such changes and share the story of why you've decided to commit to a more sustainable energy solution.

Also, as we've mentioned, be very mindful of the power of social influence. Are there marketing campaigns that you can use to encourage your team, customers or wider audiences to join you in making better energy choices? One study involved people being publicly praised each week for their energy-efficiency efforts, engendering a sense of pride amongst participants. This group saved more energy than a group that was given a small $5 weekly financial reward (Handgraaf et al, 2012). This shows that perhaps a simple 'energy champion of the week' or 'energy superstar customer' of the month recognition scheme on the company's intranet could have a big impact.

From a very practical perspective, there are a number of ways you and your organization can review your energy consumption. These range from manufacturers seeking more innovative and truly sustainable solutions, to the basics of questioning current energy supplies and practice and generally becoming more conscious of energy consumption, along with renewed awareness of the very real relationship between our use of non-sustainable energy and climate change. When it comes to such an enormous topic as energy, it's easy to feel overwhelmed and unsure about where to start to make a conscious impact, but awareness is a great start – it drives questions and starts the conversation, and opens up opportunities to seek and source better solutions for your business, your audiences, yourself and the world.

9.6 Action points to consider

No.	Action	Considerations	Next Step
1	Consider your marketing messaging.	Undertake an audit of the current position in your own organization regarding sustainable energy. Do you have good news stories to share with your audiences, both internally and externally?	What, if anything, is planned for the development of sustainable energy in the future? Commit to building this into relevant marketing campaigns to align with brand.
2	Switch energy suppliers.	Is there opportunity to switch energy supplies or introduce some sustainable energy practices?	Consider sustainable energy to heat and light offices. Could car fleets and transportation, where relevant, shift to vehicles powered by electricity?
3	Explore positive partnerships.	Are there any key partnerships throughout your supply chain that mean you could collaborate in a joint venture to improve energy efficiencies and support the reduction of your carbon footprint?	How could you develop partnerships if none are currently in place?
4	Take a stand.	Is there scope for your organization or brand to take a stand on sustainable energy?	Create a campaign to encourage others to increase their awareness and bring about change – or indeed, as in the case of the *Guardian*, remove partnerships that no longer align with your brand values?
5	Review how the coronavirus pandemic has changed your energy strategy.	Consider how the coronavirus has affected your energy strategy.	Have there been any unintended improvements as a result of coronavirus?

9.7 Chapter 9 references

Balch, O. (2015). 'Turning waste into energy'. *Guardian*. Available at: https://www.theguardian.com/sustainable-business/2015/feb/23/future-of-waste-five-things-look-2025 (Accessed: July 2020)

Bulk, S. (2020). 'GoodFuels Successfully Complete Trial of Sustainable Marine Biofuel'. Available at: https://www.prnewswire.com/news-releases/stena-bulk-and-goodfuels-successfully-complete-trial-of-sustainable-marine-biofuel-301055533.html (Accessed: July 2020)

Camero, F. (2020). 'Renewable Capacity Statistics Report 2020'. IRENA. Available at: https://www.irena.org/publications/2020/Mar/Renewable-Capacity-Statistics-2020 (Accessed: July 2020)

Carrington, D., Ambrose, J. and Taylor, M. (2020). 'Will Corona Virus Kill the oil industry and help save the climate?'. *Guardian*. Available at: https://www.theguardian.com/environment/2020/apr/01/the-fossil-fuel-industry-is-broken-will-a-cleaner-climate-be-the-result (Accessed: July 2020)

Doyle, A. (2013). 'Biofuels cause pollution, not as green as we thought'. Reuters Study. https://www.reuters.com/article/us-climate-biofuels/biofuels-cause-pollution-not-as-green-as-thought-study-idUSBRE90601A20130107 (Accessed: July 2020)

Dudley, D. (2019). 'Renewable Power Generation Costs Report'. *Forbes*. https://www.forbes.com/sites/dominicdudley/2019/05/29/renewable-energy-costs-tumble/#388e7a8de8ce (Accessed: July 2020)

European Environment Agency (2019). 'Greenhouse gas emissions from transport in Europe' – https://www.eea.europa.eu/data-and-maps/indicators/transport-emissions-of-greenhouse-gases/transport-emissions-of-greenhouse-gases-11 (Accessed: July 2020)

European Environment Agency (2020). www.eea.europa.eu (Accessed: July 2020)

Farmbrough, H. (2020). 'Why the Coronavirus Pandemic is Creating a Surge in Renewable Energy'. *Forbes*. https://www.forbes.com/sites/heatherfarmbrough/2020/05/05/why-the-coronavirus-pandemic-is-creating-a-surge-in-renewable-energy/#6bf01803534b (Accessed: July 2020)

Goodfuels.com (2020). 'Stena Bulk and Goodfuels successfully complete trial of sustainable marine biofuel'. https://goodfuels.com/stena-bulk-and-goodfuels-successfully-complete-trial-of-sustainable-marine-biofuel/ (Accessed: July 2020)

Handgraaf, M. J. J., Van Lidth de Jeude, M. A. and Appelt, K. C. (2012). 'Public praise vs. private pay: Effects of rewards on energy conservation in the workplace'. Available at: https://doi.org/10.1016/j.ecolecon.2012.11.008 (Accessed: July 2020)

IEA (2020). 'IEA and Denmark Ministerial Roundtable Discussion'. Available at: https://www.iea.org/news/iea-and-denmark-host-ministerial-roundtable-discussion-on-making-clean-energy-a-key-part-of-the-global-economic-recovery (Accessed: July 2020)

Jobert, M. (2016). 'Palm Oil Production Up, As Forests Pay the Price'. *Journal de L'environment*, Available at: https://www.euractiv.com/section/climate-environment/news/palm-oil-production-on-the-up-as-forests-pay-the-price/ (Accessed: July 2020)

Jones, J. (2018). 'Biofuels Marketing Size Will Reach USD 218.7 Billion by 2022, Globally.' Zion Market Research. Available at: https://www.globenewswire.com/news-release/2018/01/09/1285912/0/en/Biofuels-Market-Size-Will-Reach-USD-218-7-Billion-by-2022-Globally-Zion-Market-Research.html (Accessed: July 2020)

Keating, D. (2018). 'Biofuels – good or bad for the environment'. Available at: https://www.dw.com/en/biofuels-good-or-bad-for-the-environment/a-44354834 (Accessed: July 2020)

Kennedy, H.T. (2018). 'Global Biofuels market to exceed $218.7B by 2022'. *Biofuels Digest*. https://www.biofuelsdigest.com/bdigest/2018/01/07/global-biofuels-market-to-exceed-218-7b-by-2022/ (Accessed: July 2020)

Majid, A. (2018). 'WHO reveals 7 million die from pollution each year in latest global air quality figures'. *Telegraph*. https://www.telegraph.co.uk/global-health/climate-and-people/estimates-7-million-die-pollution-year-reveals-latest-global/ (Accessed: July 2020)

Mason, M. (2019). 'Renewable Energy: All You Need to Know'. *Environmental Science*. https://www.environmentalscience.org/renewable-energy (Accessed: July 2020)

Nair, J. (2009). 'How sustainable are biofuels? Answers and further questions arising from an ecological footprint perspective'. *Science Direct*. Available at: https://www.sciencedirect.com/science/article/abs/pii/S0960852409000947 (Accessed: July 2020)

Potenza, A. (2017). 'In 1952 London 12,000 people died from smog – and here's why'. *The Verge*. Available at: https://www.theverge.

com/2017/12/16/16778604/london-great-smog-1952-death-in-the-air-pollution-book-review-john-reginald-christie (Accessed: July 2020)

Ritson, M. (2020). 'Marketers must follow guardian and ban ads from fossil fuel'. *Marketing Week*, January 2020. Available at: https://www.marketingweek.com/marketers-follow-guardian-stop-enabling-oil-brands-hypocrisy/ (Accessed: July 2020)

Ruiz, I.B. (2018). 'Energy in Demand'. Available at: https://energyindemand.com/2018/05/ (Accessed: July 2020)

Science Media Centre, (2020). 'Expert reaction to study looking at recalculating human-generated methane emissions'. https://www.sciencemediacentre.org/expert-reaction-to-study-looking-at-recalculating-human-generated-methane-emissions/ (Accessed: July 2020)

Sevenko, M. (2016). *Guardian*, 'Power to the poop – One Colorado city is using human waste to run its vehicles'. https://www.theguardian.com/environment/2016/jan/16/colorado-grand-junction-persigo-wastewater-treatment-plant-human-waste-renewable-energy (Accessed: July 2020)

Storrow, B. (2020). Global CO2 Emissions Saw Record Drop During Pandemic Lockdown, Scientific American. https://www.scientificamerican.com/article/global-co2-emissions-saw-record-drop-during-pandemic-lockdown/ (Accessed: July 2020)

UN.org (2019). 'Sustainable Development Goals Knowledge Platform'. Available at: https://sustainabledevelopment.un.org/sdg7 (Accessed: July 2020)

United Nationals, Economic and Social Council (2019). 'Report of the Secretary General'. Available at: https://sustainabledevelopment.un.org/sdg7 (Accessed: July 2020)

Waterson J. (2020). '*Guardian* to ban advertising from fossil fuel firms amidst climate crisis'. *Guardian*. Available at: https://www.theguardian.com/media/2020/jan/29/guardian-to-ban-advertising-from-fossil-fuel-firms-climate-crisis (Accessed: July 2020)

Watts, J. (2020). 'Oil and gas firms have had far worse climate impact that thought'. *Guardian*. Available at: https://www.theguardian.com/environment/2020/feb/19/oil-gas-industry-far-worse-climate-impact-than-thought-fossil-fuels-methane (Accessed: 6 July 2020)

White, K., Hardisty, D. and Habib, R. (2019). 'The Elusive Green Customers'. *Harvard Business Review*. Available at: https://hbr.org/2019/07/the-elusive-green-consumer (Accessed: July 2020)

World Energy Council (2019). 'World Energy Trilemma Index Report'. Available at: https://www.worldenergy.org/assets/downloads/WETrilemma_2019_Full_Report_v4_pages.pdf (Accessed: July 2020)

CHAPTER TEN

Sustainable Yet Innovative Packaging

10.0 Chapter introduction

As consumers, we're becoming more aware than ever of our personal consumption and regard for the sustainability of packaging. You may have found yourself making purchasing choices over the past few months in relation to how a product is packaged and the biodegradability of the materials, the information on the pack, or the branding or messaging around the stance the organization or brand takes on sustainability. You may even have had an internal conversation with yourself, such as: 'Why can't this packaging be designed to be used again?' or 'Why this unnecessary, elaborate packaging? What a waste of resources.'

When visiting the expansive topic of sustainable packaging and the role we play as consumers, as well as the role you play as a responsible marketer, it's useful to consider the topic through the measured lens of the three key pillars of sustainability: 1) the economy, 2) our society and 3) the environment.

Whilst from a consumer level (society) we may feel emotional when exposed to heartbreaking images of polluted seas and overseas communities making their homes amongst the miles and miles of landfill sites – to the extent that we want to become part of the change, stamping out single-use plastic, calling on brands to do more about the reduction of elaborate and unnecessary packaging and upping our recycling game – the solution is far from simple. As we demonstrate with other topics, and particularly in our chapter on plastic, when it comes to packaging, there is a complex balance to strike – a balance that has to be driven by wider systemic thinking that considers all three pillars of sustainability. Can packaging be created economically, bearing in mind costs to source, produce, ship and distribute? Then, the societal concerns – is it safe and still attractive for customers? After all, even if consumers have the best of intentions, price is still a key deciding factor for the majority. And last, but not least, the environment: does the packaging hit the agreed and necessary carbon footprint targets?

Whilst consumer unrest may be driving manufacturers, brands and organizations to prioritize sustainability and effect change, and even provide pressure for new legislations to be enforced, the reality is that we have to consider the wider implications of packaging and why we use certain types. For example, as highlighted in Chapter 7, in some cases, plastic is the most sustainable choice, particularly for some foods – eradicating contamination, disease and wastage. And in industries such as the medical profession, the use of plastic packaging from a safety and hygiene perspective is less about convenience but rather provides a highly innovative solution – and importantly, may also be hitting both the economic pillar (being the most cost-effective solution to produce) and the environment pillar (being the most environmentally friendly solution), having less of a carbon footprint than an alternative.

Then there's e-commerce. The growth of global e-commerce continues year on year and is expected to account for 14.4 per cent of all retail spending by 2022 (www.statista.com). With more e-commerce, the need for packaging to be lighter and smaller to save space in shipping trucks and reduce overall shipping costs also continues to drive packaging innovation.

In this chapter, then, we will look at innovations in packaging and developments around the practicalities of 'reduce, reuse and recycle', the circular economy and who should take responsibility for packaging.

We'll also examine from a marketing perspective how packaging plays a role in communication with consumers, including schemes that enable consumers to play their part in the solution.

10.1 Where are we?

The packaging industry has long been driven by innovation; as early as the early 19th century, the French government offered a prize of 12,000 francs to the inventor who created the best container for preserving food for Napoleon's army (Hamilton, 2018). The result … the tin can. Since that time, we've continued to innovate, and design packaging solutions which have moved beyond simply acting as a container. Indeed, packaging today fulfils a number of roles: protecting, preserving, promoting and educating.

Packaging plays an integral and significant role when it comes to commerce. As described by Sealed Air's president and CEO, Ted Doheny: 'Packaging is the focal point of everything. Everything is put in a package. Packaging is also a communication device for people who want to know what's inside, when it was filled, how much it weighs, nutritional properties and whether the contents are nearing their expiration' (Varanasi, 2019).

To give some context to the size and significance of the packaging industry, the industry generates about $900 billion in annual revenues worldwide and has been growing year on year since 2013, growth driven by the desire for innovation around more sustainable packaging options. The industry is highly fragmented, with the top 25 to 30 companies accounting for less than 25 per cent of the market; the majority of the industry is made up of thousands of smaller, often innovative packaging players covering a range of different packaging forms (Santhanam and Varanasi, 2019).

Packaging takes many forms: corrugated board, folding cartons, liquid paperboard, rigid plastics, flexible plastics, foil, paper, metal, glass, wood, bamboo, cork and jute to name but a few, and our growing desire as consumers to support ever more sustainable packaging options continues to drive innovation, creating a whole industry dedicated to innovative sustainable alternatives, some of which we'll turn to later. Packaging is also a key player when it comes to brand – just think about the ease with which you can quickly spot a can of Coca-Cola amidst a crowded shelf of soft drinks. And then there's the alignment of consumer and brand values. Take, for instance, the Oatly milk brand and their stance on health and the well-being of the planet, with their educational and community-driven packaging messaging, such as their 'You're one of us now' thank you message to customers, which provides stats and facts to inform consumers about how their purchasing habits are helping the planet (www.oatly.com). Packaging is being used not only to make customers aware of the recycling properties of the packaging but also to communicate how they are effecting change.

When it comes to the role consumers play in pressurizing brands and packaging organizations to prioritize sustainability, according to new research from Trivium Packaging in partnership with Boston Consulting Group, 74 per cent of consumers are willing to pay more for sustainable packaging and nearly a quarter willing to pay an increased cost of 10 per cent or more (Holbrook, 2020). Their report findings also show that 60 per cent of consumers say they are less likely to buy a product in harmful packaging, with 80 per cent associating plastic as being more harmful than metal.

Closer to home, a study of 2,000 adults across the UK, conducted by The Chartered Institute of Marketing (CIM), revealed that 88 per cent think their shopping comes with more packaging and wrapping than is required – with children's toys, mobile phones and cosmetics associated with the most elaborate and unnecessary packaging – and consumers reporting that they would like to see more done by large companies to provide more sustainable packaging. Over-packaging is also seen to reduce appetite for consumers to return to brands and providers both online and in store, with 33 per cent stating they were put off from purchasing by the sheer volume of unnecessary packaging, and 36 per cent stating that reputational damage can ensue, as consumers judge an organization's commitment to sustainability by their approach to packaging. Furthermore, in line with the role played by the consumer, more than a quarter of respondents advised that they would be willing to spend more on products if they knew the packaging used was sustainable (CIM, 2019).

From a consumer perspective, there is a growing appetite for more sustainable packaging, and from a brand-reputation perspective, it make sense that brands and organizations preserve sales and repeat purchases by providing customers with what they want. And then of course there are legislative commitments and global pledges, goals and targets regarding packaging, that organizations and manufacturers are challenged to comply with. As we touched on in Chapter 7, in recent years we've seen a global commitment to eliminating plastic waste and pollution. Alongside all that is the requirement to meet both the United Nation's SDGs and the New Plastics Economy Global Commitment. The latter, led by the Ellen MacArthur Foundation in collaboration with the UN Environment Programme, is a pledge signed by many of the world's largest packaging producers, brands, retailers, recyclers, governments and NGOs.

The pledge sets out to create a new normal for plastic packaging committing to:

- eliminate problematic or unnecessary plastic packaging and move from single-use to reuse packaging models;
- innovate to ensure 100 per cent of plastic packaging can be easily and safely reused, recycled or composted by 2025;
- circulate the plastic produced by significantly increasing the amounts of plastics reused or recycled and made into new packaging or products. (www.ellenmacarthurfoundation.org)

Another collaboration concerning sustainable packaging is CEFLEX (www.ceflex.eu), a consortium of European companies and associations representing the entire value chain of flexible packaging. The CEFLEX mission is to enhance the performance of flexible packaging in the circular economy by designing and advancing systemic thinking and solutions through collaboration. Packaging targets focus on: waste prevention, resource efficiency, elimination of leakage and the recycling of flexible packaging materials.

Global manufacturing solutions provider Jabil surveyed more than 200 key packaging decision-makers across a variety of industries – including food, beverage, personal care and home care – to better understand the role sustainability played as part of packaging solutions. Their report (Jabil, 2019), identified that 93 per cent of some of the largest packaging manufacturers in the world face challenges in delivering sustainable packaging, with the biggest obstacle being the lack of necessary infrastructure. Other findings include:

- 38 per cent of consumers refuse to pay for the available solutions;
- 38 per cent of retailers are not set up to handle changes;
- only 24 per cent of companies consistently calculate the carbon impact of products when evaluating packaging options;
- a whopping 81 per cent won't sacrifice any level of product protection for sustainability.

Any sustainable packaging option must provide equal or greater product protection as non-sustainable options – a clear catalyst for driving innovation.

10.2 Why do companies need to do something about this now?

Whilst it's encouraging that there is strategic intent from organizations and brands, targets to reach, and pressure and appetite from consumers, the reality of delivering sustainable packaging is complex, and to do so relatively quickly is even more so. When we consider the New Plastics Economy Global Commitment pledge (as outlined on page 208), with its roadmap and targets for 2025 and the UN SDGs with climate targets for 2030, 5–10 years is but a heartbeat, particularly given the fast, convenient consumption culture consumers have adopted as 'normal'.

The shift in consumerism post World War II has been significant. For the past 70 years we've aligned with the mantra of 'out with the old and in with the new', which has created a global throwaway society. As we've admitted, marketing and advertising has played a significant role in encouraging consumers to consume more, faster and quicker than ever before. Convenience food, convenience beauty, convenience cleaning, convenience living, convenience clothing … the list goes on. We're now inherently conditioned to buy, use and throw out. If something is broken, we no longer try to fix things, we simply scrap them and order a new one! And of course, it may be that the product isn't even broken; it could simply not be the latest version – and marketing and advertising play a role in luring us into the 'faster, better, newer' purchasing cycles.

In addition, there's the issue that products are designed and made so that they deliberately become out of date or useless within a known time period – a term referred to as 'planned obsolescence'. The main goal of this type of production is to ensure that consumers have to buy a product multiple times rather than only once, naturally stimulating demand. And of course, not only does this stimulate more production and more revenue, but it also generates the need for more packaging.

Technology and innovation

Whilst it's only relatively recently that consumers have woken up to the brutal consequences of our throwaway mentality, this awareness, often referred to as the 'Attenborough Effect' (McCarthy and

Sanchez, 2019) – relating to Sir David Attenborough's educational climate wake-up call in the form of the *Blue Planet II* series, and also his powerful 2020 film release, *A Life on Our Planet* – comes at a time where marketers, brands, organizations and customers can really harness technological developments to effect change more collaboratively and more quickly.

In line with packaging regulations and our growing awareness, the amount of material used in packaging has been in decline for a number of years: between 2004 and 2014 the average plastic packaging weight fell by 28 per cent (BPF, 2020). This has been brought about not only by regulation but also by improved technologies and design that enables a similar product or package to be produced with smaller amounts of material (which, as we will explore a little later, isn't always a good thing).

In the sustainable packaging report by GlobalWebIndex, 'Lifting the Lid on Sustainable Packaging', research findings state that three out of 10 consumers don't feel they have enough information about packaging, particularly in terms of what can be recycled, with 41 per cent saying the latter is because brands don't give them enough information (Gilsenan, 2019). Further, according to a recent survey of more than 10,000 consumers across France, Germany, Italy, the Netherlands, Spain, Sweden, the UK and the US, 75 per cent of consumers support carbon labelling on products. Consumers want more education, steer and advice. And it's not just about education, it's good for brands too, with 64 per cent of consumers stating that they are more likely to think positively about a brand that can demonstrate it has lowered its carbon footprint (Packaging Europe Survey, 2020). And what better way to demonstrate that position to consumers than communicating it directly via the packaging?

When it comes to sharing messaging about a brand's stance on sustainability, digital technologies aligned with packaging enable a direct line of communication with customers for manufacturers, brands and organizations. For example, a quick scan via a smartphone of a QR code displayed on packaging can help a customer to find out more about the brand's position and progress in relation to sustainability or indeed share advice, ideas and information about how to reuse the product, and/or provide clear recycling instructions – whilst at the same time advising on the brand's sustainability stance. Technology therefore provides a significant opportunity for packaging manufacturers, brands and marketers to better communicate and engage with consumers and also to drive sustainable packaging innovation, particularly when it comes to labelling, educating, traceability and even theft. For instance, Rémy Martin, the premium cognac brand, embeds a near-field communication (NFC) chip in its bottles so users can scan the chip on their smartphones to guarantee authenticity (Smith, 2015).

Reuse

Samsung is set to introduce new packaging across its Lifestyle TV product portfolio with the intention to reduce its carbon footprint and also encourage reuse. Their packaging includes a dot matrix design allowing customers to cut the boxes more easily and assemble them into various other uses – small side tables, houses for pets and magazine racks, to name a few. They provide a user manual that is accessed by scanning a QR code on the box. This is a great example of systemic thinking in practice, developing packaging at the outset with a reuse function in mind and providing tools and resources to enable the user to participate in successful fulfilment; a partnership between brand and consumer. Their executive VP of strategy, Kangwook Chun, states: 'Consumers are more likely to purchase from a brand that shares similar fundamentals and values as they do, we can provide customers with a new experience that considers the environment as an important way to express themselves' (PackagingEurope.com).

Reusable packaging can also play a key role in reverse logistics, whereby packaging is recovered and redistributed after being used by the end consumer and absorbed into the supply chain for reuse. When it comes to innovations around reuse, there's one organization that's stepping back in time to drive innovation. Launched at the World Economic Forum in Davos in 2018, and the brainchild of TerraCycle's founder Tom Szaky, Loop (www.loopstore.com) is an online shopping concept modelled on the traditional 'milkman' idea. It is currently operational in the Mid-Atlantic US and Paris, but is set to expand both nationally in the US and internationally. Loop delivers consumers products in customized, durable packaging that is subsequently collected for reuse rather than recycling. Loop's vision is that rather than passing all the responsibility on to the customer to manage the recycling or reuse of packaging, the packaging becomes part of the brand experience, with brands retaining ownership of it. This concept not only benefits sustainability but presents an opportunity for brands to invest at the outset in high-end, fully branded materials that enhance the consumer experience and indeed drive loyalty, repeat purchase and positive state of mind – all key elements of any successful marketing strategy.

The Loop concept is based on the economic depreciation of reuse: basically, that expensive packaging grows cheaper the more times it is used. And Loop claims the costs are in line with single-use plastic even when collection and washing are factored in. Their carbon footprint 'Life Cycle Assessments' have been carried out under usage pattern assumptions – and it's reported that they reach parity with single-use packaging after three lifecycles. Brands participating in the Loop initiative so far include: Procter & Gamble, Nestlé, PepsiCo, Unilever, Mars Petcare, Coca-Cola, Danone, BIC, Carrefour, Jacobs Douwe Egberts, Lesieur, Beiersdorf and Mondelēz International (Sykes, 2019).

Reduce

The idea of sustainable packaging encompasses a combination of factors that reconsider how products are produced, distributed, preserved and consumed. Of course, one way to reduce packaging is to opt for zero-waste solutions. PepsiCo is exploring ways to move beyond the bottle and the bag for their brands. Their acquisition of SodaStream is part of the approach to bring zero waste product directly into the home (Sykes, 2019). Also, a US-based company, Cleanyst (www.cleanyst. com) has created a home appliance that makes custom-made cleaning and hygiene products. Cleanyst compares to a Keurig or Nespresso in terms of ease of use, mixing batches of product in minutes, using a reusable container, tap water and packets of concentrates. The waste is minimal, and packets are recyclable.

And then of course, there are a wide range of sustainable material innovations being introduced to the packaging industry, with manufacturers, inventors and brands considering production, distribution and end-of-life compostability. One example is Lush, the British cosmetics company, which has developed 'carbon-positive' packaging. The packaging is made from cork instead of plastic. In addition to having a lower carbon footprint, cork offers antibacterial properties, is water-resistant, strong and can even be composted. Cork comes from bark, which is harvested every 10 years and does not require the cutting down of trees during the process (Watkiss, 2019).

And Lush is not alone. Fuelled by their frustration that 80 billion plastic bottles are produced every single day, of which 80 per cent end up in landfill where they take 800-plus years to biodegrade, Paper Water Bottle (www.paperwaterbottle.com) created an alternative, more eco-friendly way of consuming water. Their Eco 100 bottle is made from 98 per cent compostable materials, which biodegrade 4,000 times faster than plastic bottles. The remaining 2 per cent are recycled materials, meaning the bottle creates zero waste. Fast food chain KFC (Kentucky Fried Chicken) made headlines in 2017 when it announced plans to create edible packaging. Since that time, they've created edible bowls, wrappers and coffee cups – the ultimate solution to packaging with zero waste ('Structural Packaging' blog, 2019). In 2018, Tetra Pak, the world's leading food processing and packaging solutions company, started to restructure their innovation strategy to deliver packaging that contributes to a low-carbon aim and ultimately moves towards a climate-neutral circular economy, made entirely from renewable and/ or recycled materials that is fully recyclable, without compromising on food safety requirements (Greenbiz, March 2020).

Innovation

Sustainable packaging challenges continue to pique the interest of conscious designers. For example, Hungarian designer Ágnes Gyömrei has engineered the VitaPack, a flexible, clever and 100 per cent recyclable cardboard alternative to plastic packaging of fresh fruit (www.packagingoftheworld.com, 2015). Pippa Bridges, meanwhile, a graduate from Loughborough University in the UK, conscious of the fact that 1 billion mascara tubes are sold worldwide every year and pretty much directly end up in landfill, was driven to develop a more sustainable solution. Her Infinity Mascara, which features a reusable, refillable capsule, alongside a 3D-printed fingertip applicator, presents a fully closed-loop solution. All components last longer (up to 10 years), function more effectively and are more financially efficient (www.springwise.com).

In fact, we could have dedicated a whole book to the pursuit and commitment towards sustainability across the packaging industry and the many alternatives and innovations being explored – including natural materials such as jute, bamboo and pineapple leaves, to name but a few – as well as efficiencies around biodegradability, and overall reduction, reuse and recyclability. And when it comes to innovation and reduction, packaging that is designed to totally disappear has become a reality.

Innovative sustainable packaging start-up Notpla (www.notpla. com) has created a flexible packaging material, ideal for beverages and sauces, that is made from seaweed and plants. The packaging biodegrades in four–six weeks, or you can simply just eat it! Their latest product, the 'Notpla Liner', tackles the problem of lined cardboard, which we covered in Chapter 7. They've developed a coating for takeaway food packaging that is natural, biodegradable and even re-pulpable. Another solution that disappears on use – water-soluble bags – comes from Aquapak (www.aquapakpolymers. com). We discovered their innovative 'disappearing' packaging via an article highlighting laundry bags for infection control on the BBC News in 2020. Hydropol by Aquapak is a ground-breaking technology that dissolves completely in commercial washing machines, reducing the risk of cross-contamination. This notion led us to investigate further. Aquapak and their plastic technology, which has full functionality as a packaging solution in the modern world, and is recyclable and environmental friendly, has been designed for a circular economy and has a number of practical applications across the fashion industry, hospitality, airlines, hotels, fill-and-seal packaging, food waste and pet food. You'll find a highly insightful interview with Mark Lapping, Aquapak's founder and CEO, a little later in this chapter.

10.3 Things that need to be acknowledged as not perfect

Whilst technology, innovation, targets and consumer pressure are certainly bringing more awareness to the importance of systemic thinking and positive steps are being taken, there's still a lot of ground to be conquered. According to the GlobalWebIndex report, consumers identify recyclability as the most important factor when it comes to packaging. Their report also states that when consumers play a role in the recycling process, they feel that they are taking action in protecting the planet, adding even more reason for ensuring there is transparent labelling and indeed clear instruction as to what can and can't be recycled. Take a moment to ask yourself how sure you are that the packaging that goes into your recycling (assuming you're a good citizen doing your bit for society) is actually recyclable?

And this is where things can get rather misleading. For example, a quick look at the Andrex UK website (www.andrex.co.uk/sustainability) will advise you that their products (including their packaging) are 100 per cent sustainable and recyclable. At first glance, as a consumer you can align with these positive brand values and feel that you're supporting sustainability. However, on closer inspection, you'll find that you can't actually recycle their plastic wrapping via the usual household recycling process, referred to as 'kerbside' recycling. In order to recycle the packaging, the consumer is instructed via the packaging to 'recycle with carrier bags at larger stores'. The challenge here is that to make the packaging truly sustainable, the onus is fully on the not-always-conscious consumer to a) read the small print and be educated that the plastic isn't recyclable kerbside and b) locate, find and drive to one of the larger stores/supermarkets that provides such a facility. Andrex, one of the many FMCG brands under consumer product giant Kimberly-Clark, certainly aren't on their own when it comes to this practice – it's a challenge faced by the entire consumer goods industry.

In terms of packaging, most companies focus on two priorities (and not always in this order): 1) the marketing/advertising/branding one – how can this packaging attract and drive consumers to my product? 2) what does it cost? Environmentally friendly packaging alternatives often have higher costs attached to them, particularly if this means making investment in packaging infrastructure and changing operations. Manufacturers and brands are keen to avoid passing these additional costs on to consumers – because, although consumers state they are happy to pay more for sustainable products, price points still need to be appealing. And of course, from a playing the sustainability card perspective to attract consumers, brands are having to be ever more cautious about the claims they publicly make about sustainability. The everyday and highly connected 'Joe' can now kick up a thunderstorm pretty quickly on social media and expose or challenge brands about 'greenwashing' in ways previously not possible, and the speed and momentum with which social movements can take root is much more rapid thanks to how connected and dependent on digital communication channels we are.

From a consumer perspective, we're all likely to have been guilty at some point of 'wish-cycling', the act of putting a non-recyclable item in the recycling bin in the hope that it will magically be recycled. Giving full responsibility to the consumer for what can and cannot be recycled removes ownership and responsibility from the brands and organizations that supply the packaging. And even if labelling and packaging includes details about recycling, the onus is still on the customer to read it. Further, whilst consumers are becoming more conscious and questioning, the global food service packaging market is expected to showcase a growth rate of 5.23 per cent between 2020 and 2027 (Global Newswire, 2020).

Food companies increasingly favour bendable, smashable packaging for being lightweight and therefore low-carbon when it comes to shipping. However, although the product may be lighter, that's often due to the utilization of mixed materials, which are commonly totally impossible to separate at the recycling phase without sophisticated recycling infrastructures (that are rare or non-existent) and, importantly, a market for the material. As Lawrence Black, director of global business development at Waste Management, states: 'It all comes back to is there a market for the material. If there's not an ongoing market for the material it won't get recycled' (Wu, 2014). If there is no market, packaging becomes unrecyclable and continues to contribute to landfill and polluting our oceans.

What's more, whilst recycling is critical, it doesn't solve core waste problems, as TerraCycle's Tom Szaky states: 'One of the starting points for Loop was questioning the idea of consumers owning the packaging of the products they buy. This provides an incentive to make packaging cheaper, and the cheaper and lighter it is, the less economical it is to recycle, whereas, if the manufacturer takes ownership and responsibility, packaging starts to be treated as an asset in the P&L' (Sykes, 2019). From a marketing perspective, packaging being accounted for as a brand asset in the profit and loss rather than a production cost certainly aligns with the overall value of the brand. However, again, this poses another significant area where transformational change is required.

Revisiting the Jabil manufacturer research, whilst sustainability certainly appears to be on the agenda, there are very real challenges to overcome. Planning for packaging regulations and compliance is deemed as the most difficult challenge for manufacturers to address, with 52 per cent of companies opting to find a partner with sustainable packaging expertise, 51 per cent stating that they are investing in in-house innovation centres and 49 per cent saying they are training existing staff to address sustainable packaging needs. When it comes to the sustainability solution manufacturers favour, 47 per cent assert that biodegradable packaging will be the ultimate solution to sustainability, 30 per cent state reusable packaging, 14 per cent support mechanical recycling and only 9 per cent support chemical recycling.

Sustainable packaging, then, is clearly on the agenda. The big challenge is that whilst consumers are starting to become more aware and take more responsibility with regards to sustainability and turn to packaging to research and make better purchasing choices, there's a far bigger systemic infrastructure challenge to overcome. However, on the upside, manufacturers have recognized that they need to start planning for sustainability and so whilst it may be a little bit like turning a tanker, at least the steering has started.

10.4 Case study – Aquapak

We interviewed CEO Mark Lapping about Aquapak's stance on sustainability and the packaging challenges they are endeavouring to overcome. Mark is a hugely informed and passionate environmentalist, and shares an impactful overview of how innovation, consumer appetite and investment can play a part in driving effective change – and how they are partnering with enlightened brands, such as the surfing brand Finisterre (a B Corp), to meet their sustainability desires, with their 'leave no trace' packaging.

Interview – Mark Lapping

As a passionate environmentalist, after 20 years in the packaging industry, I was growing increasingly embarrassed by the negative aspects of packaging on sustainability. I got to a point in my life where I wanted to do something positive towards sustainability and recyclability – something that would contribute towards moving the dial, even just a little bit, to make the wider planet a better place. And that's how Aquapak was born.

There are so many issues across the whole packaging chain and we have an enormous problem and a huge mountain to climb, and as consumers, mainly out of convenience, we have chosen to ignore the severity of the problem. Since David Attenborough got on to our TV screens and brought some of the reality to light, we've become more aware, but even now, we still really don't understand the iceberg that lurks beneath the water. Whilst the general public is growing increasingly aware of the problem with visible plastic, we're largely blissfully unaware of the toxicology of microplastics and the impact they have on human and animal health. We're involved with some fascinating research currently being done around the toxicology of microplastic, with government support and the Heriot-Watt University – but it's new and there needs to be far more done in this area. A recent study from Stirling University found that cholera stuck to microplastic from India was washed up on a beach in the west of Scotland. The toxicology of microplastics is new and emerging news, it's a timebomb waiting, ticking all around us.

Another key challenge lies with the fact that there's no general consensus around effective measurements for sustainable packaging. There are a lot of groups, schemes and associations, you need an 'ology' just to make your way around it all – but the reality is, there's no consensus, which means it's not easy to measure or for people to understand where organisations sit on the sustainable packaging scale. And this creates a problem, particularly for products like ours, because as a nascent technology, not previously seen before, it's difficult for brands and manufacturers to easily understand where we fit in and the impact we can create. A classic example is biodegradability. What exactly does biodegradability mean? Well, on its own, it doesn't mean anything. You have to frame it with time and environment, will it biodegrade in 6 days or 6000 years – it needs context and explanation of how it behaves in certain conditions over a period of time. Yet, the world has become fixated on a compostability standard, EN13432 – regardless of whether anything made to the EN13432 standard actually gets composted, because in reality, there is no industrial capacity or capability to compost such items. It's good marketing, as brands can stamp their products as compostable, and consumers feel better about their purchase – and it's a good revenue generator for the standards agency, which provide the standard and charge up to $20,000 every time you need to get approval, but effectively, it's has a very small impact on sustainability, it doesn't improve recyclability and ultimately will cause methane in landfill, which is exactly where the majority of these items go.

In reality we need systemic thinking. Designing products with end of life in mind. But it's going to take consumers to start behaving differently to force big industry to make the necessary changes. There are of course brands and organizations that want to do the right thing, they've taken on board what's happening in the world and have made a decision to make a conscious choice – and are taking the lead. We've been approached by a few brands from the fashion industry looking to improve their packaging. Finisterre, a UK-based B Corp surfing brand, design functional, sustainable products for those that share a love of the sea. They came to us to help solve their packaging problem, as whilst they were creating beautiful sustainable products in line with their sustainable values, they were still packaging them in polyethylene bags designed to hang around the world for at least 700 years and break down into microplastics that could carry toxins around the planet if released into the natural environment. To align with their brand values, they wanted us to make a truly 'leave no trace' garment bag to replace the polyethylene one. They fully understood that making this sustainable choice came at a cost for them – because it's a more expensive material to produce, but it has the same functionality, protecting and carrying the garment anywhere – but the main positive is that it's designed with the end of life in mind: the consumer can simply pop the bag we produce into their food waste bin, compost it or dissolve it in their dishwasher or boil a kettle and watch it dissolve before their eyes. And even if it does get to landfill, both the brand and the consumer can sit comfortably with the knowledge that it will dissolve safely and leave no toxic microplastics. So, Finisterre's packaging that states 'Leave no trace' – is an absolute reality.

Other brands are coming to us now too, some really big brands, and what's really interesting is which ones do stuff and which talk about doing stuff. If you're serious about making a change, then yes, leaving no trace may cost more, but if you're not serious then you have to do it in the knowledge that you are carrying on polluting the planet. You're making a binary choice – if you want polyethylene, then carry on polluting the planet.

Scarily – 350,000 million tonnes of polymer is produced annually of which less than 2 per cent comes from biosources, the alternatives to standard hydrophobic (polluting microplastic), and products like ours, which are hydrophilic (non-polluting), is part of that, so there's such a huge mountain to climb. Of the 350,000 million tonnes of polymer produced annually globally, 140,000 million tonnes goes into packaging, and the packaging industry is the biggest polluter because of a lack of closed loop (how the consumer uses it, how the consumer disposes of it) as to how consumers dispose of it. And if you look at the global population, 7 billion, 40 per cent of those people do not have a waste disposal system – and many don't have other basic infrastructure in place either, so investing in waste disposal just isn't a priority, so they are going to carry on disposing of stuff in a way that doesn't fit with a 'recycle this' argument. Many will tell you that all this hydrophobic stuff is fine, because you can make it into something really useful and then you can just recycle it – well you can three or four times but capturing it is less than 10 per cent in the UK – so how on earth are you going to capture all the shampoo pouches, milk packaging pouches around India and all this other convenience stuff that big consumer brands are pushing into all corners of the globe to continue their marketing efforts everywhere? And just saying you can recycle your way out of this isn't true, it can't be done – you have to find alternative end of life solutions that fit the environment that these products are being used in. Even in Europe, if you go and speak to the sophisticated brands, which have sophisticated supply chains, they will tell you they have at least 3 to 4 per cent leakage when it comes to packaging.

We believe there's a significant opportunity for brands, as packaging after all is a key communication channel, it meets, attracts and educates consumers. Manufacturers may tell you that they can't use a more sustainable product because they can't print on it, or it's not safe – but the reality is that now, with packaging innovation, everything is possible, they're just not moving quick enough to switch to a truly sustainable option. Yes, it may look a bit different, and yes, it is likely to cost more – but they do not have to lose functionality – all things are possible. If cost wasn't such a driver all of this could change very quickly. The packaging element of a product is a few per cent of the value of the product, so when consumers say they are happy to pay more for sustainable products, that gives enormous scope for brands to invest in the packaging to make it sustainable. But at the moment – packaging isn't designed with end of life in mind and the consumer isn't telling the brand to make those shifts and in my opinion, most brands won't make the shift until the consumer forces them to move. But consumers aren't fully aware of the realities, and large consumer brands will advise customers that their product is recyclable and sustainable, but it's not a reality. If every consumer fully understood that less than 9 per cent of consumer plastic packaging ends up going through a recycling system, it would perhaps make a difference.

But it doesn't need to be that way, you can have a healthy economy and still make good choices and achieve a healthier climate – we all have the opportunity to effect change. From a brand perspective, you can't sell anything without packaging and so there's a huge marketing opportunity for organizations to make sustainable packaging part of the offering, communicating what they do, protecting what they've made and also differentiating themselves, advising their customers that you cannot pollute by using our product because we've thought of the end of life and you are part of the solution. At Aquapak we're taking fantastic innovative materials and making a difference and we have capacity to scale, delivering viable long-term solutions to brands that want to do the right thing. Our focus is on knocking down all the reasons why large consumer brands can't make the switch towards genuine sustainable solutions.

10.5 Chapter summary

Going back to the roots of the humble and still highly practical tin can, packaging has always served to drive solutions to our problems. The significant problem of climate change, waste management, plastic pollution, recycling challenges and energy consumption is that whilst it can't all be completely resolved through packaging innovations, it certainly requires a rethink about the role and ownership of packaging. Technological advances are supporting innovation and with brands and major consumer product organizations starting to take responsibility for packaging, there is hope that targets set by the likes of the Ellen MacArthur Foundation and CEFLEX are not only met, but surpassed. But it takes a symbiotic partnership between producer and consumer to really make 'reduce, reuse and recycle' a reality. And although consumers are increasingly putting pressure on brands and making more conscious purchasing decisions, the real scale of change has to come from the producers: a change of strategic endeavour, starting with the end in mind and planning sustainability at the outset, applying practical systemic thinking and designing products with a focus on 'end of life' to make the circular economy a reality.

As we've stated throughout this chapter, over the last few decades marketing has played a significant role in changing consumer habits to create the throwaway society we are faced with today. Packaging plays a key role in brand identity, attracting, engaging and educating consumers – as Mark outlines, it's part of every product sold. And so there's a significant opportunity for marketers to harness packaging as a direct line of communication, using the power of technology and social technologies to connect more creatively and personally to collaborate with consumers and bring them on board to play an even more significant role in reducing, reusing and recycling. What's more, they can even champion the cause, and put pressure on manufacturers to invest in more sustainable practices. Innovation is out there, investment to scale it just needs to become a priority, and that is likely to be driven by purchasing behaviour.

As stated by Chris Daly, CEO of The Chartered Institute of Marketing: 'The onus is on the marketing industry to take what consumers are telling us and help organisations fully buy-in to sustainability led strategies' (CIM, 2019).

10.6 Action points to consider

No.	Action	Considerations	Next Step
1	Audit marketing messaging.	Undertake an audit of how you are communicating sustainability in terms of recycling, reusing and reducing packaging.	Do you have any campaigns dedicated to sustainability advising customers of the steps you're taking or your position?
2	Educate yourself and your target market.	From a marketing perspective, audit the messages you are sharing with your audiences about sustainable packaging. Do you practise clear carbon labelling?	What opportunities are there for you to consider and explore in this area?
3	Recycle, reduce, reuse.	What creative marketing campaigns/initiatives could you embark on to collaborate with customers to educate or encourage them to recycle or reuse?	How can you amplify the outputs of this campaign further (for example, sharing on social media or in store)?

No.	Action	Considerations	Next Step
4	Consider collaboration.	Do you have core competences internally with regards to marketing sustainability when it comes to packaging, or like the manufacturers cited in the Jibal research, is there a need for you to look beyond and build partnerships?	Run a needs assessment in this area – what key issue can you address with your partners?
5	Work with your consumers.	How can you create a 'symbiotic partnership' between your company and your consumer to make reduce, reuse and recycle a reality?	Start with the end in mind when planning a sustainability initiative with your consumers. What would represent a significant change?

10.7 Chapter 10 references

Andrex (2020). 'Make our pawprint greener'. Available at: www.andrex.co.uk/sustainability (Accessed: July 2020)

Baldesi, N., Feber, D., Santhanam, N., Spranzi, P., Tewari, A. and Varanasi, S. (2019). 'Packaging solutions: Poised to take off?'. Available at: https://www.mckinsey.com/industries/advanced-electronics/our-insights/packaging-solutions-poised-to-take-off (Accessed: July 2020)

BBC (2020). 'Coronavirus: Thousands of dissolvable laundry bags given to NHS'. Available at: https://www.bbc.co.uk/news/uk-england-birmingham-52384672 (Accessed: July 2020)

BPF (2020). 'Why do we need plastic packaging?'. Available at: https://www.bpf.co.uk/packaging/why-do-we-need-plastic-packaging.aspx (Accessed: July 2020)

CIM (2019). 'Consumers demand sustainable packaging'. Available at: https://www.cim.co.uk/newsroom/release-consumers-demand-sustainable-packaging/ (Accessed: July 2020)

Gilsenan, K. (2019). 'Lifting the Lid on Sustainable Packaging'. GlobalWebIndex. Available at: https://blog.globalwebindex.com/chart-of-the-week/lifting-the-lid-on-sustainable-packaging/ (Accessed: July 2020)

Global Newswire (2020). 'Food service packaging market to expand', https://www.globenewswire.com/news-release/2020/06/09/2045457/0/en/Food-service-packaging-market-to-expand-at-5-23-CAGR-over-2020-2027.html (Accessed: July 2020)

Greenbiz (2020). 'Tetra Pak's Mustan Lalani on the company's move towards a low-carbon circular economy'. Available at: https://www.greenbiz.com/video/tetra-paks-mustan-lalani-companys-move-toward-low-carbon-circular-economy (Accessed: July 2020)

Hamilton E. (2018). Available at: https://www.thevintagenews.com/2018/04/06/napoleon-food-2/ (Accessed: July 2020)

Holbrook, E. (2020). 'New Report Finds Overwhelming Majority of Consumers Are Willing to Pay More for Sustainable Packaging'. Environment + Energy Leader. Available at: https://www.environmentalleader.com/2020/04/new-report-finds-overwhelming-majority-of-consumers-are-willing-to-pay-more-for-sustainable-packaging/ (Accessed: July 2020)

Jabil (2019). 'Sustainable Packaging Trends: A Survey of Packaging and Sustainability Stakeholders March 2019'. Available at: https://www.jabil.com/dam/jcr:2adf6bb4-dc81-4dbf-97bb-21d6abd2333b/sustainable-packaging-survey-report.pdf (Accessed: July 2020)

McCarthy J. and Sanchez, E. (2019). 'The "Attenborough Effect" is Causing Global Plastic Pollution to Plummet'. Global Citizen. Available at: https://www.globalcitizen.org/en/content/attenborough-effect-plastics/ (Accessed: July 2020)

Notpla (2020). 'Edible and biodegradable. The alternative to plastic.' Available at: https://www.notpla.com/products-2/ (Accessed: July 2020)

Packaging Europe (2020). 'Samsung introduces cardboard packaging that becomes furniture', https://packagingeurope.com/samsung-introduces-cardboard-packaging-that-becomes-furniture/ (Accessed: July 2020)

Packaging Europe Survey (2020). 'Research shows sustained consumer support for carbon labelling on products'. Available at: https://packagingeurope.com/research-shows-sustained-consumer-support-for-carbon-labelling/ (Accessed: July 2020)

Packaging of the World (2015). Available at: www.packagingoftheworld.com (Accessed: July 2020)

Smith, M. (2015). 'Remy Martin thinks an NFC bottle cap is the key to authentic cognac'. Available at: https://www.engadget.com/2015-07-02-remy-martin-nfc-cognac.html (Accessed: July 2020)

Springwise. 'Pippa Bridges – Case Study – Springwise'. Available at: https://www.springwise.com/sustainable-production-mascara/ (Accessed: May 2020)

'Structural Packaging' blog, 2019. Available at: http://structuralpackagingblog.com/en/packaging-comestible/ (Accessed: July 2020)

Sykes, T. (2019). 'Recycling or Reuse? Will Loop Redefine the Circular Economy?'. Packaging Europe. Available at: https://packagingeurope.com/reuse-vs-recycle-loop-radical-vision-redefine-circular-economy/ (Accessed: July 2020)

Sykes, T. and Munford, L. (2020). 'Live from Davos: TerraCycle & Global Brand Owners Launch Retail Platform Based on Reusable Packaging'. Packaging Europe. Available at: https://packagingeurope.com/live-from-davos-terracycle-global-brand-owners-launch-retail/ (Accessed: July 2020)

Varanasi, S. (2019). 'Opportunities in Packaging'. McKinsey. Available at: https://www.mckinsey.com/industries/advanced-electronics/our-insights/opportunities-in-packaging-an-interview-with-sealed-airs-president-and-ceo-ted-doheny (Accessed: July 2020)

Watkiss, C. (2019). 'LUSH confirms its Cork Pots are carbon positive'. Available at: http://www.climateaction.org/news/lush-confirms-its-cork-pots-are-carbon-positive (Accessed: July 2020)

Wu, A. (2014). 'Good Product, Bad Package, Waste Management'. *Guardian*. Available at: https://www.theguardian.com/sustainable-business/2014/jul/18/good-product-bad-package-plastic-recycle-mistakes (Accessed: July 2020)

CHAPTER ELEVEN

The Importance of Effective Partnerships

11.0 Chapter introduction

Corporate social responsibility is no longer a nice-to-have or a tick-box exercise. As we have discussed throughout this book, there is far more focus now from consumers, investors, governments and non-governmental organizations on the detail and actions that underpin how organizations will meet their sustainable development plans. When it comes to sustainability, we have spoken extensively about the size and complexity of the subject and how it requires multiple parts to come together if change is going to happen. Whilst business is seen as the catalyst for change, organizations need further support, such as access to expertise and insight, means to increase reach and awareness, and additional capability to execute schemes in order to help meet the objectives they set. NGOs play a vital role across environmental, social and human rights issues. Although the word 'government' is in their name, the term 'non-governmental organization' was actually created in Article 71 of the Charter of the newly formed United Nations in 1945. An NGO can be any kind of organization provided that it is independent from government influence and is not-for-profit (World NGO Day, 2020). NGOs are important partners to business. The 'Edelman Trust Barometer 2020' report showed that: 'business and NGOs remain tied as the most trusted institutions for the third year in a row (each at 58 per cent)', yet neither institution is seen as both competent *and* ethical – two distinct considerations that build trust in society. Throughout this chapter we will discuss why partnerships are important in the pursuit of sustainability and what the benefits are for organizations that partner with NGOs and vice versa.

11.1 Where are we?

As sustainability continues to work its way to the top of organizations' agendas, NGOs have become a growing key influencer and partner to which businesses look for advice and expertise in building and executing their sustainability strategies and business growth plans. NGO partnerships have become even more important since the increased visibility of high-profile campaigns and setting of global initiatives and agreements, such as the UN 2030 Agenda, the introduction of the UN SDGs and the Paris Agreement. And, with the rise of the conscious consumer, organizations are more likely to be held to account if they are viewed as not doing their part for the environment. Partnerships with NGOs are beneficial on multiple levels and we will discuss these in more detail later in this chapter. However, the current landscape as laid out by the 'NGO Partnerships Barometer 2019' (C&E Corporate, 2019) shows there is a shift towards deeper, more impactful partnerships driven by the sheer volume of issues that we are now faced with, with more organizations and NGOs realizing that they are far more effective when they work together.

Why form partnerships and what's the value exchange?

Looking again at the barometer, it clearly shows that for business, 'reputation and credibility' (cited by 91 per cent of companies) remain top priorities, with innovation also a key motivation and access to new markets seen as increasingly important. For NGOs, 'access to financial support' (cited by 100 per cent of NGOs) remains the primary driver, but access to people and contacts and securing long-term stability and impact are also seen as key benefits.

The barometer also highlights:

- 90 per cent of companies aspire to or are already engaged in such partnerships, with 76 per cent of NGOs reporting similar status in the quest to address core mission-relevant or purpose-led issues in ways that create value for society;
- one of the core contributions that business engagement with the non-profit sector can bring is greater proximity to, and improved business understanding of, social and environmental contexts, issues, trends and stakeholders, in local or international arenas;
- both corporates and NGOs (96 per cent and 90 per cent respectively) are very confident that their partnerships have enabled corporations to improve their understanding of the social and/or environmental issues partnerships aim to tackle;
- NGOs have an important stakeholder role to play in holding business to account.

It is interesting to see how partnerships have evolved over time, moving beyond just putting a brand's name on your website as part of a 'badging' exercise, with NGO partnerships now taking many forms.

Some partnerships enable the organization to meet a specific need, such as the LEGO and WWF partnership whereby the WWF work with LEGO's global supply chain to look at where LEGO can cut the amount of energy it uses. In 2016, LEGO joined the 'Bioplastics Feedstock Alliance' (WWF, 2017) – an alliance that was founded by WWF to help with the sharing of information about renewable, plant-based plastics. The WWF continues to work with LEGO to provide technical guidance to enable LEGO to meet its '2030 goal of using sustainable materials for all packaging and core products'. This type of relationship has developed a wider set of objectives and has long-term goals on both sides.

Other partnerships can look to meet specific goals at a local level. HSBC and WaterAid, another example of a long-term partnership, work together on water and sanitation issues in underdeveloped countries. They have specific targets, such as their three-year programme to deliver essential water and sanitation services in apparel factories and nearby communities in Bangladesh and India. 'HSBC's eight-year $150 million partnership brings WaterAid's expertise together with WWF and Earthwatch to tackle the global water challenge' (WaterAid, 2020).

It is clear that partnerships are an important strategic investment, and businesses and NGOs see the value of working together. The very nature of these partnerships provides the opportunity to be more impactful and this plays a key part across many areas, both internally and externally.

The 2019 GlobeScan/SustainAbility Leaders Survey highlighted the valued contributions of NGOs, showing the importance they can bring and supporting why partnerships are increasingly becoming stronger and longer term: 'The private sector, institutional investors and national governments are called out by experts as making the poorest contribution to sustainable development globally. In contrast, experts view the contributions NGOs are making to the transition to sustainable development very positively and point to WWF, Greenpeace, WRI, Oxfam and the Nature Conservancy as leading the charge.'

External impact

We know from research that consumers want to engage with brands that are serious about sustainability and have a positive impact on society. Accenture's 'From Me To We, The Rise Of The Purpose-led Brand', global research of 30,000 consumers, revealed that: '62 per cent of customers want companies to take a stand on current and broadly relevant issues like sustainability, transparency or fair employment practices' (Barton et al, 2020). The findings also demonstrate that consumers will walk away from brands that aren't taking action. Partnerships with NGOs provide a way for organizations to demonstrate that their actions are well planned, and they mean what they say. With trust being at an all-time low globally, with fake news and social media platforms adding to the huge waves of noise and opinion, it is sometimes difficult to get a clear and informed view on what the facts are. As discussed, consumers now play a much bigger part in the stakeholder chain, and it is critical that brands retain trust and loyalty. Partnerships with NGOs provide brands with another voice, one that sits independently and is neutral – NGOs sit alongside businesses as being 'the most trusted institution', as reported by the 'Edelman Trust Barometer 2020' report (Ries, Edelman et al, 2020). It's a good balance, as NGOs are seen as ethical but not competent, whilst businesses are seen as competent but not ethical.

Internal impact

As well as looking externally, it is also important to consider the impact that partnerships can have internally. Working effectively with NGOs can have a positive impact on employees. It can be used as a means to educate, increase engagement and instil a sense of motivation and 'feel good' factor, all of which create a more efficient and effective workforce. The Deloitte Global Millennial Survey (2019) highlights that millennials and Gen Z are disillusioned; they have multiple areas of their lives that they aren't satisfied with across social, economic and political landscapes. The findings show that when it comes to business they are: 'skeptical of business's motives. Respondents do not think highly of leaders' impact on society, their commitment to improving the world, or their trustworthiness' (Deloitte, 2019). Whilst this workforce of the future has evolved in terms of what is important, the climate and environment continue to be a top concern by a considerable margin, with 29 per cent citing it as a worry, seven points more than the next-highest concern of income inequality/distribution of wealth. There is a spotlight on governments across many pieces of research that points to growing distrust and puts blame for the lack of social progress firmly at their doorstep. The upcoming generations are future employees, and organizations need to provide them with a reason to engage on both a consumer and employee level. The findings further highlight that: 'Millennials and Gen Zs show deeper loyalty to employers who boldly tackle the issues that resonate with them most, such as protecting the environment and unemployment'. And as consumers: 'they are inclined to spend their income on products and services from brands that speak to these issues'. It's not enough to just have a set of values; businesses need to live by them and ensure their employees also understand and live by them too.

11.2 Why do companies need to do something about this now?

The many roles of the NGO

As well as the areas previously mentioned, NGOs play key roles in many other areas, and in a way that no other partner can, due to their neutral position, their global and local presence and their knowledge. Most importantly, they have earned the trust of the communities they serve and they have demonstrated the impact they can have on the ground. This makes them a critical part of the stakeholder chain and an effective business partner. As stated in the 'NGO Partnerships Barometer 2019' (C&E Corporate, 2019), 'one of the core contributions that business engagement with the non-profit sector can bring is greater proximity to, and improved business understanding of, social and environmental contexts, issues, trends and stakeholders, in local or international arenas.' So, let's explore a little further the many roles that NGOs play and the very real value they can bring.

Facilitator and advisers

NGOs are important in the facilitation of communication between society and governments, they act as the voice on both sides informing and providing feedback. They share information about what is happening as well as what is required both upwards from the 'grass roots' and downwards from the policymakers. Indeed, much research has highlighted the important roles NGOs have played in promoting and influencing the negotiation of a wide variety of international agreements on issues of global concern, whether they be the environment, public health, human rights or debt, trade and development (Crowley and Persbo, 2006). One such example is, the 'Healthy forests = equitable livelihoods, inclusive development and a resilient climate' briefing (Lepitak, S., 2018). This briefing, which was endorsed by a number of NGOs, provided detail on what the EU could do to ensure healthy forests contributed to local communities and how they lived, improved governance, and mitigated the impact of climate change. They recommended that the European Commission, in co-operation with EU Members States:

1) Reinvigorate support for Voluntary Partnership Agreements (VPAs) and the EU Timber Regulation implementation.
2) Uphold human rights including gender equality in VPAs.
3) Adopt additional regulatory measures to tackle the deforestation crisis and protect rights.
4) Strengthen linkages between FLEGT and the climate and Sustainable Development Goals agendas.
5) Use trade as a lever to support human rights and protect forests.

(Lepitak, 2018)

The above example shows the level of knowledge and influence NGOs have and the value they can bring to a partnership. They take what are often highly complex issues that require understanding across multiple areas and bring expertise to enable the right recommendations, legislation and course of action. There is a lot of work being done globally to protect forests from deforestation and degradation. Forests are critical to sustaining life, stabilizing the climate and provide economic opportunity. Through working together with shared intention to protect and restore forests, NGOs can meet their societal objectives ensuring wildlife, communities and the climate have the opportunity to survive and grow. Organizations have the opportunity to review business practices, create improved and more efficient processes, and innovate new products and ways of working. They open up the opportunity for longer-term economic growth and strengthen their brand and purpose.

There are many examples of organizations successfully working with NGOs in this area, such as McDonald's, which partners with the WWF and aligns its sustainable development plan to the UN SDGs, stating: 'We're committed to eliminating deforestation from our global supply chains, and promoting responsible forestry and production practices that benefit people, communities and the planet' (McDonald's Corporate, 2019). Food and drink production have a significant impact on forests, and those businesses that recognize this have the opportunity to work towards more sustainable businesses in a more stable environment.

Innovation and opportunity

The 'NGO Partnerships Barometer 2020' report highlights that innovation and accessing new markets is a key motivation when partnering with NGOs. NGOs, through their experience of working with local communities, provide knowledge and can act as a trusted partner, building relationships with commercial organizations that may not have been possible via other means. This opens up opportunities for organizations to gain insights into potential new markets and design products specifically to meet the needs of those markets. GlaxoSmithKline, for instance, has partnered with Save the Children since 2013 (GSK, 'Save the Children', 2013) and, over the years, they have gained insight and knowledge that has enabled them to develop life-saving products. Innovation is at the heart of the partnership, demonstrated by the commitment to the research and development of medicines to help save the lives of mothers and babies in developing countries:

'The research and development work conducted by the partnership has reformulated chlorhexidine (CHX), an antiseptic commonly used in mouthwash, as a gel in a sachet for the prevention of umbilical cord infection in low-resource settings. The newly cut umbilical cord is a common entry point for bacteria that can cause neonatal sepsis – a blood stream infection. CHX is listed as one of the WHO's Essential Medicines and prior to the partnership, GSK had begun to explore its reformulation to help prevent infection and improve postnatal care. Once the two organizations started working together, we were able to harness in-country expertise and insights gained from research to advise on how this new formulation could be made accessible to mothers and babies in the hardest to reach areas. Through the partnership, over 30,000 newborns in Bungoma County, Kenya, have so far benefitted from the new chlorhexidine gel. GSK has made the details of the new formulation and quality specifications available to other manufacturers, in addition to making the medicine available on a "not-for-profit" pricing basis.'

(GSK, 'Save the Children', 2019)

This type of innovation is invaluable, and it is through effective partnerships that it is able to happen.

Communication and communities

As well as facilitating communication up and down and throughout the stakeholder chain, NGOs play a critical role on the ground. They communicate at a local level and build trust amongst communities, allowing them to gain a deeper understanding of the local issues and social values. They also work with the local communities, educating them on how they can work towards a more sustainable future. One example is the Better Cotton Initiative (BCI) (www.bettercotton.org) – the largest cotton sustainability programme in the world. Working across the total cotton supply chain on a global level, they have trained 2 million farmers across 21 countries on more sustainable agricultural practices and their goal is to reach 5 million farmers. The Better Cotton Initiative, like many sustainable initiatives, is a long-term project, and began in 2005. They are a strong example of an NGO that has worked effectively with countries, communities and partners. They've set standards, the 'Better Cotton Principles and Criteria', which set criteria against key principles, and they work on the ground to support and educate farmers in local communities in monitoring and evaluating progress. BCI created the 'Claims Framework' to enable their partners to spread the word. BCI say of their framework: 'The Better Cotton Claims Framework makes it simple for BCI Members to make credible and positive claims about Better Cotton and allows flexibility in how to communicate about your commitment. Many other communications resources are available, such as quotes, images, Stories from the Field and promotional artworks. By combining claims in the framework with these other resources, a member can articulate a compelling story which is meaningful to them and their customers' (Better Cotton Initiative, 2019).

Communication is a key part to the success of a partnership. By effectively communicating the objectives, intentions and progress on a continuous basis it not only shows that you are taking your sustainable development seriously, but it also acts as a way of highlighting and educating employees and consumers about what the issues are and how you are helping to make progress. This leads to more informed decisions on engagement and purchases and creates further awareness through word of mouth. The more society is aware, the more they can get involved to effect change. It is therefore important for marketing teams on both sides to be actively engaged and have a solid understanding on why the partnership exists and what it is setting out to achieve.

An example of this is Marks & Spencer, a partner of BCI, which convey their partnership through a dedicated page on their website that explains all elements of the partnership and why they support the Better Cotton Initiative. The use of social marketing, as already discussed, is an effective way of raising awareness with the objective to change societal behaviours. In this case, there are two elements at play: 1) raising awareness and educating consumers about the environmental impacts that the production of cotton has, with the objective of changing how people effectively 'consume' clothes; 2) being able to sell their products with a sustainable proposition that is better than their competitors. However, whilst the message that their cotton is sustainably sourced also appears on product pages that it applies to, it is only mentioned further down the page, with no links to their sustainability pages, and can be easily missed. Unless a customer is proactively looking at how Marks & Spencer sources their cotton, they are unlikely to notice it. As sustainability continues to move up the ranks of what consumers care about and influences their purchase decisions, these messages need to sit alongside other key marketing messages and reasons to buy, such as price and quality.

NGOs' knowledge and insight into what the issues are and what projects and local initiatives are needed are also key to partners when developing more effective campaigns on both a strategic and tactical level. Effective partnerships enable an organization to build initiatives that work, deliver better results and ensure what they are doing is having the impact where it is intended. NGOs can become advocates for the projects and campaigns, making them more credible, which again will build trust and influence both employees and society.

As the 'NGO Partnerships Barometer' shows, meaningful, longer-term relationships are increasing. In order to make progress, organizations of all types need to work together as development goals (SDGs) become more urgent and the deadlines for change become ever more critical and draw closer. As with the previous example of leading investor BlackRock, investors are making it a priority to invest in those organizations that are making progress with their sustainable development and divesting from those that are not. Furthermore, the wants and needs of consumers and society are looking towards those brands that are focused on the triple bottom line.

11.3 Things that need to be acknowledged as not perfect

Partnerships with NGOs can be a strong and successful strategy to follow, though there are challenges also associated with such partnerships, which need to be acknowledged – from imbalances of power through to the need for stronger communication. When it comes to effective partnerships with NGOs, communication, as we have already discussed, is key. However, whilst communication is happening as relationships become longer term, and sustainability becomes more of a priority, there are areas that need improving, and marketing plays a vital part in ensuring the messages work and the awareness grows.

Alignment of goals and objectives

As discussed at the start of the chapter, the 'NGO Partnerships Barometer' showed that 'reputation and credibility' is the top priority for business when it comes to NGO partnerships, whilst 'access to financial support' was the top priority for NGOs. Given the differing nature, objectives and culture of these organizations it should come as no surprise that their priorities are different. However, it is important that this does not lead to a potential imbalance of power that could damage progress. Like any joint venture or partnership, it is so important that the intention of the partnership is understood at the beginning. The value exchange between the organizations needs to be compatible so the NGO can meet its social goals and the organization its business goals. For the NGO, the risk of losing funding can put them in a vulnerable position due to their 'not-for-profit' status they rely heavily on such funding from business to carry out their work, which is often very complex and can cover multiple areas, all of which requires resource and financial support. For the corporate partner, their vulnerability lies in damage to their reputation, which could lead to loss of business. The influence an NGO can have can be incredibly powerful and their reach in some cases both at a global and local level means again that partnerships need to be considered and entered into with transparency and agreed intentions. In addition, how progress is reported also needs to be agreed to ensure that it meets the needs of both partners. Unlike financial reporting, which has to go through auditors, because there are so many different bodies, frameworks and targets, sustainability measurement and reporting varies and is not verified, which can make it impossible to compare. Whilst effective partnerships are delivering results, what is seen as success by a business may be different to the view of the NGO. Removing some of the complexity when it comes to measurement and reporting could make it easier to communicate.

Cause marketing

Cause marketing has benefits for both sides of a partnership. The commercial organization can use it to drive sales of a product or products and raise awareness of its values and support for good causes. The NGO benefits financially from the donations, which come from the sales of product, and has its profile and the work it does amplified as a result of the marketing activities. Rise of the belief-driven consumer is a key driver of cause-related marketing's success. The '2019 Edelman Trust Barometer Special Report' (Ries et al, 2019), which was conducted across eight countries and with more than 25,000 people, highlights that: '81 per cent of consumers must be able to trust a brand to do what is right.' It goes on to show that only: '34 per cent trust most of the brands they buy or use.' Most notably, 56 per cent think that: 'too many brands use societal issues as a marketing ploy to sell more product'. It is critical that trust is built in order for a cause marketing campaign to work. The majority of consumers only want to engage with brands they trust, and to do this they need to understand the motivation behind the campaign and know that their money is going direct to the cause. Cause marketing allows marketers to show a side to their organizations that goes beyond selling products.

The Co-op Group, has a long-running partnership with the One Foundation (www.coop.co.uk/our-suppliers/water) whereby for every litre of its own-brand Fairbourne Springs bottled water sold it donates 3p, and for all other water bottles sold it donates 1p per litre to the One Foundation to fund clean water, sanitation and hygiene projects around the world. This initiative encourages consumers to buy Co-op's own brand of water, which directly helps fund water projects and raises awareness of the One Foundation. You could certainly argue that promoting the sales of bottled water whilst helping fund such projects also results in increasing the world's plastic problem. However, given that the market for bottled water shows no signs of slowing, buying a brand that at least gives back and saves lives is better than nothing.

One of the most recent examples of a poorly thought-out and executed cause marketing campaign was MasterCard's 'goal-for-meals' campaign. The credit card company announced it would donate the equivalent value of 10,000 meals to the World Food Programme (WFP) for children in Latin America and the Caribbean each time the football stars Messi and Neymar Jr netted a goal between the start of the campaign in summer 2018 and the end of March 2020. This campaign was likened to the Hunger Games and faced a serious backlash across social platforms, which resulted in MasterCard pulling the campaign. MasterCard went on to contribute two million meals in 2018 with the United Nations World Food Programme (Lepitak, 2018).

There are always going to be questions such as 'Where does my money go?' when it comes to cause marketing. Conversations over the years have been raised over whether cause marketing is just another driver of pointless purchases and in fact adds to the waste problem.

One of the ways organizations also try to get consumers involved is to ask for a charitable donation as part of the checkout process. For instance, Domino's Pizza has worked with Pennies, the digital charity box (Domino's Pizza, 2020), since 2010, when the long-standing partnership was formed, whereby: 'customers use our website and app to round up their orders to the nearest pound. Almost 93 per cent of the money raised goes to our charity partners, while the rest goes towards achieving Pennies' charitable objectives.' Many organizations have used this approach, both through e-commerce and in store. However, whilst successful for some partnerships, it has faced some criticism. Consumers can feel uncomfortable (more in-store/in-person) when they are asked if they want to make a donation, as they feel obliged. Second to that, there are also questions raised about passing the responsibility down to the consumer, especially if the organization in question does not match or contribute to the donations. The risk is that business is seen as taking all the rewards in the form of promoting themselves as doing good, stronger brand reputation and tax write-offs, all whilst the consumers pay.

To counter just this, Amazon, through AmazonSmile, have a process whereby consumers can choose a charity at the start of the shopping process and then: 'Amazon donates 0.5% of the net purchase price (excluding VAT, returns and shipping fees) of eligible purchases to the charitable organization of your choice.' This means the donation isn't at the cost of the consumer. AmazonSmile is a simple and effective process; consumers have the choice to opt in and they can choose from a range of charities, which are growing all the time. They can also change the charities they choose to support, which means it is a more personalized initiative. AmazonSmile has: 'raised over $150m for charities worldwide and over £1.9m for UK charities since launch – as of July 2019' (Blum, 2019).

When executed correctly, therefore, cause marketing can be highly effective. The right partners can provide credibility. Critically, though, how the organization chooses to design the campaign and process needs to ensure that offence isn't caused, it isn't passing the cost and responsibility to the consumer and, most importantly, that the donations go to the causes they are intended for. It is marketing's role to amplify the message, be involved in the design to ensure the right customer journey and to take the opportunity to have a different conversation with its audience and ensure every employee is an advocate.

11.4 Case study – GSK

Communicating effectively and making your employees advocates is vital. GlaxoSmithKline's approach to its Save the Children partnership has therefore focused on ensuring its employees are not only aware of the work that it is doing, but that they are a key part of it as well.

The global GSK employee workforce of over 100,000 are encouraged to support the partnership through award-winning Orange United fundraising campaigns, as well as by contributing their time and expertise through GSK's skill-based PULSE volunteer engagements (PULSE, 2020). So far, over 100 GSK employees have been placed in Save the Children roles, drawing on their professional expertise to provide valuable skilled services.

In March 2017, select GSK employees participated in a global Trek for Kids. Building on the enthusiasm, 40 GSK employees from 25 countries trekked the Simien Mountains in Ethiopia in March 2019, where Save the Children has been working for decades to support programs that provide education, health, food security, HIV/AIDS prevention and lifesaving care for children.

GSK employees have always been at the heart of our partnership. Employees in over 70 countries have raised millions for Save the Children's work globally, which is also matched by GSK.

(GSK, 'GSK and Save the Children: A U.S. Disaster Response Partner')

By taking their partnership throughout the organization, GSK is ensuring that it is more than just a 'tick in the box' or a partnership that is siloed off and managed by one part of the business. By involving employees in roles and fundraising activities, they are not only advocates but they also play an active part in the direction and the success of the partnership and its progress. This is a partnership that is communicated effectively and with multiple people and parts working together. By doing this, GSK has created an environment whereby more ideas can be fuelled, innovation is possible, and lives are being saved.

11.5 Chapter summary

Partnerships with NGOs have increased and developed into longer-term relationships over the years and the outlook is that this will continue to strengthen moving forwards, with both sides seeing the value and impact that it can have both to business and society. The expertise and knowledge that NGOs bring and their ability to effect change both within communities and in advising and driving legislation at a government level is invaluable. As shown in the 'Edelman Trust Barometer 2020' report (Ries, Edelman et al, 2020), businesses are seen as the catalyst for change, but they are not seen as ethical; NGOs, whilst trusted, are not seen as competent. By working together with transparency on what the intentions, priorities and objectives are on both sides, a successful partnership can bring about change to business practices, brands' purpose and provide valuable insight that can open up opportunities in new markets and deliver a more meaningful customer experience.

And, it is not only the organization itself that can benefit; a clearer understanding of supply chains, how they operate and where they source their products from can be gained, which is where the real impact for change and progress at the source of many of the issues can take place. Palm oil, tea, cotton, food products – all have far greater impacts on the environment than we realize and it is through effective campaigns, consistent communication and working together to meet sustainable goals that more informed decisions can be made.

NGO partnerships, when done well, can open up opportunities beyond just awareness: they enable organizations to build and access new and developing markets, become more efficient in their business practices and create the appropriate market conditions for growth. For NGOs, there is the opportunity to help, educate and improve local communities in less developed countries. Research and learnings are gained that go towards educating and steering governments and leaders of the world to come together and form policies that can drive positive change. And, together with a more informed understanding of how we all need to play our part to effect change, that is more important now than ever.

11.6 Action points to consider

No.	Action	Considerations	Next Step
1	Decide whether an NGO partnership is right for your organization.	Be clear on why you want to work together, on both sides. It cannot be a vanity measure, or a 'tick box' exercise. Values must align or they risk not being taken seriously.	Work closely together to review and align your goals and objectives.
2	Allocate the time, resource and funding.	Be sure of the time and effort that is required at the start of the partnership.	Agree the different roles each partner will have. Commit people, teams and senior leaders to the partnership to ensure accountability.
3	Make sure the targets are realistic.	The end goal may be the same but how you get there needs to be planned carefully. Plan targets and timeframes based on realistic assumptions.	How will the partnership will be monitored and measured to benefit both the NGO and the business? Remember that success will look different to each party.
4	Keep going.	The situation is changing all the time, so be prepared to change direction and evolve. Be prepared also to make mistakes and learn from them.	Not every part of the partnership will work all the time. Be prepared to bring in new resources or remove older ones. Review the status and objectives on an ongoing basis.
5	Communicate effectively.	Use all the expertise within your marketing function to amplify your messages. Use your employees as advocates. Communicate outside of the 'sustainability' section on your website.	Take your message to society, do not make them have to look for it.

11.7 Chapter 11 references

Barton, R. Ishikawa, M., Quiring, K. and Theofilou, B. (2020). 'To Affinity And Beyond: from me to we, the rise of the purpose-led brand'. AccentureStrategy. Available at: https://www.accenture.com/_acnmedia/Thought-Leadership-Assets/PDF/Accenture-CompetitiveAgility-GCPR-POV.pdf (Accessed: 11 April 2020)

Better Cotton Initiative (2019). 'Better Cotton Claims Framework'. Available at: https://bettercotton.org/resources/better-cotton-claims-framework/ (Accessed: 26 April 2020)

Blum, J. (2019). 'AmazonSmile: you shop, Amazon donates'. Available at: https://blog.aboutamazon.co.uk/in-the-community/amazonsmile-you-shop-amazon-donates (Accessed: 24 April 2020)

C&E Corporate (2019). 'NGO Partnerships Barometer'. Available at: https://www.candeadvisory.com/sites/candeadvisory.com/files/FINAL_C%26E_Corporate-NGO_Partnerships_Barometer_report2019.pdf (Accessed: 24 April 2020)

Co-op (2020). 'Funding clean water projects' Available at: www.coop.co.uk/our-suppliers/water (Accessed: 10 April 2020)

Crowley and Persbo (2006). 'Thinking Outside the Box in Multilateral Disarmament & Arms Control Negotiations'. Available at: https://www.peacepalacelibrary.nl/ebooks/files/UNIDIR_pdf-art2588.pdf (Accessed: 11 April 2020)

Deloitte (2019). 'The Deloitte Global Millennial Survey 2019'. Available at: https://www2.deloitte.com/global/en/pages/about-deloitte/articles/millennialsurvey.html (Accessed: 28 May 2020)

Domino's Pizza (2020). 'Domino's Pizza works with Pennies, the digital charity box'. Available at: https://corporate.dominos.co.uk/pennies-become-pounds (Accessed: 24 April 2020)

GSK (2019). 'Save the Children: helping to save one million children's lives'. Available at: https://www.gsk.com/media/2756/save-the-children-partnership-progress-brochure.pdf). (Accessed: 24 April 2020)

GSK (2020). 'GSK and Save the Children: A U.S. Disaster Response Partner'. Available at: https://www.savethechildren.org/us/about-us/become-a-partner/corporations/gsk (Accessed: 25 April 2020)

GSK (2020). 'Pulse Volunteer Partnership'. Available at: https://gskpulsevolunteers.com/ (Accessed: 24 April 2020)

Lee, M. and York, B. (2019). 'The 2019 GlobeScan/SustainAbility Leaders Survey'. GlobeScan. Available at: https://globescan.com/unilever-patagonia-ikea-sustainability-leadership-2019/ (Accessed: 24 April 2020)

Lepitak, S. (2018). '"The worst marketing I've ever seen" – MasterCard's World Cup children's meals campaign stirs debate'. Available at: https://www.fern.org/news-resources/healthy-forests-equitable-livelihoods-inclusive-development-and-a-resilient-climate-2009/ (Accessed: 11 April 2020)

Lepitak, S. (2018). 'Healthy forests = equitable livelihoods, inclusive development and a resilient climate' briefing' Available at: https://www.fern.org/news-resources/healthy-forests-equitable-livelihoods-inclusive-development-and-a-resilient-climate-2009/ (Accessed: 11 April 2020)

McDonalds Corporate (2019). 'Conserving Forests'. Available at: https://corporate.mcdonalds.com/corpmcd/scale-for-good/our-planet/conserving-forests.html (Accessed: 26 April 2020)

Ries, T. et al (2019). '2019 Edelman Trust Barometer Special Report: In Brands We Trust?'. Available at: https://www.edelman.com/sites/g/files/aatuss191/files/2019-06/2019_edelman_trust_barometer_special_report_in_brands_we_trust.pdf (Accessed: 24 April 2020)

Ries, T. et al (2019). '2019 Edelman Trust Barometer: In Brands We Trust?'. Available at: https://www.edelman.com/sites/g/files/aatuss191/files/2019-06/2019_edelman_trust_barometer_special_report_in_brands_we_trust.pdf (Accessed: 24 April 2020)

Ries, T. et al (2020). 'Edelman Trust Barometer 2020'. Available at: https://www.edelman.com/sites/g/files/aatuss191/files/2020-01/2020%20Edelman%20Trust%20Barometer%20Global%20Report_LIVE.pdf (Accessed: 10 April 2020)

Save The Children (2019). 'GSK Helping to save one million children's lives'. Available at: https://www.savethechildren.org.uk/about-us/who-we-work-with/corporate-partners/gsk (Accessed: 28 May 2020)

'Structural Packaging' blog (2019). Available at: http://structuralpackagingblog.com/en/packaging-comestible/ (Accessed: 28 May 2020)

WaterAid (2020). 'HSBC Partnership'. Available at: https://www.wateraid.org/uk/get-involved/hsbc (Accessed: 24 April 2020)

World NGO Day (2020). 'World NGO Day'. Available at: https://worldngoday.org/ (Accessed: 10 April 2020)

WWF (2017). 'Building a Brighter Future: The LEGO Group and the Bioplastic Feedstock Alliance journey towards a future built with sustainable materials'. Available at: https://www.worldwildlife.org/blogs/sustainability-works/posts/building-a-brighter-future-the-lego-group-and-the-bioplastic-feedstock-alliance-journey-towards-a-future-built-with-sustainable-materials (Accessed: 24 April 2020)

CHAPTER TWELVE

Summary and Next Steps

As we said at the very beginning, we took the decision to write this book following numerous conversations with fellow marketing professionals and business leaders, increasing numbers of whom were and still are seeking to embrace a profits-with-purpose approach to their marketing strategy. As with our journey in writing this book, with every chapter we have met the complexities that come with sustainability and the challenges of navigating the sheer volume of information to gain understanding.

We've looked at the stakeholder chain, leadership and the global goals, such as the SDGs, that are in place to drive sustainable development and living. We've discussed the numerous frameworks for reporting and the different calculations used that get us there, all of which are not wrong per se, but highlight the lack of a unified approach to address a unified problem. We've talked about the labels, badges and terms on products, which although designed to provide clarity and direction, in some cases just confuse or, even worse, deliberately mislead. We've explored the agreements and processes put in place to support a more sustainable world and then the lack of infrastructure to support them. We've talked about the difficulty in comparing progress and results in order to make informed decisions. And then there is the issue of trust – trust, or the lack of it, has come up repeatedly throughout this book, with society continuing to lose trust, fuelling the need for transparency.

Throughout this entire book, our focus has been on educating you about the facts and trying to help you to not only practise more responsible marketing, but also how marketing sustainability effectively can improve your organization and lessen its impact on the environment. As well as highlighting the complexities and challenges, we hope you've taken inspiration from the many ideas, examples, interviews and case studies we've shared on where and how progress can be and is being made.

We hope through our research and writing that we've shown how aligned marketing is to sustainability – how it also needs to sit at the heart of your brand, communication strategy, stakeholder management and the supply chain involved in your product development.

Here's a recap of the main conclusions and take-outs from this book before we offer a suggestion on how to structure your action plan based on their recommendations.

12.0 Chapter 1 – Introduction summary

In Chapter 1, we explored how developing a corporate responsibility strategy in your business is closely linked to brand and reputation, and how as marketers we can 'own' making a difference to the environment with the company we are working for. We identified that sustainability can apply to many different areas of your company's activity, and touches everyone – from your employees to your immediate local community to the wider marketplace you operate in.

We hope it is also clear that active management of sustainable practice is now essential for every business. Now that you have come from Chapter 1 to this final chapter, you have begun your journey towards more sustainable marketing practice and leadership of it in a wider business capacity. This involves managing what sometimes seem to be conflicting positions, as ultimately our companies' operations will always have an environmental impact; leading this is a big responsibility.

It will be difficult, and not everyone will share your enthusiasm, but the point is key: your company can change, and does not need to do things as it has 'always done it', but you must help to drive that transformation.

12.1 Chapter 2 – Sustainability and Leadership summary

This chapter explored what it means to begin your journey as a sustainable leader, leading with purpose, and beginning to set the agenda for sustainability in your organization. We show that it is possible for companies to undertake sustainable practice, as well as driving shareholder profit. However, it is clear that truly delivering a purpose-led strategy starts at the very top of the organization, and requires significant buy-in and investment of time and resources from a company's leadership team.

In order to be impactful and action-orientated, sustainability needs to be baked into organizational culture in order to be able to be a true long-term focus. It is also clear that there will be significant challenges with delivering it – another reason why management teams need to be fully behind achieving the desired end result. Clarity about organizational values that align with sustainability and SDG goals are key – alongside all departments and team members being fully accountable.

12.2 Chapter 3 – The Importance of Stakeholder Engagement summary

In this chapter we outlined the significant importance of a proactive and detailed approach to stakeholder engagement, which is key to delivering a successful sustainability strategy. We discussed how the stakeholder chain has evolved, with society, consumers and employees now playing a more important and empowered role, and how the role of investors is turning to focus, for the first time, on sustainability and the environment.

Clear communication is key, and this is where marketing teams can play a crucial role in creating impact and value, acting as both a facilitator and enabler in delivering their company's sustainable development plan to all parts of the stakeholder chain. Each part of your company's stakeholder chain will have a multitude of different reasons for wanting engagement, different communication requirements and, perhaps most important, different levels of view on the desired impact they wish to see.

Key to managing this complex mix is a recognition that no single stakeholder can effect change in isolation. Collaboration and collective action are vital, as is trust – made all the more difficult by the significant increase in fake news. Consistency and transparency are essential if a business is to be effective.

12.3 Chapter 4 – Sustainable Supply Chain summary

This chapter outlined that in order to be a truly effective initiative, supply chain sustainability needs to be a board-level topic for any company that works with external partners to deliver its end product or service. It is also clear that companies therefore need to address the impact on the environment created by their production process, in order to produce a material reduction in carbon emissions and waste.

Key for marketing teams to deliver is ensuring that companies do not just look to their supply chain sustainability because it is 'the right thing to do', but also because it can deliver strong commercial results. A brand's reputation is paramount to its future success. Rapidly shifting consumer attitudes in the younger generation of buyers mean they now expect sustainable practice to be a given at the companies they are buying from, and will increasingly not tolerate poor performance or negative environmental impact.

However, in undertaking even a base audit of a company's supply chain, marketers and leaderships teams need to be prepared and able to commit resources to dive deep into operational parts of the business. As we explored in depth, the business case for sustainably managing your supply chain is a daunting and complex one, and all companies should approach it from a partnership perspective. A sound commercial basis is clearly required. However, companies need to be ready to question the premise that the best sources of manufacture are those producing goods at the lowest cost base – why is this? Finally, marketers should work with procurement teams to ensure best practice in sustainability is built in all contracts – and key areas such as human rights, modern slavery and environmental improvement are addressed and assessed at all times.

12.4 Chapter 5 – Beyond Corporate Social Responsibility summary

Moving beyond the basic constructs of corporate social responsibility in developing your marketing sustainability practice is key. As the natural custodians of brand reputation, employee engagement and owners of the end-to-end 'customer journey', marketing should be the champion for developing sustainable practice.

Careful management of a brand's reputation, sponsoring conscious consumerism and ensuring employees are engaged in turn can deliver enhanced brand reputation and image, customer loyalty and employee satisfaction. Combined together, this will deliver a significant bottom line impact to the financial position of the company.

There is little choice but to adopt this philosophy. As highlighted in this chapter, multiple brands and organizations have encountered a backlash from their consumers – greatly amplified by social media – when seemingly cause-related initiatives aren't seen as being delivered authentically, and don't align with their values.

Marketing must also take an active role in helping to evidence a company's impact, alongside leading an ever-greater understanding of what is considered important by their customers as well as their company's objectives. Aligning their business's purpose and values will help all business functions take practical steps in relation to packaging, plastic, energy, the climate, waste, partnerships and supply chains – each aspect is part of the economic, social and environmental umbrella of CSR.

12.5 Chapter 6 – Reducing Waste in the Workplace summary

Here, we overviewed the need to adopt a target-led approach to reducing waste, and recognize that change can and should begin in the environments closest to you – your company's own workplace. As discussed in Chapters 4 and 5, effective waste management is key to any contemporary corporate responsibility strategy and, if implemented well, will enhance the performance of your company.

As with the majority of this book's suggestions, truly dealing with reducing waste in the workplace requires the entire leadership team to adopt the principles of a 'circular economy'. As custodians of communication, marketing professionals must lead in signposting, promoting and encouraging team members to actively reduce, reuse and recycle as part of in-office waste reduction.

Many principles are surprisingly easy to implement, and companies will also begin to see a real reduction in costs over time – from offering reusable containers rather than single-use ones, to reducing the use of unnecessary printing through using more digital means.

As in other chapters, there does however need to be a recognition that eliminating all waste is an extremely difficult issue for many companies to handle. This is especially difficult for marketers – many readers will be promoting consumption of new items and using a variety of materials in their marketing efforts that are single-use, or of limited value as they date. You can, however, make a significant difference by considering waste in all planning and reducing it through more considered purchases.

12.6 Chapter 7 – Plastic: Reduce, Reuse, Recycle summary

Here we tackled the complex area of plastic production and where it ends up. Despite being much maligned, there is a recognition that not all plastic produced is inherently bad, although in some areas such as food packaging, plastic waste is growing at an unacceptable rate.

Addressing single-use plastics is key for every single businesses out there. There are many sustainable alternatives, but we acknowledge cutting through high levels of misinformation can be difficult. As some governments bring in new laws and regulations to govern the use of plastic, organizations and their marketing teams must embrace the opportunity to innovate, help change direction in their packaging, and influence behaviours throughout their company and in the wider world (i.e. their customers).

Marketers should also draw on emerging best practice; for example, the growing trend of some supermarkets moving to sell more loose produce instead of packaged goods and providing refill models. Companies must ensure their own recycling labelling is made clearer and support delivery of a better recycling infrastructure. Marketing needs to consider how it manages its broader message on plastic when influencing behaviour, and can no longer be based solely on promoting the sale of product. Marketers must also focus on changing the stories that sit behind the products they help sell, increasing transparency – ultimately, the manufacturing, reasons to purchase and the means of disposal must all be marketed effectively, as much as the usage.

12.7 Chapter 8 – Climate Change and the Carbon Challenge summary

In this chapter, we attempted to cover the vast, complicated topic of climate change and outlined how only a co-ordinated global effort will change its current direction. Governments need to deliver more than ever on their commitments to the Paris Agreement and provide clear reporting on progress and how they are adjusting their targets.

It is clear that organizations need to work closely with government, continuing to innovate and invest in new technologies that increase progress towards a more sustainable ecosystem. Companies also need to focus on contributing to escalating the pace of change, sharing any case studies and stories of success to help others implement best practice, and fuelling new ideas across industries.

With companies, individuals and government increasingly working towards a common purpose, there is also a need for greater transparency, investing in long-term social marketing-focused campaigns built on fact. As such, marketing can, and must, play the key role here – helping to educate and inform all of its stakeholders about climate change, and emphasizing the need to change behaviours on a mass scale.

A key action area for readers of this book to focus on is navigating the complex world of carbon offsetting, noting that internal targets are equally as important as external ones. Start with understanding your own carbon footprint and then look at implementing a sustainable plan of action to reduce and offset, partnering with only credible providers that offer only certified projects.

12.8 Chapter 9 – Sustainable Energy summary

In this chapter we explored that the 'end' of the peak of the use of fossil fuels such as coal and oil may be as close as 2023, just a handful of years away from our writing of this book. There is a possibility that the global Covid-19 pandemic has brought the 'peak' earlier – advising us that now is a time for real change. Regardless of 'when', we hope that this chapter has inspired you to begin innovating towards greener, renewable energy solutions immediately – at the very least switching to more sustainable suppliers.

As with many areas of this book, we strongly encourage you to share any results from opting for more renewable energy solutions with your employees, customers and wider stakeholder community – don't let this be something that is buried in an annual report. Build your responsible energy position into your brand values and use your marketing campaigns to encourage the same audiences to join you in making better energy choices themselves. There are a number of practical ways to review their energy consumption. Work with your manufacturers to develop more innovative and truly sustainable solutions, question your current energy suppliers on their sustainable practice and look to reduce your own energy consumption where possible.

12.9 Chapter 10 – Sustainable, Innovative Packaging summary

Packaging, whilst in many cases essential, is also a significant contributor to climate change – impacting waste management, creating plastic pollution, often prohibiting recycling and creating additional energy consumption.

Companies are increasingly taking an innovative approach to packaging and rethinking its role in products. Technological advances are helping, and major consumer product brands take more responsibility for packaging, and are supported by being set targets from entities such as the Ellen MacArthur Foundation and CEFLEX.

This chapter also details how essential a symbiotic partnership between the product producer and its end consumer is in order to ensure that the principle of reduce, reuse and recycle becomes a reality. Ultimately, this can only be delivered through planning in long-term sustainability from the outset in order to make the circular economy a reality.

It can't be avoided that marketers have spent most of the last century playing a significant role in changing consumer habits to create the 'throwaway' society we are faced with today – however, now it can be a major sponsor of the change that is needed, harnessing packaging innovation as a method of communication and collaboration with consumers.

12.10 Chapter 11 – The Importance of Effective Partnerships summary

This chapter discussed how NGO partnerships, when executed well, can help companies develop incredible opportunities for growing their business and help others in a sustainable manner. NGOs can support through enabling organizations to access new and developing markets, become more efficient, and support the appropriate market conditions for growth. In turn, companies can help, educate and improve local communities in underdeveloped countries.

The key responsibility here is for all parties to work together towards educating and steering governments and world leaders to form policies that drive positive change. It is encouraging to see business partnerships with NGOs increasing and developing into longer-term relationships that help them and the societies they serve to grow.

Management of a brand's reputation in this area is essential, as we have shown in research such as the Edelman Trust Barometer reports (Ries, Edelman et al), with all business now needing to be seen as a catalyst for change. This is particularly the case since many companies are seen as not being ethical and the NGOs they work with, whilst trusted, are often seen as not being competent. Provided that both parties work together with transparency about their intentions, priorities and objectives, they can develop a successful partnership that can bring about change to business practices and brand purpose and provide valuable insight that can open up opportunities in new markets, refine sustainable practice in supply chains and deliver a more meaningful customer experience.

12.11 Taking action: marketing sustainability action plan model

The following model is a summation of the topics and themes we've covered in this book and is also our proposal for a framework in which you can actively manage sustainability in your organization.

Marketing Sustainability Action Plan Model

KEY ACTIONS:

❶ Commit to keeping the conversation on the strategic agenda.
❷ Adopt Systemic Thinking. Design any products with 'end of life' in mind.
❸ Run an audit of supply chain and partners to optimize.
❹ Communicate the real changes. Align sustainability with brand values.
❺ Run a waste management audit, set targets to improve your product footprint wherever possible.
❻ Look for alternatives, Reuse and Recycle responsibly.
❼ Run analysis as to where you currently sit, set targets and develop projects to meet them.
❽ Run an energy assessment audit. What can switch? Develop a phased plan of continuous development.
❾ Aim to 'leave no trace' optimize this key asset for brand communication.
❿ Look to build long term momentum through relevant partnerships.

Our marketing sustainability framework is designed to provide you with a practical starting point and helpful reference for ensuring that all of the topic areas we've addressed in this book can be pulled together to create a framework for planning and implementation.

You may also find it useful to go through each of the action points we've outlined for you at the end of each chapter to create practical tasks that align with the framework. We've highlighted some key actions in the framework, but there are a number of others we suggest too. And of course, you can adapt the framework as necessary to create your own marketing sustainability framework, using ours as a starting point.

12.12 Closing thoughts

Thank you for joining us and reading *Sustainable Marketing*. We know you are busy, and we really appreciate it. We hope we've emphasized the crucial role marketers play in the critical issue of marketing sustainability – from a brand, communication, stakeholder, product development, advertising, promotion, pricing and partnership perspective, in your organization and with your consumers, and in the wider world. The role of marketing and those who work in it continues to grow and evolve with the changing landscape in which we operate. Our ability to inform and educate across all parts of the stakeholder chain is becoming more important as we move forwards.

As we finished writing this book, the world found itself in the middle of an unprecedented global pandemic – coronavirus. The impact on the economy at time of writing was already colossal and millions have suffered as a consequence, and our hearts go out to everyone affected. Conversely, as we've touched on in some of the chapters, the impact it also had on highlighting climate change is also extraordinary. As manufacturing greatly reduced, modern aviation stopped almost overnight, and travel in cities paused. The earth took a breath and showed some slim recovery with reduced emissions. Whether or not restricted movement and social distancing have become the norm as you read this in 2021 and beyond remains to be seen, so too does the question of whether or not we have managed to take this moment to address the damage we have been doing to our planet and have 'awakened' to prioritizing climate change, or perhaps the inevitable global recession that may have followed has put climate change to the bottom of the world's agenda. Only time will tell.

We fully recognize that marketing sustainability is no easy task. As marketers ourselves, we are all fully aware of the challenge of influencing boardrooms and the rest of the organization you work within. Our view, however, is that there's no one better placed to drive and effect HOPE than a marketer with a responsibility to drive sustainability within their organizations.

As a responsible marketer we suggest you continue to think about the following:

- Where are you now? Where do you want to be? Do some simple gap analysis and evaluation.
- Is there an organizational purpose that employees can align with? Review the vision/mission – is there a purpose that you're aligned with – and is it authentic?
- What's your specific role in driving activity within the organization – what resources and who do you need to align with? Can you pull together an action group to take responsibility for driving change?
- Is your organizational purpose clearly part of your brand story – and if not, how can that be addressed? What practical actions need to be taken? Can you canvas the views of senior leadership teams, employees, customers, stakeholders?
- What does responsible marketing/ethical marketing mean for your organization?

- What changes can you make aligned with the prioritization of the marketing sustainability framework?
- How will your organization be fully accountable? Will you make a pledge or brand promise that is transparent and visible?
- How will you practically communicate what you do so that consumers and employees are aware?
- How will you track brand sentiment and the impact of the changes you implement?

We hope that you can use the contents of this book to help develop habits that become part of your brand story. As you progress, remember to share your good news stories – especially those that align with your consumers' own desires. Help all of your company's employees feel good about the organization they work for with internal communication on the topic as well, but most of all, please take this opportunity to own and drive sustainability in your organization.

As a planet, we really can't wait any longer.

Afterword

The purpose of most non-fiction books is to bring awareness and educate – indeed, in many ways, that purpose aligns with many endeavours of 'the marketer' and is a perfect marketing vehicle to meet our objective of raising awareness and providing practical solutions.

We hope that we've achieved our goal of making you more aware of and educated about the various topics. The journey of writing this book over the past year has been a revelation for the three of us; we've learned a great deal about things we had vague ideas about and had our ideologies, viewpoints and passions both stimulated and challenged. It's important to reiterate that whilst we're all highly experienced and experts in marketing, we're by no means experts when it comes to the topics we have tackled in this book and sincere thanks is due to those who have kindly given their time to share their views with us, namely: James Perry, Sarah Walker-Smith, Sarah Kauss and Mark Lapping, The Chartered Institute of Marketing, Alex Cullen and Victoria Page.

What's been interesting for us, from the perspective of a marketer, is the realization of the role marketing has played in developing a throwaway society, and the role it is currently playing and can lead on in order to develop a more conscious society.

And whilst, as we've summarized, there needs to be a total rethink about how we approach sustainability and protect our planet – focused, systemic thinking, with products designed and manufactured with sustainability and end of life in mind, as Mark Lapping states: 'It's going to take consumers to start behaving differently to force big industry to make the necessary changes.' And in our view, there is no one better placed to effect change, align with and influence customers and drive hope for a better, more sustainable future, than an 'educated and aware', responsible marketer.

Gemma, Michelle and G. X

Marketing sustainability action plan

The below is a summary of the suggested actions we have made throughout this book. We hope these are highly practical for you to consider, and provide perspective and help you form an 'audit' against implementing each of the framework (chapter) areas.

Not all of these actions will be appropriate for your business, but do take the time to evaluate each of them and prioritize what you are going to focus on, coming up with your own version of the marketing sustainability action plan:

Chapter 1 actions

No	Action	Considerations	Next step
1	Review your company's current publicly stated CR/CSR position (whether it is in annual reports etc).	What areas does your company focus on? What does it not mention?	Write down three areas in which your company is making good progress – and three in which it is not.
2	Review your competitors' current CR/CSR positions.	How do you differ? Is there anything you can learn from – or seek not to do?!	Write down a key observation from each of your competitors that warrants further investigation or an issue in your own business that this work has highlighted you need to address.

No	Action	Considerations	Next step
3	Put yourself in your customers' shoes – what would they think about your current reputation?	Would your customers consider you to be an ethical brand? Would they be aware of your impact on the environment?	Do a simple SWOT analysis of your company's current position from a customer perspective. What are your strengths and weaknesses from their perspective? Where do you have opportunity to do more? What threats do you see?
4	How is CR/CSR reflected in your internal culture?	What initiatives do you have internally that reflect your publicly stated strategy?	Write down three initiatives that would really improve your company's working environment.
5	Are you clear on the UN's SDGs, the Paris Agreement and the Ellen MacArthur Foundation's 'Pledge'?	Can you develop a deeper awareness of and education about what's expected regarding key targets and challenges?	Start researching the wider concepts and targets sustainable goals. Run a quick audit internally to understand awareness of these from your colleagues and leadership team. Commit to developing an awareness communication.
6	What would be your equivalent of Ben & Jerry's three missions?	What would your product, social and economic mission be in your ideal view?	Write down draft versions of your company's new mission in the three areas.

Chapter 2 actions

No	Action	Considerations	Next Step
1	Explore SDGs in more detail.	Where are your knowledge gaps when it comes to SDGs and how do they apply to your company? Make a list of what more you need to be doing, prioritize them and then take courageous steps to drive change.	Make one target a commitment to continuously learn.
2	Develop a sustainability action group.	Identify those within the organization who are driven to make change aligned with SDGs, collaborating and sharing responsibility, and who have a sense of purpose across the organization.	Set clear targets and accountability and work as a collective task force.
3	Review your reporting model.	How are you reporting on sustainability and SDGs now?	Consider how to embed SDG targets into your reporting.
4	Research best practice.	Look at practice by other organizations in your industry, and further afield.	What are three practical lessons you can apply to your business based on what others are doing?
5	Create or join a leadership best practice task force.	Find ways to collaborate with other leaders from other organizations to share best practice and continuous learning.	Reach out to three people on LinkedIn whom you respect in the area of SDG and invite them to join a call to discuss the issue.

Chapter 3 actions

No	Action	Considerations	Next Step
1	Collate a list of all internal stakeholders connected to your organization.	Consider which departments should be involved in developing your sustainability strategy. Should it be all of them? Add them to a visual plan to help you map all stakeholders.	Begin to identify the key stakeholders who can help sponsor change in your organization.
2	Collate a list of all external stakeholders connected to your organization.	What groups and individuals may have an active interest in how your company approaches developing your sustainability strategy? How do they connect to your internal stakeholders?	Begin to decide whether and how the external stakeholder will be involved – will they be an active participant or just informed of your plans?
3	Create a stakeholder communications plan.	Once you have mapped all of your stakeholder groups, develop a plan for how, and with what media, you will aim to engage with them throughout the next year.	Have you considered your customer yet? How are you going to engage with them in this process? Remember – give your consumers context and reasons to engage with your brand. Remember that your internal customers are just as important as your external customers.
4	Create an engagement timing plan.	Consider whether it is useful for your company to have a calendar of events, including key meetings, to ensure that sustainability is being considered.	What other meetings should sustainability be a part of? For example, is it a standing item on your management team/board meeting?

No	Action	Considerations	Next Step
5	Create an annual impact summary for your stakeholders on your company's progress in meetings.	Remember, your role is to act as a catalyst for change – establish your key KPIs and track them to show that you are progressing and the company is effecting change.	Consider whether bringing all stakeholders together to discuss your annual summary might help you further explain the direction of your sustainability objectives.

Chapter 4 actions

No	Action	Considerations	Next Step
1	Review your company's current supply chain sustainability objectives and KPIs.	What areas does your company focus on? What does it not mention?	Write down three areas of supply chain sustainability where your company is making good progress – and three it could do more on. Try to set targets to measure against wherever possible.
2	Review your company's current publicly stated supply chain sustainability position (whether it be in annual reports etc).	How much are you publicly committing to changes or new standards over the next year?	Write up a new summary of what you are doing as a business for your board to approve to release as public information.
3	Consider how you currently work with your procurement function on supply chain sustainably.	Were you ensuring that your procurement team consider your impact on the environment?	Come up with a practical way you can ensure that supply chain sustainability is a regular topic that is discussed – for example, set up a standing meeting on it with your procurement team each month.

No	Action	Considerations	Next Step
4	Consider the Intel case study – how are you auditing your suppliers and sharing sustainability best practices?	What initiatives could you create internally that set your company up for future success|?	Write down three ways technology might support the future growth of your company – how can they be used to improve your sustainability position?
5	How are you working with your company's employees and the employees of your suppliers on sustainability?	What would be your equivalent of Intel's 'Code of Conduct' that guides the actions of their employees, directors and business partners?	Work with other members of the senior leadership team to create your own 'code of conduct' for how your company expects itself and its partners to act.

Chapter 5 actions

No	Action	Considerations	Next Step
1	Assume corporate social responsibility.	How can cause-related marketing initiatives fit into your CSR plan? And if they're in there already, are they authentic?	Commit to taking the lead to drive two cause-related marketing initiatives that align with purpose and audiences.
2	Be aware of conscious consumers.	Do you understand the purpose and values of your audiences?	If not, perhaps you could develop a survey and undertake some consumer research to better understand their views around sustainability and issues that are close to their heart – so that you can learn more about what they're basing their purchasing decisions and choices upon.

No	Action	Considerations	Next Step
3	Aim for employee engagement.	An internal marketing initiative – could you lead and champion an initiative with your HR department to better understand the needs of employees? How do they feel about the organization's CSR efforts? How diverse is the workplace? Are employees kept up to date and aware of the CSR work the organization embarks on?	Run an internal audit to identify any 'gaps' and develop a structured action plan to improve activities or initiate communications.
4	Do a B Impact Assessment.	Take the B Impact Assessment – whilst you may not be considering B Corp accreditation, the assessment will give you a benchmark and stimulate thinking around what's possible for your organization. It will also help you to better understand any potential gaping holes.	Complete the B Impact Assessment at https://bimpactassessment.net/ and see how your business compares.
5	Work with other companies.	How can you take inspiration from B Corp companies?	Review the case studies or look for organizations similar to yours. What ideas and best practice can you implement?

Chapter 6 actions

No	Action	Considerations	Next Step
1	Walk around your office and make some notes on what you see being used on a daily basis.	Where is waste being created that could be avoided?	Write down 10 suggestions your company can implement in the next 30 days.
2	What is this waste costing your company?	Try to estimate the monthly costs of the items you've identified.	Write a mini business case for what making some changes looks like.
3	Make it a boardroom discussion.	It is amazing how seldom the 'office environment' is referred to at board level (maybe because the senior team often don't face the same challenges as team members do!).	Ask to show senior management a simple presentation on what you've found, and what you are going to drive in terms of change. There's no need to make it a big 'ask' – more of an FYI!
4	How sustainable is your marketing practice?	What initiatives do you have planned or underway that are going to create waste?	Write down ways you could improve or really reduce the amount of waste you are producing.
5	How can you mitigate the inevitable ways you are creating waste?	How can you avoid creating more and e-waste?	Come up with three practical ideas for how you can avoid sending more e-waste from your office to landfill this year. Can you recycle old computers and office furniture in some proactive way (i.e. donating it to charity/ schools etc)?

Chapter 7 actions

No	Action	Considerations	Next Step
1	Consider the whole journey from manufacture to disposal and beyond.	Consumers do not sit and think about the entire journey. They rely on what they read and see. What do you want them to know and how can you be more transparent?	Map out each part of the journey and how you intend to tell the story in a way that doesn't complicate the matter. Use your knowledge to educate your customers too. Provide reason and context behind why you are doing what you are doing so they too can make informed decisions.
2	Understand the regulations that are in place and coming in the future.	What changes are coming? Do they/ will they impact your products? Is your messaging in line or will it require change?	Plan ahead. Don't wait for the rules to take effect. How can you use these to innovate how you do things or inform on your marketing communications to stay ahead of your competitors and evolve your sustainable development?
3	Consider your use of plastic.	Identify any areas of your products and services that may be using plastic that is not necessary or cannot be recycled.	What sustainable alternatives could you introduce to reduce or remove these entirely?
4	Review your recycling labelling on your products and services.	Consider how you can make the recycling options on your packaging clearer?	What ways can you use to encourage your consumer to also reuse and repair?
5	What exciting innovations could you develop with other partners?	What start-ups and other partner companies could you work with to produce innovative new ideas?	What companies could you help solve a problem with your products and services?

Chapter 8 actions

No	Action	Considerations	Next Step
1	Review the commitments of the Paris Agreement in the context of your own company.	Develop your own method of reporting on your progress towards achieving the targets.	Consider how you might set more ambitious targets than are suggested by the agreement.
2	Consider how your organization could work with government to innovate and lead the way.	Investigate if any government support is available to help invest in new technologies that can support your sustainability strategy.	Consider if your ways of working are set up to ensure continued progress towards your objectives.
3	Share your progress.	Consider what stories of success you have that could be shared, with a view to creating best practice and fuelling new ideas.	How could you provide even greater transparency on your progress?
4	Articulate your company's carbon offsetting commitment.	Start with gaining a clear understanding of your own carbon footprint and implement a plan of action to reduce it.	In what way can you offset your carbon emissions? What certified projects or organizations could you partner with to further reduce your emissions?
5	How has the coronavirus pandemic changed your strategy?	Consider how the coronavirus has affected your carbon emissions.	Have there been any unintended improvements as a result of coronavirus? For example, less travel – how could this be developed further?

Chapter 9 actions

No	Action	Considerations	Next Step
1	Consider your marketing messaging.	Undertake an audit of the current position in your own organization regarding sustainable energy. Do you have good news stories to share with your audiences, both internally and externally?	What, if anything, is planned for the development of sustainable energy in the future? Commit to building this into relevant marketing campaigns to align with brand.
2	Switch energy suppliers.	Is there opportunity to switch energy supplies or introduce some sustainable energy practices?	Consider sustainable energy to heat and light offices. Could car fleets and transportation, where relevant, shift to vehicles powered by electricity?
3	Explore positive partnerships.	Are there any key partnerships throughout your supply chain that mean you could collaborate in a joint venture to improve energy efficiencies and support the reduction of your carbon footprint?	How could you develop partnerships if none are currently in place?
4	Take a stand.	Is there scope for your organization or brand to take a stand on sustainable energy?	Create a campaign to encourage others to increase their awareness and bring about change – or indeed, as in the case of the *Guardian*, remove partnerships that no longer align with your brand values?
5	Review how the coronavirus pandemic has changed your energy strategy.	Consider how the coronavirus has affected your energy strategy.	Have there been any unintended improvements as a result of coronavirus?

Chapter 10 actions

No	Action	Considerations	Next Step
1	Audit marketing messaging.	Undertake an audit of how you are communicating sustainability in terms of recycling, reusing and reducing packaging.	Do you have any campaigns dedicated to sustainability advising customers of the steps you're taking or your position?
2	Educate yourself and your target market.	From a marketing perspective, audit the messages you are sharing with your audiences about sustainable packaging. Do you practise clear carbon labelling?	What opportunities are there for you to consider and explore in this area?
3	Recycle, reduce, reuse.	What creative marketing campaigns/initiatives could you embark on to collaborate with customers to educate or encourage them to recycle or reuse?	How can you amplify the outputs of this campaign further (for example, sharing on social media or in store)?
4	Consider collaboration.	Do you have core competences internally with regards to marketing sustainability when it comes to packaging, or like the manufacturers cited in the Jibal research, is there a need for you to look beyond and build partnerships?	Run a needs assessment in this area – what key issue can you address with your partners?
5	Work with your consumers.	How can you create a 'symbiotic partnership' between your company and your consumer to make reduce, reuse and recycle a reality?	Start with the end in mind when planning a sustainability initiative with your consumers. What would represent a significant change?

Chapter 11 actions

No	Action	Considerations	Next Step
1	Decide whether an NGO partnership is right for your organization.	Be clear on why you want to work together, on both sides. It cannot be a vanity measure, or a 'tick box' exercise. Values must align or they risk not being taken seriously	Work closely together to review and align your goals and objectives.
2	Allocate the time, resource and funding.	Be sure of the time and effort that is required at the start of the partnership.	Agree the different roles each partner will have. Commit people, teams and senior leaders to the partnership to ensure accountability.
3	Make sure the targets are realistic.	The end goal may be the same but how you get there needs to be planned carefully. Plan targets and timeframes based on realistic assumptions.	How will the partnership will be monitored and measured to benefit both the NGO and the business? Remember that success will look different to each party.
4	Keep going.	The situation is changing all the time, so be prepared to change direction and evolve. Be prepared to make mistakes and learn from them.	Not every part of the partnership will work all the time. Be prepared to bring in new resources or remove older ones. Review the status and objectives on an ongoing basis.
5	Communicate effectively.	Use all the expertise within your marketing function to amplify your messages. Use your employees as advocates. Communicate outside of the 'sustainability' section on your website.	Take your message to society, do not make them have to look for it.

Full interview with Sarah Walker-Smith

With reference to the quote you shared recently on Twitter, 'Business can be both purposeful and profitable at the same time, indeed one leads to the other', what's your experience of profit with purpose in action – one leading the other?

'Despite having qualified in accountancy, marketing, strategy and change, my role now largely focuses on people. I listen to what they have to say, I increasingly see the need for alignment of people's personal values with their organization's and their roles having capacity to make a difference in order for them to feel truly happy and fulfilled at work. This isn't just a generational thing, although it's increasingly prevalent in people coming into the workforce for the first time. We see it in the questions we are asked before people join us through to the traffic via our digital presence and the activities people want to engage in when they get here. This equally applies to clients, too, who want to work with brands who share at least some of their values and who they are proud to be associated with. For a while now I've referred to this intersection of purpose and commercialism as "good business" – indeed the recent CBI manifesto also alludes to this – they call it a "new kind of inclusive capitalism". Put simply, I believe purpose will enable organizations to remain competitive in an increasingly volatile and competitive market given changes in social attitudes and demographics. Plus, it's more fun!'

As CEO of Shakespeare Martineau have/are your own personal views and values about sustainability driven/driving the culture and mission of your business?

'They are very much aligned – the leader sets the tone! However, our values and strategy have been developed after much consultation at all levels and corners of the business, so I am confident they are shared by many – indeed if they weren't it wouldn't work!

On a personal level, I've been influenced by my husband, who is passionate about climate change and who has retrained from being a lawyer to an environmental scientist, and also my children, who just seem to "get it" so much more than those older and "wiser" than them. Indeed, it gives me hope for the future listening to the Gen Z and Alpha populations in terms of how they see themselves as caretakers rather than owners of not only the planet, but also the businesses they develop and work in.'

Do you see yourself as a champion of sustainability within the organization – leading from the top, responsibly – and if so, how does this impact others within your organization?

'It's the only way, if it's not led this way, from the top, then it's not authentic and it just won't stick. That said (and this is where I differ from my hubby a little), that doesn't mean I need to become vegan or refuse to ever fly again. I believe the masses making small changes will be necessary and these marginal and evolving changes are easier to achieve than extreme measures overnight. We need to create new habits. But we all do need to make those changes quickly. On a personal level, I have reduced foreign holidays (especially flying), changed how I heat and insulate our home, saved energy with better appliances and shifted to an electric car, plus reduced the amount of meat I eat and paper I use. At that level, it's relatively painless, but the effect if we all did it, would be enormous.'

What practical challenges have you had to overcome to take a stance on 'profit with purpose'?

'Short term versus long term is perhaps the biggest mindset shift. Too many businesses and business commentators react to annual profit cycles rather than trends. Also explaining that this way of operating is commercially essential and not just a "fluffy aspiration", ensuring the purpose is shared and more than just generic – but becomes the critical bit in the middle of the Venn diagram of someone's role, values and organizational values, that's where you can use purpose to drive motivation and therefore competitive advantage through people.'

How do you lead by example as an organization supporting others to make changes? What sustainable practices have you implemented internally within your own business?

'So, I need to explain this in two parts – the business I ran for 15 years and the one I joined less than a year ago. It's fair to say the current business still has much to do and we have only just started; however, we can take all the best practice and learning from others and use it to rocket ahead. I was increasingly proud of where we got to in my last role, having started our Green Champions Programme back in 2005. The main ways to get ahead in the sector I am in is how we use office space, travel and paper. The key is to make the changes "business as usual" and not make life harder for people. Look for benefits beyond sustainability. In all cases we managed to make "green" changes which also saved costs and most importantly improved our employee offer.'

In practice, have you found that sustainable practice actually delivers on better profitability or cost-saving directly within your own organization, and if so, how?

'Yes – cost per person in terms of consumables, travel and office overheads was significantly reduced. In many cases allowing us to reinvest in things which matter to our people or are valued by our clients.'

Do you believe that employees are more engaged when aligned with organizational values around 'profit with purpose'?

'Yes and it's only going to increase faster in the next decade than the last – government policy as well as increased scrutiny and reporting will accelerate this, too.'

As the CEO of a major law firm, is there enough pressure on organizations/leaders to take a more responsible sustainable approach?

'They shouldn't need pressure. I do worry that the wrong kind of pressure will lead to a superficial response. Business leaders need to see the genuine, medium- to long-term business benefits in this to make the response meaningful.'

Do you feel that organizations are taking the opportunities that profit with purpose offer – such as wider stakeholder engagement (employee, customer)?

'So this one needs careful explanation, for this to really work it's about "taking wider opportunities" – in effect, this is where the purpose should come from. I possibly need to explain what I mean by purpose – it's not just the generic three Ps [people, planet, profits], (although they need to be in there,), it also needs to be a simple, clear and shared "why" for the organization, which needs to be specific and relevant to all within the organization regardless of their role – ours is "unlocking potential" (for our people, clients and investors).

Do you feel that leaders of organizations are keen to champion sustainability within their organizations? Are they embracing the 'do well and perform well' opportunity?

'To be fair I don't know. I think some are saying what they think they should – but how many really mean it? I couldn't say and nor am I too interested, it's my job to create the right conditions and environment to make it live and breathe in the DNA of my organization.'

If not, why do you think this is – and what needs to shift?

'Again I can't expect to know what's in someone else's mind or judge others without having the full facts, but I would only imagine it's because they don't yet really understand the principles of what I call "good business" and/or they are looking through a short-term and purely financial lens.'

What's your view on the future of 'marketing sustainability' within organizations? How important will it become?

'It will become increasingly important, especially as the mix of four working generations starts to further shift generations. This will be added to by a rise in progressive mindsets driven by social attitudes and policy.'

Reducing costs within a business has always been seen to be a powerful driver. Do you find that 'marketing sustainability' is only accepted if one can showcase the cost savings aligned with profit with purpose?

'I think it's a happy bonus outcome! We have to build cases for change in whichever way they are most palatable and use multiple arguments – for some, this will be a key argument, so let's not be too purist or afraid to use it alongside the other ones. It's the end result that matters.'

In your opinion – what drives what? Appetite to be more sustainable and responsible – or bottom line?

'I think it's a virtuous circle or indeed the same thing.'

Keeping in mind the challenges around being perceived to be 'green washing' or 'green sheening', in your opinion, is the appetite to be genuinely more sustainable growing?

'I think our people and clients are adults and can see through and aren't likely to believe anything which isn't authentic.'

Glossary

B Corp – Certified B Corporations are businesses that meet the highest standards of verified social and environmental performance, public transparency and legal accountability to balance profit and purpose. B Corps form a community of leaders and drive a global movement of people using business as a force for good.

Biodegradable plastic – A plastic that decomposes naturally in the environment. This is achieved when microorganisms in the environment metabolize and break down the structure of biodegradable plastic. The end result is one that is less harmful to the environment than traditional plastics.

Biodiesel – A form of diesel fuel derived from plants or animals and consisting of long-chain fatty acid esters. It is typically made by chemically reacting lipids such as animal fat (tallow), soybean oil or some other vegetable oil with an alcohol, producing a methyl, ethyl or propyl ester.

Bio ethanol – Mainly produced by the sugar fermentation process, although it can also be manufactured by the chemical process of reacting ethylene with steam. The main sources of sugar required to produce ethanol come from fuel or energy crops.

Biofuel – A fuel that is produced through contemporary processes from biomass, rather than a fuel produced by the very slow geological processes involved in the formation of fossil fuels, such as oil.

Biomass – A plant or animal material used for energy production (electricity or heat), or in various industrial processes as a raw substance for a range of products.

Bioplastic – A substance made from organic biomass sources, unlike conventional plastics, which are made from petroleum. Bioplastics are made through a number of different processes. Some use a microorganism to process base materials, such as vegetable oils, cellulose, starches, acids and alcohols.

Brand purpose – The reason for the brand to exist beyond making money. If you want a really powerful brand purpose, it needs to relate to the product or service itself. For example, if you're in the educational sector, your purpose might help children and shape their future.

Business Roundtable – An association of chief executive officers of America's leading companies working to promote a thriving US economy and expanded opportunity for all Americans through sound public policy.

Carbon dioxide emissions – A colourless, odourless and non-poisonous gas formed by combustion of carbon and in the respiration of living organisms, considered a greenhouse gas. Emissions mean the release of greenhouse gases and/or their precursors into the atmosphere over a specified area and period of time.

Carbon footprint – A carbon footprint is defined as the total amount of greenhouse gases produced to directly and indirectly support human activities, usually expressed in equivalent tons of carbon dioxide (CO_2).

Carbon labelling – A carbon emission label or carbon label describes the carbon dioxide emissions created as a by-product of manufacturing, transporting or disposing of a consumer product. This information is important to consumers wishing to minimize their ecological footprint and ascertain the contribution to global warming made by their purchases.

Carbon neutral – Making or resulting in no net release of carbon dioxide into the atmosphere, especially as a result of carbon offsetting.

Carbon offsetting – Buying carbon credits equivalent to your carbon impact.

Carbon sink – Any natural reservoir that absorbs more carbon than it releases, and thereby lowers the concentration of carbon dioxide in the atmosphere. Globally, the two most important carbon sinks are vegetation and the ocean.

Carbon Trust – An organization that provides analysis on sustainability issues to help businesses, investors and policymakers with their roles in reducing carbon and saving energy. It works with companies and governments across the world.

Cause marketing – Marketing done by a for-profit business that seeks to both increase profits and to better society in accordance with corporate social responsibility, such as by including activist messages in advertising.

Centralized procurement – Implies purchasing decisions are made either by company headquarters or some regional or divisional level.

CEO activism – When senior leaders speak out on social issues that are not directly related to their company's bottom line.

Circular economy – A circular economy is an alternative to a traditional linear economy (make, use, dispose) in which we keep resources in use for as long as possible, extract the maximum value from them whilst in use, then recover and regenerate products and materials at the end of each service life.

Clean Air Act 1956 – An Act of the Parliament of the United Kingdom enacted principally in response to London's Great Smog of 1952. It was sponsored by the Ministry of Housing and Local Government in England and the Department of Health Scotland and was in effect until 1993.

Climate Action Tracker (CAT) – An independent scientific analysis produced by two research organizations tracking climate action since 2009. They trace progress towards the globally agreed aim of holding warming well below 2°C (3.6°F), and pursuing efforts to limit warming to 1.5°C (2.7°F).

Climate risk – Refers to risk assessments based on formal analysis of the consequences, likelihoods and responses to the impacts of climate change and how societal constraints shape adaptation options.

Code of conduct – Clarifies an organization's mission, values and principles, linking them with standards of professional conduct. The code articulates the values the organization wishes to foster in leaders and employees and, in doing so, defines desired behaviour.

Compostable plastic – A plastic that is capable of undergoing biological decomposition in a compost site as part of an available programme, such that the plastic is not visually distinguishable and breaks down to carbon dioxide, water, inorganic compounds, and biomass, at a rate consistent with known compostables.

Conscious consumers – A person who concentrates on making positive decisions throughout the buying process, with the intention of helping to balance some of the negative impacts that consumerism has on the planet.

Corporate social responsibility (CSR) – This is a type of international private business self-regulation that aims to contribute to societal goals of a philanthropic, activist or charitable nature by engaging in or supporting volunteering or ethically oriented practices.

CR objective – Delivering an exemplary customer experience. Achieving top-quartile customer satisfaction whilst maintaining an effective cost structure is a key customer service objective.

'Edelman Trust Barometer Report' – Annual trust and credibility survey. The research is conducted by Edelman Intelligence, a global insight and analytics consultancy.

Electronic waste or e-waste – Describes discarded electrical or electronic devices. Used electronics that are destined for refurbishment, reuse, resale, salvage recycling through material recovery, or disposal are also considered e-waste.

Energy security – The association between national security and the availability of natural resources for energy consumption. Access to (relatively) cheap energy has become essential to the functioning of modern economies.

Environmental, Social and Governance (ESG) – Refers to the three central factors in measuring the sustainability and societal impact of an investment in a company or business. These criteria help to better determine the future financial performance of companies.

Ethical consumption – Making the connections between a product, where that product originated and in what context it has been produced. An ethically informed consumer realizes that when they buy something, they are not only buying the product, they are also making an ethical choice.

Fossil fuels – Hydrocarbons, primarily coal, fuel oil or natural gas, formed from the remains of dead plants and animals.

Fossil methane – A gas that can be emitted via natural geologic seeps or as a result of humans extracting and using fossil fuels including oil, gas, and coal.

Fracking – The process of drilling down into the earth so that a high-pressure water mixture can be directed at the rock to release the gas inside. Water, sand and chemicals are injected into the rock at high pressure, which allows the gas to flow out to the head of the well.

Gen Z – Generation Z is the demographic cohort succeeding Millennials and preceding Generation Alpha. Researchers and popular media use the mid- to late 1990s as starting birth years and the early 2010s as ending birth years.

Global warming – A gradual increase in the overall temperature of the earth's atmosphere, generally attributed to the greenhouse effect caused by increased levels of carbon dioxide, CFCs and other pollutants.

Green energy – This comes from natural sources such as sunlight, wind, rain, tides, plants, algae and geothermal heat. These energy resources are renewable, meaning they are naturally replenished. In contrast, fossil fuels are a finite resource that take millions of years to develop and will continue to diminish with use.

Greenhouse gases (GHG) – A gas that absorbs and emits radiant energy within the thermal infrared range. Greenhouse gases cause the greenhouse effect on planets. The primary greenhouse gases in earth's atmosphere are: water vapour (H_2O), carbon dioxide (CO_2), methane (CH_4), nitrous oxide (N_2O) and ozone (O_3).

Greenwashing – The process of conveying a false impression or providing misleading information about how a company's products are more environmentally sound. Greenwashing is considered an unsubstantiated claim to deceive consumers into believing that a company's products are environmentally friendly.

Hyper competition – Occurs when technologies or offerings are so new that standards and rules are in flux, meaning that competitive advantages and profits resulting from such competitive advantages cannot be sustained.

Intended nationally determined contributions (INDC) – The (intended) reductions in greenhouse gas emissions under the United Nations Framework Convention on Climate Change (UNFCCC).

International Integrated Reporting Council (IIRC) – This is a global coalition of regulators, investors, companies, standard setters, the accounting profession, academia and NGOs. The coalition promotes communication about value creation as the next step in the evolution of corporate reporting.

International Renewable Energy Agency (IRENA) – This is an intergovernmental organization supporting countries in their transition to a sustainable energy future.

Investment risk – This refers to risk assessments based on formal analysis of the consequences, likelihoods and responses to the impacts of climate change and how societal constraints shape adaptation options.

Kyoto Protocol – An international agreement that aimed to reduce carbon dioxide emissions and the presence of greenhouse gases in the atmosphere. The essential tenet of the Kyoto Protocol was that industrialized nations needed to lessen the amount of their carbon dioxideemissions.

Methane – A powerful greenhouse gas that is found in small quantities in the earth's atmosphere. Methane is the simplest hydrocarbon, consisting of one carbon atom and four hydrogen atoms. It is flammable, and is used as a fuel worldwide. It is a principal component of natural gas.

Millennials – Millennials, also known as Generation Y, are the demographic cohort following Generation X and preceding Generation Z. Researchers and popular media use the early 1980s as starting birth years and the mid-1990s to early 2000s as ending birth years, with 1981 to 1996 a widely accepted defining range for the generation.

Mission statements – Created to set the tone for an organization and act as a guide to reach revenue goals and other business objectives.

NGOs – A non-governmental organization (NGO) is any non-profit, voluntary citizens' group that is organized on a local, national or international level.

Paris Climate Agreement – Commonly called the Paris Agreement, this is the first truly global commitment to fight the climate crisis. In 2015, 195 countries and the European Union signed up to a single, sweeping agreement that aims to keep global warming to well below 2°C (3.6°F) – and make every effort to limit any increase to 1.5°C (2.7°F).

Peak coal – The year in which demand for, and therefore production of, coal was greatest, namely 2013.

Peak oil – Refers to the hypothetical point at which global crude oil production will hit its maximum rate, after which production will start to decline.

Photovoltaic – The conversion of light into electricity using semiconducting materials that exhibit the photovoltaic effect, a phenomenon studied in physics, photochemistry and electrochemistry.

Profit with purpose – A business led by a mission to achieve social, community and environmental benefit through trading and by channelling a portion of their profits towards their mission.

Project Drawdown – Not-for-profit organization that develops resource by conducting rigorous reviews and assessments of climate solutions, creating compelling and human communication across mediums, and partnering with efforts to accelerate climate solutions globally.

PPP – Triple bottom line three Ps: People, Profit, Planet.

Renewable energy – Energy that is collected from renewable resources, which are naturally replenished on a human timescale, such as sunlight, wind, rain, tides, waves and geothermal heat.

Responsible Business Alliance (RBA) – The world's largest industry coalition dedicated to corporate social responsibility in global supply chains.

Responsible sourcing – A business-critical activity, in which all participating actors are equally accountable for the ethical, social, environmental and financial impact during the trading of goods or services. This means your entire value chain needs to be committed to the cause.

Socially responsible investing (SRI) – Also known as social investment, this is an investment that is considered socially responsible due to the nature of the business the company conducts. Common themes for socially responsible investments include socially conscious investing.

Social marketing – An approach used to develop activities aimed at changing or maintaining people's behaviour for the benefit of individuals and society as a whole.

Stakeholder – A party that has an interest in a company and can either affect or be affected by the business. The primary stakeholders in a typical corporation are its investors, employees, customers and suppliers.

Sustainability – Focuses on meeting the needs of the present without compromising the ability of future generations to meet their needs. The concept of sustainability is composed of three pillars: economic, environmental and social – also known informally as profits, planet and people.

Sustainability Accounting Standards Board (SASB) – An independent non-profit, whose mission is to develop and disseminate sustainability accounting standards that help public corporations disclose material, decision-useful information to investors. That mission is accomplished through a rigorous process that includes evidence-based research and broad, balanced stakeholder participation.

Sustainable Development Goals (SDGs) – A collection of 17 global goals designed to be a 'blueprint to achieve a better and more sustainable future for all'. The SDGs, set in 2015 by the United Nations General Assembly and intended to be achieved by the year 2030, are part of UN Resolution 70/1, the 2030 Agenda.

The Attenborough Effect – David Attenborough has been credited with driving more than half of UK consumers to reduce the amount of plastic they use. This 'Attenborough effect' has played a significant role in the raising of awareness and the changing of attitudes.

The Climate Pledge – A commitment by Amazon to meet the Paris Agreement 10 years early.

World Energy Trilemma Index – Ranks country energy performance on the three dimensions based on global and national data and includes recommended areas for improvements on policy coherence and integrated policy innovation, helping to develop well-calibrated energy systems.

Triple Bottom Line – The triple bottom line (or otherwise noted as TBL or 3BL) is an accounting framework with three parts: social, environmental (or ecological) and financial. These three bottom lines are often referred to as the three Ps: people, planet and profit. Some organizations have adopted the TBL framework to evaluate their performance in a broader perspective to create greater business value.

Virgin plastic – The resin produced directly from the petrochemical feedstock, such as natural gas or crude oil, which has never been used or processed before.

VUCA – An acronym to describe or to reflect on the volatility, uncertainty, complexity and ambiguity of general conditions and situations.

Wish-cycling – Unwittingly contaminating household recycling bins with items we assume to be recyclable, but which aren't readily acceptable by domestic recycling services.

Woke washing – The appropriation of ethical and progressive values as a form of advertising just to make more profit whilst hiding the dark side.

World Health Organization (WHO) – An organization set up to direct international health within the United Nations' system and to lead partners in global health responses.

Zero carbon – No carbon emissions are being produced from a product/ service, e.g. zero-carbon electricity could be provided by a 100 per cent renewable energy supplier.

Index